coming home to eat

wholefood for the family

For my wonderful mum, Evelyn McMullen.
Mum has always considered good food to be an essential
part of family life. To this day, she still makes biscuits to
post to her dearly loved grandchildren, minestrone soup
(no other soup will do) when they are feeling poorly,
and always ensured there was
food to come home to …

 C℞

coming home to eat

wholefood for the family

Jude Blereau

MURDOCH BOOKS

acknowledgments

This book was a far more creative process than my previous book *Wholefood,* and was conceived some five years ago in Santa Fe, New Mexico. I had come across the most beautiful picture in a magazine of an older woman and two very young children (presumably her grandchildren) coming back home after picking blueberries, with laden baskets. The house was just off in the background, they were laughing and, to my mind, anticipating the delicious pie that might follow. Something about it called to me but at that time, I didn't know why.

It took until August 2006 for me to understand where my work was heading. I wanted to bring people back home into the kitchen, to help them discover how easy it really is to transform 'real' food into something wholesome and delicious, and how much capacity that food has to heal, nourish and delight.

Thus was *Coming Home to Eat* conceived, but of course, conception is only the very beginning. I am so deeply thankful to my publisher Kay Scarlett who, as before, understood my message and has enabled it to be heard. *Wholefood* had been a slightly wild but wonderful beast; that Kay so willingly opened her heart, door and resources to this new baby is deeply appreciated.

There are so many other people who, in their many different ways, enabled this book to be. Above and beyond everything, my thanks and love are for my beautiful daughter Nessie. A fabulous cook in her own right, Nessie loves and supports me unconditionally and when the going gets tough, this is a treasure indeed. I am profoundly blessed. One does not write a book alone and to all who follow, my deepest thanks and love.

To my family, who are always there for me in so many different ways — putting up shelves, moving washing machines, testing recipes … really, it goes on and on. Thank you so very much.

To my dearest Jeanie, whose passion for excellence, skill and friendship keep me sane.

To Nessa, without whom I couldn't do the amount of teaching I do. Not only does she hold the space, she keeps classes flowing and supports the work I do so generously and wonderfully. To my dearest friends Nene, Tess, Nola and Will, Julie and Peter, and Denise who are *always* there for me, no matter what, so generously giving their time, skill, love and help to me.

To Deanu, who makes me laugh and helps plug holes when they occur (this might be me ringing and saying, 'I'm a bit concerned about my worms. Help!') and around he comes for a bit of worm rescue.

To all my students, who have become good friends, for their continued support of my work, and for their questions and inputs. We are building a brave new world.

How would a baby ever grow up to become the book it was meant to be without a team of very gifted editors? I am deeply grateful to Desney Shoemark (definitely an angel disguised as one very talented editor), who took the manuscript and brought her tremendous talents to bear, overseeing the project and holding the space for it to be all it could. To Katri Hilden, who brought her very discerning eyes to the pages and continued to shape the book until it sang. To my food editor Katy Holder, such a great fairy godmother who took charge of the baby when I wasn't there and watched over it as her own. Cooking is definitely a creative process, and Katy found a way for my voice (I talk a lot in life, as on paper!) to come through, while honouring the need for precise and workable recipes — thank you so much.

To Vivien Valk, who designed the book and brought her style and many talents to the pages, reflecting the beauty I believe is inherent in good, wholesome food. Thank you so very much.

To Mary Jayne House, Noel Hammond, Emma Hutchinson, Colette Vella and all the very talented and dynamic individuals who make up Murdoch Books, thank you for all the support that allows me to write.

Every writer needs a computer guardian angel and this time it was Charles, who has so generously solved my problems and done his best to keep me up to date with technology (not always easy!).

As always, I am deeply indebted to those who continue to inspire and teach me: Annemarie Colbin, Alice Waters, Weston A. Price, Deborah Madison, Jessica Prentice, Thomas Cowan, Holly Davis and, locally, Gabrielle Kervella, Sophie Zalokar and Julie Eady.

To all the organic and biodynamic farmers who work so hard (Wayne battles tiger snakes when picking some crops) to ensure good food and sustainable farming practices continue. I believe it is the best path we have for the future. To Thom and Rossane at City Farm, who established and continue to hold the space for an Organic Farmers Market in Perth, making real food available to those of us who choose to live a city life. Thank you.

Finally, to all the mothers and fathers who are beginning to return to the kitchen, buying real food and cooking from scratch … This is the profound work at hand and one of the most valuable things you can give your children.

contents

Dear Reader,

To 'come home' is defined in the *Oxford English Dictionary* as 'to get to the very heart or root of a matter, directly, thoroughly'. We need to 'come home' to eat, where the very heart of the matter is eating food that actually nourishes us. I believe it is possible to weave wholesome, healthy and delicious food into our everyday lives. It's a bit tricky in the beginning — but truly, it gets easier as you go, becomes more than workable, and rewards you enormously.

The recipes in this book reflect the way I cook at home. They are the ones I turn to for everyday use, or 'spiff up' a bit for casual entertaining.

I've tried to concentrate on using cheaper and more easily available seasonal ingredients, but where I felt the cost and time to source a special ingredient justified the nutritional benefit, I have used that. So when you see me using kudzu (kuzu), for example, which is very expensive, you will know it's there for a good reason, even though I may suggest alternatives.

It's also true that more nutrient-dense foods (such as eggs, nuts, seeds) are more expensive, but because you eat less of them and they sustain you longer, the cost balances out. There may also be ingredients that you haven't used before or that are not readily available at your supermarket — for example, a good chilli powder. They are worth tracking down because they will make things so much easier for you in the long run, and will make the dish 'work'.

Each section in this book is fluid — you could have something from the dinner chapter for breakfast, and vice versa. The most important thing is to learn to eat in balance: that is, keeping a balance between the carbohydrates, proteins, minerals, fats, vitamins and enzymes you eat during the day.

You'll find old-fashioned cooking with a funky, upbeat wholefood thing going on — this is the way I cook. Some recipes will be quick and easy, and others will require a little more time. There's food to have on the go, and food to sit down to. There's not a lot of meat, because it's not my strength, but I hope you'll find my fish and vegetarian meals delicious options. I hope you enjoy them all, and find it's all food you long to come home to eat. ◌

With love

Jude

healthy eating

I am standing by the stove (keeping watch and stirring every now and then) while the mushrooms, leek, basil and garlic cook in a lovely knob of organic butter and the smell is talking to me — promising me a full stomach, needs met and great deliciousness. I have picked a huge bunch of young rainbow chard leaves from the garden, given them a very good wash, and chopped them … soon I will add them to the pan to sweat them down. A quick mix with some brown rice I had left over from breakfast, a dash of seasoning and an egg or two … then into the oven. Dinner is assured.

Alas, it is not always this way — I would love to say it was. Many people think I whip up delicious gourmet feasts every night but, just like you, I get worn out and uninspired too. Today's success reminds me how worthwhile and relatively simple it is to include wholesome and delicious food in my day, and how good it makes me, and those I love, feel.

Wholesome food provides our body with the fuel it requires, and it also tastes great. But incorporating it into everyday life can sometimes be tricky — it shouldn't be, but it has become so. I speak to so many people who feel confused and overwhelmed about getting it all to work in their busy 21st century lives. Should I use organic food, how can I afford it, how do I find the time to cook it, and what is healthy and wholesome food anyway? ∞

There are many confusing wisdoms about what healthy eating actually is. Really though, it is quite simple. There are certain fundamental truths that form the basis of healthy, wholesome eating:

- ◌ Food should be organic where possible. This will increase its nutrient density (nutrients are what your body runs on) and reduce the pesticide load.
- ◌ Food should be 'real' — that is, made with real ingredients, rather than chemicals that mimic them. There are many toxic chemicals in the additives, flavours, colours and preservatives used in the commercial production of food. It would be an understatement to say that these are not 'body compatible', when we consider the resulting carcinogenic, mutagenic (agents that damage DNA) and teratogenic (agents that cause birth defects) effects, not to mention the entire field of agents that disrupt the intelligent running of the cells — neurotoxins, excitotoxins (toxins that affect the function of neurotransmitters, and overstimulate the neurons), and so on.
- ◌ Food should be as close as possible to its natural state and refined as little as possible. When food is refined, there are nutrient losses, and no 'enriching' or adding back will make it whole again. But more importantly, when a food is whole, with all the 'parts' (vitamins, minerals, fat, fibre, protein, carbohydrate, and the known and unknown) nature has put there intact and in their original ratio, optimum effectiveness is ensured. Milk is a good example: fat is an essential component of milk, containing the fat-soluble vitamins A and D, which are essential for assimilation of calcium and protein.
- ◌ Food is far more than its actual physical nutrients. Fractionalizing food into its components, and eating what may be considered the 'healthiest' meal on the planet, can never satisfy, fulfil and truly nourish if it is not enjoyed. In ways I cannot understand, but know exist, deliciousness and joy invite food in and enable it to be understood by the body. Equally though, the most delicious and enjoyable meal cannot nourish if there are no nutrients present. Both aspects make up what I consider to be healthy, wholesome food.

I am a great believer that we are spiritual beings having a human experience. But while we are here on Earth, we have bodies that are cellular machines, and our cells require fuel. The fuel our cells require consists of more than refined carbohydrate — processed cereals, white bread and pasta. A vast majority of Westernized people eat nothing but refined carbohydrate and sugars, and I believe this is one of the most profound contributing causes to our epidemic of obesity: most of what we now call food is a disgrace. The beating heart of our homes — the kitchen — has been replaced by the commercial factories of food companies that simply do not care what they put in the food we eat. We need to take the prime responsibility for food back from business to the home, or at the very least, demand better.

Cells require protein, fats (including saturated), vitamins, minerals, enzymes and other numerous known and unknown factors. The carbohydrate they prefer is complex — that is, it breaks down into starch (and thus sugar) slowly.

These nutrients are found in 'real' food, and are most optimal when the fundamental truths of healthy eating (outlined on the previous page) are adhered to. This, simply put, is wholesome and healthy food. It can be meat or dairy, or not — it should be what suits your body, not someone else's. Including wholesome food in your everyday life does not mean having mung bean patties for dinner if mung bean patties aren't your thing. It does not mean having food that tastes horrible, but is 'healthy'. Wholesome and healthy food is not about being a purist; it's more about making sure you keep your food as 'real' and clean as possible, and then doing the best you can each day. This will involve the need to draw your line — to know what you absolutely will not tolerate.

I, for example, will not tolerate:

- Anything made with damaged fat (ingredients listed as vegetable oil, hydrogenated vegetable oil, vegetable shortening). This means just about all commercial food: cakes, biscuits (cookies), pastry items (including croissants and Danishes), ice cream, corn chips, potato chips, pizza, muesli bars, soups, cheese spreads, mayonnaises and dips.
- Chemicals — again, this means just about all commercially produced food, including delicatessen meats, stocks, soups and sauces.
- Any animal product coming from an animal that has not had the opportunity to live a natural life, eat their natural foods and experience a respectful processing of that life (killing). Because of this, I prefer organic animal products, preferably from grass-fed animals. Unfortunately, some organic practices for livestock have

become less than optimal. I'm open to some non-certified organic products where I know the farmer has not taken on certification, but practises organically, feeds the animals an appropriate diet and does not use antibiotics or hormones.

So, come home to eat. Come join me in my kitchen as we cook delicious food from real ingredients, shop from the bounty our local organic growers and seas deliver, set the table and share a meal. In this way, we not only enrich our lives — and the lives of those we love — with the physical nutrients of food, but with the other equally essential nutrients of connection, community and meaning. May there be much joy and deliciousness at your table.

Incorporating wholesome food into your daily life

It is a fabulously worthwhile goal to want to include wholesome, nourishing food in your everyday life, and you will notice real changes when you start to eat more of it. But don't think you have to start at a purist level — for example baking with wholegrain flours, rice or barley malt — if you are not yet up to that stage. You will probably end up with a disaster that no-one eats. What you make at home with butter, eggs, even raw sugar and white flour is still light years ahead of many commercial foods full of chemicals. If you have managed to use organic ingredients, you have done stunningly well.

If you buy commercially prepared foods, look for options that use real ingredients. Numbers and words you can't understand on an ingredient list are not a good sign. Consider this simple guideline: if you don't know what something is, don't buy it.

Without doubt, the best advice I can give you is this: expect the transition to take some time. It doesn't happen overnight — I consider one to two years normal. It takes time to source appropriate foods, and to find your own cheaper and more workable options. It also takes a while before you fully understand the whole idea of real food, adjust your approach to meal preparation and cooking and work out your own shortcuts.

THE QUESTION OF COST:
ORGANIC VERSUS NON ORGANIC

I am a big advocate for organic food, but I do accept that in many cases — not all — it is more expensive. In many places it is also difficult to source. The cheaper price of much conventionally produced food is an illusion — we do not see the indirect costs of loss of biodiversity, damage to the soil and waterways, the resultant necessary clean-ups, and subsidies paid to the farmers from taxes, to name but a few. The higher price charged for most organic foods reflects the true cost of producing it — it is generally more labour intensive, and the 'real' inputs involved (as opposed to chemicals) are also more expensive.

You might need to decide how much you can afford to spend on organic foods. I strongly recommend that all animal products you buy be organic — meat, bones, milk, yoghurt, eggs, cheese, cream, butter. Secondly, buy organic unrefined oils — always more expensive, but undamaged. I also prefer fruit and vegetables to be organic (especially strawberries, carrots and broccoli) — but if it is a choice between conventional or none, I heartily endorse conventional.

Having said this, there are always ways to work within a limited budget and still buy organic food.

- ✂ Cooking from scratch — this is always far cheaper than buying food pre-prepared (pastry, for example).
- ✂ Buy and eat seasonally. Every time I see organic food at the same and even cheaper price than its conventional counterpart, it is because the product is in season.
- ✂ Buy direct from the grower — from a farmers' market, for example. This simple act also reduces your impact on the environment by reducing the kilometres food needs to travel. Food travelling long distances costs more — for you and for the environment. When we eat food that has been produced locally, we reduce both the amount of energy required to transport the food and the resulting pollution.
- ✂ Buy direct from the farmer at the farm — this is often even cheaper than the farmers' market.
- ✂ Join a CSA (Community Supported Agriculture) group. The model varies enormously from farm to farm, but the general idea is you pay to join. This

money then gives the farmer a stable income to plant and produce his/her crop. The return to the contributor is the crop, which can be distributed in a variety of ways — it might be a weekly box of vegetables and fruit. Some farms offer the return of food for volunteer labour.

- ෨ The alternative to this is a co-op. I know many groups of families who form a simple co-operative, taking turns to pick up the fruit and vegetables from an organic wholesaler or organic farm and then pack a box for each member — your investment is generally time.

- ෨ Buy in bulk — grains, legumes, flours. Anything bought in bulk is cheaper than buying it packaged. It's also a great way to buy meat.

- ෨ Buy a whole chicken and cut it yourself into portions of legs, thighs and breasts, and save the carcass for stock. This is far cheaper than buying ready-cut portions.

- ෨ Buy cheaper cuts of meat — beef cheeks, shin and shanks, lamb shoulder, and neck or bacon bones, for example.

- ෨ Balance out meat dishes with more vegetable, grain and legume dishes.

- ෨ Grow some of your own vegetables.

- ෨ When fruit is in season, buy seconds in bulk — they might be slightly misshapen, but are often still wonderful, and much cheaper. Use this bulk to make your own jams, chutneys and bottled fruit.

- ෨ Plan the menu for the week ahead — this makes a huge difference to cost, avoids wastage, and saves a lot of time by enabling you to 'dovetail' your meals by making extra to use later in the week.

- ෨ Keep your eyes out for nature's bounty, freely given. Next door to me is a very old, enormous mulberry tree. There are probably more mulberries there than the entire neighbourhood could eat, and my neighbour is happy for all to share. After eating them fresh and making a pie for dinner, I make the rest into jam.

- ෨ Pick your own: in summer we go picking organic blueberries. This works out so much cheaper, because you supply the labour. My favourite thing about picking them is seeing all the family groups joining together to harvest — many hands make light work. Young and old join together for the good of the family, and in the doing, learn where food comes from. Again, we eat the blueberries fresh, freeze them for later, have blueberry tarts, cakes and smoothies, and make jam. I rarely buy jam for two reasons: first, because I prefer mine, and secondly, it is so expensive to buy decent jam.

FINDING TIME

The single easiest way to make this lifestyle workable is to plan your menu the week ahead. Making a menu plan enables you to do two or three things at once. For example, if you bake extra vegetables — capsicum (pepper), zucchini (courgette), eggplant (aubergine), sweet potato — the extra can be used in a frittata or sandwich the next day. Extra grain from dinner can be used tomorrow as stuffing for vegetables. *Extra is good*. This works for a family of one or of many.

Allow everyone to have their tastes catered for — with a few guidelines. If your children want pasta, make sure the pasta meal balances with the rest of the week (that is, you are not having refined carbohydrate in lots of meals) and use good-quality pasta (whether bought or made). Show your children the delights of delicious, real pasta with an excellent (and this can be a simple) sauce. Serve it with a large salad and let them know they have to eat it too — *this* is how we teach our children. You might like to take this a step further and buy a quality pasta book with a pasta machine for Christmas or a birthday.

Involve everyone who lives in the home, even the young. It is here children learn to come together for the common good, share the responsibilities of everyday life and, most importantly, learn to cook. It might be as simple as peeling, measuring or stirring. And because I know that sometimes this can be more trouble than it's worth (especially after a crazy day), maybe just letting them set the table, even finding some flowers to put in the middle, is enough. Everyone should also be involved in the cleaning up. If everyone in the house is working, all should share the running of the home. Where possible, everyone should share in the cooking, taking turns. Again, this is how they learn.

Having a back-up plan is very important. I am a big fan of cooking one or two meals (such as a soup or pie) and having them on hand in the freezer. Some say freezing food diminishes its nutrition and life force, and I agree, but I would rather have something wholesome and real than nothing. Having nothing means you are starving, stressed out and ready to eat anything that crosses your path — usually commercially inferior and damaged snacks made from refined carbohydrate. Freshly cooked food is optimal, but is not always a viable option. Knowing you have something on hand saves much stress during the day.

Some simple tricks up your sleeve to help you save time include:

- ∝ Soak your grains, use quicker-cooking legumes (red, green and brown lentils, mung dahl, black-eyed peas), and choose quicker-cooking grains (quinoa, hulled millet).
- ∝ Cook extra — again, extra is good... Extra grain to turn into a pudding, mix into a salad, or use in a porridge. Extra legumes to quickly mash into a dip, enrich a stew or anchor a salad. Extra baked vegies to use tomorrow in a salad, a wrap or tomorrow night's tart. Extra salsa from tonight's nachos in tomorrow's dahl. Extra stewed fruit from tonight's fruit crumble to use in porridge or on a pancake tomorrow; extra crumble mix to put in the freezer for another time. Extra pastry in the freezer for a quick tart or pie.
- ∝ Have a well-stocked pantry. You don't have to have lots of everything, but small amounts of a wide range of items will give you options.
- ∝ Use a crockpot — the original slow cooker ... wonderful for making soups and legume dishes.

It's true that cooking is not rocket science, but skill and knowledge should not be underestimated. This does not mean you have to be a chef — it means you keep on being you, doing the best you can and when you do muck something up, you learn from it. As you learn how new ingredients behave and how a recipe works, wholesome cooking gets easier and quicker.

∝

foundations

Solid foundations are the bedrock upon which a strong house is built. And building a wholesome, vital relationship with real food also requires solid foundations. In this section you will find a mix of the 'why' and the 'what' that underpin my approach to healthy food. Knowing why something is good lays the foundations for understanding and keeps you motivated; knowing what ingredients to keep on hand ensures you can produce delicious, healthy meals that don't cost the earth or take forever to prepare.

Establishing sound foundations will make your adjustment to wholesome cooking and eating so much smoother and easier.

We'll start by considering the major food groups and their main sources in a 'wholefood' diet, then look at the best way to store staple ingredients to get the most from your cooking and your pantry. ❧

Fats

Fats are easily damaged by heat, light and oxygen. Damaged (rancid) fat is highly dangerous to the body. The less saturated fats are, the more fragile they are. Fats (particularly saturated) are often viewed in a bad light, yet most people have no understanding of the many critical roles they play in good health. Many people consider a low-fat diet a healthy diet — I am not one of these.

The following are the fats I stock and use in my kitchen.

SATURATED ANIMAL FATS

All animal fats are saturated fats and are highly stable when exposed to light, heat and oxygen. They all contain cholesterol. Saturated fats have an extremely valuable role to play in good health. They are essential for the proper usage of the fat-soluble vitamins A, D, E and K, boost immune function, allow the proper usage of omega-3 essential fatty acids, hold our organs in place and protect them, give integrity to cell walls and aid the absorption of calcium — the list goes on. They are also a good source of conjugated linoleic acid (CLA). Current research shows CLA has potent anti-cancer properties and a powerful ability to reduce heart disease.

The fats (and all other animal products) from grass-fed animals will be more potent than fats from their grain-fed counterparts and are well worth sourcing and paying for.

I consider it almost essential that any animal fat should be organic.

Organic butter for cooking and baking

Butter is a rich source of the fat-soluble vitamins A, D and E, as well as CLA. You could view the cost of organic butter (as I do) as a wise investment — a small amount delivers great benefits. A portion on steamed vegetables not only makes them taste delicious, but ensures optimum absorption of vitamins and minerals.

Ghee

If you remove the milk solids from butter you will end up with ghee — the ancient Indian medical wisdoms of Ayurveda consider ghee one of the most 'satvic' (body-compatible and nourishing) foods there is. Because the milk solids are removed, people on a casein-free diet can readily use ghee. Ghee is an excellent choice for frying at high temperatures and can be used for baking. It's easy to make your own ghee — see the recipe on page 239.

Drippings

Drippings are leftover hot fat from roast meat poured into a small dish to set, and kept for cooking. Lard (pork fat) is renowned for making some of the best flaky pastry available, and is an extremely rich source of vitamin D.

SATURATED NON-ANIMAL FATS

Like saturated animal fats, these are extremely stable when exposed to light, heat and oxygen; unlike animal fats, they do not contain cholesterol.

Unrefined coconut oil

Sometimes called coconut butter, this is a fabulous and very flexible fat. It is rich in lauric acid, which has many beneficial properties — it is a known anti-viral, anti-fungal and anti-microbial agent (mothers' milk is a rich source of lauric acid).

With a smoke point of approximately 170°C (325°F), unrefined coconut oil is an excellent choice for baking and frying.

I use two kinds of unrefined coconut oil: extra virgin, expeller pressed; and virgin, expeller pressed. Extra virgin has a strong fragrance of coconut, which some people dislike. Virgin is also called by many other names including refined. It has been deodorized (generally by running it through clay) to remove the strong coconut fragrance and is a good choice when you don't want that cooked coconut aftertaste.

UNSATURATED FATS

Monounsaturated and polyunsaturated fats are called oils, and are liquid at room temperature. Some, like olive and macadamia oil, can also become solid when chilled. The more unsaturated fats are, the more unstable they are when exposed to heat, light and oxygen. Most commercially available oils are refined by a process using chemical solvents and high heat. The resulting oils are highly damaged and will equally damage your body. Margarine is made from highly damaged oil mixed with nickel oxide, then pumped with hydrogen atoms — a process that creates very dangerous trans fatty acids. It is worth noting that this hydrogenated oil (margarine/shortening) is used in pretty well every commercial cake, pastry, croissant, Danish and biscuit.

The following are the oils I keep and feel comfortable using.

Almond oil
With its high (approximately 61%) level of oleic acid, I like to use almond oil for baking as a substitute for butter or coconut oil. I do not use it for frying.

Linseed (flax seed) oil
This is one of the richest land-based sources of omega-3 essential fatty acids. It should always be stored in a dark glass bottle (or tin) in a fridge. Like walnut oil, it is highly unstable and should never be heated.

Olive oil — extra virgin, cold pressed
This healthful oil is high in vitamin E and antioxidants. More importantly, because it has a high amount of oleic acid (approximately 71%), it is relatively

stable when exposed to heat, light and oxygen. I buy expensive organic extra virgin olive oil (unfiltered) for 'cold' work (as in a salad dressing) and a cheaper non-organic extra virgin cold-pressed olive oil for heating (including frying). If I come across a good deal, I use the organic oil even for hot work.

Unrefined organic sesame oil

This is not as stable as olive oil, but because it contains its own antioxidant (sesamin), it can withstand gentle heating. It's also great in a salad dressing.

Walnut oil

If I can find this oil fresh, in a tin or dark glass bottle and from a fridge, I snap it up and store it in my fridge for cold use. It is highly unsaturated and has a good amount of omega-3 essential fatty acids.

Fruit and vegetables

If you find yourself captivated by the latest nutritional buzz words relating to phytochemicals (plant nutrients) — antioxidants, lycopene, lutein, anthocyanins — please don't rush to a pill, but turn instead to fruit and vegetables. Fruit and vegetables are packed with phytochemicals as well as numerous vitamins, minerals, fibre and fats, in a far cheaper and more body-compatible form than a pill. I like mine seasonal, local and preferably organic.

Shopping at farmers' markets lets me know what's in season where I live, and enables me to buy my food freshly dug or picked. It also lets me get to know the taste of each farmer's land. I love Sean and Hua's strawberries, prefer Sona's apricots, adore Bee's figs … and so it goes. I also grow vegetables in the inner city — and though I am by no means a green thumb, the small amount I grow helps to reduce my costs. It also helps reconnect and ground me to the earth. It helps me to remember again where and how my food is grown and reminds me not to take our wealth of available food options for granted.

I try not to be a fruit and vegetable snob — so, while I like my produce fresh (that is, seasonal) I think it is only common sense (and so much cheaper) to extend and preserve the bounty for the leaner times. Freezing, bottling, drying and preserving into jams, relishes, sauces and chutneys are all just plain old-fashioned good sense. All those blueberries we pick on a hot summer day go into jam or into the freezer for smoothies and pies, and hopefully last us until mid-winter. What I won't do is buy those blueberries fresh from the opposite hemisphere for me to have in winter. If I have none left in the freezer, then I will turn to what I have bottled, or the apples that abound at that time.

Grains

Unprocessed whole grains are excellent sources of many valuable nutrients; none of the goodness has been removed or oxidized. Best of all, when bought from a bulk bin they are incredibly cheap — even the organic variety. Not only do you pay a premium price for any processing whatsoever (including 'rolling' oats or other grains), but the nutritional content is also reduced. This premium price can range from 50% to 300% more! It's also far cheaper (and far more delicious) to make your own muesli and porridge mixes from whole grains.

One of my favourite books is called *The Splendid Grain* by Rebecca Wood, and whole grains — with only the inedible husk removed, leaving the germ and bran intact — are, indeed, splendid. Within this wondrous package nature has provided vitamins (especially the B family, and vitamin E), minerals, proteins (though not complete), good fats (including essential fatty acids and unsaturated fats), phytonutrients and phytochemicals, fibre and carbohydrate. This carbo-hydrate is in the form of starch, which breaks down to sugar, one of the basic fuel sources for the body. Both the fibre and fat in a whole grain help to slow the breakdown of this starch.

Fractionalized grains (for example, wheatgerm, white flours), no matter how fortified by added nutrients, will not give optimum health benefits. If you're looking for more vitamin E, for example, eating a wholegrain porridge with a dollop of cream or butter, or using a whole-wheat grain, will provide far better nutrition than wheatgerm added to your bowl, cakes, smoothies or muesli.

Grains are best soaked to reduce their phytic acid levels, enabling maximum availability of minerals such as zinc, calcium, magnesium and iron, which are otherwise bound by the phytic acid. Soaking also decreases the enzyme inhibitors in whole grains, and increases the vitamin content (most notably B vitamins).

BREAD

'Bread and butter' is how we describe the absolute basics of life — our bread and butter is what keeps us going, both metaphorically and literally. A piece of bread made from freshly ground grain is rich in vitamins, minerals, proteins, carbohydrate and good fats. The butter — especially when made from the milk of cows that graze on pasture rather than grain — is also mega-rich in nutrients, especially vitamins A and D, to name but a few. Unfortunately, much of the bread available today can no longer keep us going, and is doing more harm than good. Commercial bread is highly refined — all those good vitamins, minerals and fibre you read about are removed, and no amount of adding back or enriching can make it whole again.

What is good bread? The most nutritious bread is made from freshly ground whole grains. Stone-ground grain is better than grain ground on a steel mill, as the heat from the steel oxidizes the highly desirable fats.

The other aspect of bread is the rising agent — sourdough is definitely favoured over commercial yeast. Sourdough will break down the whole grain's phytic acid (which combines with iron, calcium, zinc and phosphorous and blocks their absorption) and 'pre-digests' the grain, making it easier for us to digest. Given a nice slow ferment and rise, sourdough will also break down gluten — not entirely, but it certainly makes a wheat bread more digestible. Breads made from sprouted grains follow the same principle and are much easier to digest. As my friend Kingsley (who makes the delicious bread I use) says, all you should see on a bread label is flour, water, salt and the yeast used (baker's yeast or sourdough) — anything else and the bread's a bit dodgy.

I don't actually make bread myself, but I go to great lengths to buy *good* bread. I don't always buy a freshly ground, wholemeal loaf as they are hard to find where I live. I go for the best I can find — an organic white wheat bread made with a wholemeal sourdough. It's wood fired and lovely and chewy, with a slightly sour tang.

FLOURS AND BAKING POWDER

Spelt is my preferred medium for all general baking — it behaves much the same as wheat flour, but is easier to digest because the gluten is not as hard. Spelt has a darker colour and produces a darker crumb. *Where wheat or spelt has been suggested* *in the following recipes, I have used spelt; thus they will be wheat free but not gluten free.* Also take into account that white spelts vary enormously — some are fine with little germ or fibre, and some are more similar to a light wholemeal. This matters, because the more 'wholemeal' your white spelt is, the more liquid it will absorb.

If you would prefer to replace the spelt (either the white or wholemeal) with wheat you can, but bear in mind that wheat is a harder gluten to digest, and some wheat flours can be very 'hard' (high protein) — great for pizza and pasta, but bad for cakes and pastry. In some places you can buy a 'cake' or 'pastry' wheat flour, which indicates it is a low-protein wheat flour, and will give softer results. Some other wheat flours include **atta** — a wholemeal wheat flour that has been sifted to remove some of the heavier bran. It is, so to speak, a light wholemeal wheat flour.

If you are looking for a wheat- and spelt-free alternative for baking, **oat flour** and **barley flour** are the best alternatives, but note that they are only available as a wholemeal flour, and oat flour will give a chewy consistency to the crumb. Oatmeal and oat flour are not finely ground rolled oats, but the coarse and fine grinding of the oat groat or kernel.

The best gluten-free flour is **brown or white rice flour**, which is always best 'softened' by mixing in some desiccated coconut or ground nuts. Small amounts of other gluten-free flours can be included — buckwheat, amaranth or quinoa. **Buckwheat** makes a beautiful-tasting flour, but is always best used in combination with brown rice flour. It absorbs large amounts of liquid and becomes quite viscous when left to sit. **Amaranth** and **quinoa flours** are both very assertive in flavour, and again are best used in small amounts with brown rice flour. **Millet flour** has a strongly astringent taste, and is also best used in partnership.

I never use commercial gluten-free baking flours. They are generally highly refined starches (potato, tapioca, corn) with gums thrown in to help it all stick together — they will do the same thing in your stomach.

Maize flour (sometimes called cornflour) is another flour I love to use. Made from 'flour corn', this gluten-free flour looks like a fine wholegrain flour, and is a beautiful pale yellow. It is a great choice for dredging patties in before pan-frying. The cornflour (cornstarch) commonly sold as a thickener for sauces is actually the pure white starch inside the grain.

Masa (or maseca) is a corn flour (thus gluten free) treated with lime and is used for making authentic corn tortillas. When dried it is called masa harina or maseca.

Baking powder is used to rise cakes and is best bought from a health or natural foods store. Most commercial brands use fast-acting alkalines and acids (sodium bicarbonate, sodium aluminium sulphate, phosphate aerator and sodium aluminium phosphate) which are often not body-compatible. Choose brands that use potassium bicarbonate and calcium phosphate as the rising agent.

Protein

Proteins are the building blocks of life, and are used by the body for numerous processes. Proteins are involved in making muscles, nerves and organs, and are essential for the formulation of hormones. Antibodies and enzymes are examples of specialized proteins.

Animal products — meat, fish, whole milk, cheese and eggs — are the best source of protein. While nuts, whole grains, legumes and sea vegetables (such as kombu) also contain protein, they do not carry the full range of amino acids, so the protein they provide is incomplete. Thus, one cannot thrive on either legumes or whole grains alone. Paired together, they complement each other, creating a more complete protein, although it is never as perfect as the protein from an animal product. This is why it is especially important for vegetarians to eat a wide range of protein foods. Tofu and tempeh are popular replacements for protein in a vegetarian diet, but they are not complete proteins either (tempeh is the better protein source), and must be used with care (see 'Soy products' on page 30).

EGGS

Eggs make an extremely sustaining and nutrient-rich meal. They are the most perfect of proteins — indeed, the quality of proteins in all other foods is rated against that in eggs. Among their many virtues are sulphur-containing proteins for cell membrane integrity; antioxidants; the amino acid tryptophan for a robust nervous system; and B vitamins for healthy nerves. Most importantly, they are rich in the fat-soluble vitamins A and D, and the essential fatty acid, omega-3. It pays to buy organic eggs — their omega-3 content is markedly higher than that of others. Please do not be afraid of good eggs, yolk and all.

Above and beyond the simple poached, fried, boiled and scrambled eggs, I like to include vegies with them, to extend the nutrients and fuel.

FISH

There is no better example of a nutrient-dense, cheap, delicious and easy-to-prepare meal than fish. Fish are a stunning source of protein, minerals and, in many cases, the long-chain omega-3 essential fatty acids. Sadly, though, our fish stocks are in serious trouble, with many fish facing extinction within our lifetime. The seafood you choose will have a profound and far-reaching impact on the future of our oceans, our rivers and the Earth. Three-quarters of the world's oceans are officially over-exploited or fished to their limit. Scientists recently warned that only 10% of our large, predatory fish (tuna, swordfish, marlin) and ground fish (cod, halibut, skate and flounder) remain.

You can make a difference by choosing fish that are sustainable, local, seasonal and unfarmed. I know there are many who feel farming is the way of the future, and the way in which we can save our oceans — I am not one of those. I see this as an ethical as well as an environmental issue, and feel that resorting to fish farming simply disconnects us from the consequences of our actions. We are short-sighted to think we can overfish the ocean, then turn to another way of raising fish when the ocean can no longer meet our demands.

For this reason you won't see recipes for salmon in this book — I live in Australia, and all our salmon is farmed. In fact, salmon farming has turned a majestic fish into 'the chicken of the sea'. If you live in a country that offers sustainable, wild-caught salmon, please enjoy it, but don't demand it all the time.

Very often the fish that meet the criteria of local, sustainable, seasonal and unfarmed are not 'poster' fish — easy to use and sweet tasting. Many are the oily, strong-tasting poorer cousins such as herring and mullet. The upside is that they are cheap — in many cases, very cheap. They are also packed full of omega-3 essential fatty acids. The recipes in this book offer ways to temper their assertive flavours and make them entirely delicious.

It's important to understand that the fish I am using here in Perth, Western Australia, may differ from the ones you have available to you. To find out which fish meet sustainable criteria in your country, check the internet for your relevant Marine Conservation Society, which will generally have a booklet you can download or buy.

LEGUMES — BEANS, SPLIT PEAS AND LENTILS

These are some of my favourite foods. A rich source of protein, legumes contain all eight essential amino acids, although they are less usable than those found in meat, eggs and poultry. Traditionally, legumes are served with some grain, which helps the plant proteins to complement each other's amino acid low point.

Legumes are an excellent source of complex carbohydrates, B complex vitamins, and minerals including iron, calcium, phosphorous and potassium, among others. It is important to note, however, that the iron contained in legumes (and all vegetable foods) is of the non-haem variety, which is not absorbed as readily as the haem iron in meat. However, eating food rich in vitamin C — for instance tomato, capsicum (pepper) and parsley — dramatically increases the amount of iron absorbed from plant sources.

Legumes are also an extremely rich source of fibre, beneficial in helping to maintain blood glucose levels. All legumes contain both omega-3 and omega-6 fatty acids. Red kidney beans and pinto beans are high in omega-3s; pinto beans are also high in omega-6.

The legume family is split into two groups: beans on the one hand, and lentils and split peas on the other. These two types of legumes require different preparation methods:

ଓ **beans** require pre-soaking and a long cooking time
ଓ **lentils** and **split peas** do not require pre-soaking (but can be pre-soaked) and have a shorter cooking time.

Beans contain long sugar chains (oligosaccharides) that cannot be digested by the stomach. These sugars ferment in the stomach and cause the most common problem of eating beans — wind. Soaking beans overnight in lots of water, then draining and cooking them for a long time breaks down these long sugar chains and solves this problem. Cooking beans with a piece of kombu sea vegetable will also help make them more digestible.

MEAT AND POULTRY

Meat is one of our best sources of complete protein and vitamin B12. Good meat comes from animals and birds that have had the opportunity to express their natural instincts — for example, calves weaned naturally from their mothers, or chickens that have foraged for insects and greens. Good meat comes from animals that eat their natural diets: for cows, sheep and goats this is grass, not grain.

Good meat has its fat intact — fat enables the body to utilize protein, and contains the fat-soluble vitamins A and D (pork fat is one of the richest sources of vitamin D). Do keep the fat on your meat. Fat from grass-fed animals is often yellow because of beta-carotene from grass. Most organic grass-fed meat is naturally lean, and requires less and lighter cooking than commercially produced meat.

Good meat also includes the organs from the animal, which are intensely rich sources of fat-soluble vitamins A and D.

I cannot express enough how important it is to choose organic meats, raised on grass or pasture. Most animals today are reared on grains and other foods such as genetically modified soy, corn or wheat — or worse, animal, factory and bakery waste. These foods are either incompatible with the animals' digestive systems or are not foods at all. Large amounts of antibiotics and hormones are also often included in their diets.

I have in the past been strongly opposed to meat. These days I understand that it was not the meat itself I was opposed to; it was the way in which it had become 'commodified'.

Learn to understand how the rearing of animals is labelled where you live. With chickens, 'free range' can mean anything — it may simply mean that the chickens have five minutes of 'freedom' per day. Appealing words and pictures are widely used by advertisers, but my best advice is to know where your meat comes from. If possible, buy it from the farmers or their direct outlets.

Good bacon or ham

Good bacon or ham starts with organic or biodynamic pigs, preferably grazing and eating their preferred foods. Nitrate- and preservative-free bacon or ham is made using a variety of natural ingredients including sea salt, water, sometimes honey, and herbs such as bay leaves or rosemary and smoke from local wood.

MILKS

Organic, non-homogenized full-cream milk will always give the best results when used in cooking, with a preference for non-pasteurized varieties. If you are using non-pasteurized milk, you absolutely must be sure that it is organic. If you can't tolerate cow's milk, a full-cream goat's milk is a great option.

If you require a dairy-free option, soy and oat milk are good replacements, but you will need to increase the fat to accommodate them. Rice milk is especially good; I always add coconut milk to give it fat, body and flavour. If a recipe calls for 250 ml (9 fl oz/1 cup) rice milk, one-third of that — 80 ml (2½ fl oz/⅓ cup) — should be coconut milk. Coconut milk in its own right is excellent, but its full flavour will need to complement what you are making or it will overpower the dish. Soy, oat and rice milk should never have any added minerals or vitamins such as calcium or vitamin D. Your body won't absorb that calcium out of context and the vitamin D will be synthetic.

SOY PRODUCTS

Because soy is considered to be very high in amino acids, soy products are a popular protein addition to many vegetarian diets. It is essential, however, that you understand the pros and cons of soy, and choose wisely.

There are many problems with soy: it is very high in phytates that bind with minerals and reduce their availability to the body; it is high in enzyme inhibitors, including one that inhibits trypsin (which is essential for digestion); it depresses thyroid function and is an endocrine disruptor; it is very high in phytoestrogens (which have a possible link to an increased risk of breast cancer).

Fermented soy products such as tempeh, natto, miso, tamari and shoyu are preferred over 'raw' soy in the form of milk and tofu, as fermenting breaks down phytates and some of the enzyme disrupters. It also makes the protein more digestible. Any soy product you buy should always be made from whole, organic soya beans, and never from soy protein isolate (SPI) or protein extract. It should always be first-generation — i.e. tempeh, natto, miso, tamari, shoyu, tofu or milk — and never processed items such as soy dogs, sausages or patties.

When used as a replacement for dairy or protein, soy can play a great role, but should be used with care. Because of its phytoestrogens it should only be used in small amounts by children, and by women during pregnancy or breastfeeding.

Salt

Real salt is an important part of healthy eating — I keep and use three kinds.

Celtic sea salt

This is hand harvested, containing approximately 80 minerals in ionized form — it is these minerals that give the salt its grey colour. This salt is beautiful, and a powerful aid to digestion.

Herbamare

This is sea salt infused with biodynamic herbs and vegetables. I choose this salt when I want to add flavour — for example, when making a béchamel sauce.

Umeboshi plum — whole or paste

These are plums (sometimes apricots) that are pickled with salt and leaves from the herb 'shiso' (also called perilla). I use it when I want the addition of fruit to help balance the dish.

Sweeteners

I use a range of sweeteners for cooking, especially when making cakes, biscuits (cookies) and desserts. I really dislike the flavour and harsh sweetness of refined white sugar which is, essentially, bleached pure sucrose. You might be surprised to know that whole sweeteners — the ones I prefer to use — are good sources of vitamins and minerals.

Rapadura sugar, maple syrup (two of my favourites) and cane sugar are all sucrose-based sweeteners.

I never use fruit juice concentrates for baking, and am not a big fan of fructose-based sweeteners as they are highly disruptive to body chemistry, especially for children. However, I do keep both apple juice concentrate and pear juice concentrate for balancing out savoury dishes. **Apple juice concentrate** is an especially good counterpart for tomato, and makes beautiful chutney. **Pear juice concentrate** has a higher 'top note' than apple juice concentrate, and more fruit flavour — it's wonderful to balance out the astringency of lentils, and is delicious in curries and dal.

I rarely use **stevia**, even though it is entirely body-compatible and has been used as a sweetener for centuries and as a remedy for diabetes. It is available as a liquid, a white powder (where the sweetening components are separated) and in a more whole form, where the leaves are ground into a fine powder. Stevia is intensely sweet — but use too much and you will end up with a very bitter result. It is excellent in sweetening fruit desserts, but not as good in baked goods.

Rapadura sugar

Rapadura is made from organic cane sugar, where the cane juice is filtered, the fibre removed, and what remains is crystallized. It retains its valuable vitamins and minerals. Brands vary — some are quite moist, some are quite dry. Because it is so unrefined, rapadura sugar colours the product it is cooked with, and contributes less sweetening. Rapadura contains approximately 75% sucrose, compared with 99% sucrose in a white sugar.

When a little more sweetness and less colour is required, I use the lighter-flavoured, slightly more refined sugars that have been washed (sometimes referred to as 'sifted') to remove the colour and flavour that molasses gives. It also concentrates the sucrose and the end result is about 85% sucrose. It's important to understand this — 1 cup of white sugar will sweeten more than 1 cup of a lighter unrefined, washed sugar (such as unrefined raw sugar), which will in turn sweeten more than 1 cup of rapadura sugar.

Brands vary but a wide range of these unrefined, less coloured sugars are available. They vary in crystal size — from very fine icing (confectioners') and caster (superfine) sugars, to the fine and larger all-purpose varieties, to the larger demerara sugar.

Maple syrup

This is probably the easiest whole sweetener to use — you only need a small amount for wonderful flavour and sweetness, and it's rich in trace minerals, including calcium. It's far cheaper to buy it in bulk, but be particular about the brand you use — I prefer organic varieties, as many can contain formaldehyde traces from the pellets used in the trees to extend the sap flow. (This is not permitted under organic certification, or by the Canadian government.)

Palm sugar (jaggery)

This is the concentrated sap made from the coconut palm, and has the most beautiful flavour. It is also sometimes called coconut sugar. Grades and colours vary, but I prefer the darker varieties. It can be sold as a small log, wrapped in paper, and is best cut off in thin slivers using a sharp knife. Others brands are set into a small plastic container — I prefer not to use these as the sugar can be very hard. Look for a brand that crumbles and slices easily.

Brown rice syrup

Also called brown rice malt, this is a highly body-compatible, maltose-based sweetener. It's sticky and difficult to use, but has its place. It retains its syrupy consistency even when cooked, but tends to crisp (like toffee) when directly exposed to heat — crusts of a cake cooked with it will be crisp, and the insides a bit chewy. It's great in biscuits (cookies), excellent in 'creams' and works well when cut with maple syrup. It's also wonderful drizzled over porridge and pancakes.

Barley malt

Barley malt is another maltose-based sweetener, wonderfully body-compatible, but very sticky and difficult to use. It's very strongly flavoured (think beer) but also has its place, generally mixed with brown rice syrup and maple syrup.

Raw honey

Raw honey is much sweeter than processed honey and contains both sucrose and fructose. I do adore good honey, but prefer not to bake it and destroy its enzymes. Always choose raw honey — unfiltered, unprocessed, unrefined and unheated — as it will still have its enzymes intact, and use it anywhere it doesn't need to be heated. Raw honey must not be used for children under 12 months as their digestive and immune systems are not yet fully developed.

Agave nectar

This is a wonderful, light and sticky syrup (sap, so to speak) from the agave plant. It is good in 'crème' desserts instead of maple syrup, which tends to darken the end result.

Thickening agents

Cornflour (cornstarch), tapioca, arrowroot and kudzu (kuzu) are all starch-based thickeners and have their uses. Of these thickeners, I prefer to use kudzu. Agar, a sea vegetable, is another useful gelling agent.

Kudzu (kuzu)

Made from the root of the kudzu plant, kudzu is well known in Japan and China for its medicinal qualities, where it is traditionally used to treat digestive problems such as upset stomach and to soothe the nerves. Kudzu is gluten free. When used to thicken sauces it imparts a beautiful, clear sheen to the finished sauce. It will also set soft puddings. It must be completely dissolved (generally in a little liquid) before using, and then gently brought to the boil while stirring constantly. As a guide, 2 teaspoons will set 250 ml (9 fl oz/1 cup) of liquid to a sauce consistency, while 2–2½ tablespoons will set liquid to a soft pudding consistency. Kudzu is usually sold in solid form. To measure it, simply grind it up in a bowl using the end of a rolling pin, or using a pestle and mortar.

Arrowroot

Similar in appearance to cornflour (cornstarch), arrowroot comes from the root of a tropical plant and is gluten free. It can be used to thicken sauces, but I rarely use this product because true arrowroot isn't readily available where I live. It is most often tapioca (cassava) flour, which behaves a little differently to true arrowroot as it gives a more viscous and 'gooey' sauce.

Cornflour (cornstarch)

An extremely finely ground gluten-free starch, cornflour is particularly useful where some 'structure' is required in the finished product, such as baked goods as opposed to a sauce. In small portions it is also used as a flour, to aid binding. Check the packet when you buy cornflour as it is often actually made from wheat.

Agar

This nutrient-rich, high-fibre, flavourless sea vegetable acts as a gelling agent and is invaluable for making dairy-free creams and mousses. Agar will set at room temperature and can be boiled and reheated without losing its gelling ability. Agar is sold in flakes, powder and bars; I have specified powder in most recipes as it gives more reliable results. Some batches of flakes are stronger than others, and the consistency of their setting can vary enormously.

To achieve a good (but not too solid) jelly, the basic equation is 3 teaspoons agar flakes or ½ teaspoon powder to 250 ml (9 fl oz/1 cup) liquid. For a very firm jelly (when you want to turn out the jelly and cut it into shapes), use 1½ tablespoons agar flakes, or ¾ teaspoon powder.

Agar dissolves best in high-pectin juices like apple, but works in most fruit juices. It does not dissolve very easily in milk. When using the flakes and powder in recipes, they need to be dissolved slowly over a very gentle boil and stirred very frequently to stop them clumping or sticking to the bottom of the pan.

Agar will not set in distilled and wine vinegars, or in food containing large amounts of oxalic acid (such as chocolate, rhubarb or spinach).

Storage

The foods you need to store most carefully are those that contain fat, as fat becomes rancid when exposed to heat, light or air.

All **whole grains, wholemeal flours**, **seeds** and **nuts** contain fat. The reason grains were originally refined was to extend their shelf life by removing the germ, which contains fat. In warm weather these items should be kept in a cool place — preferably the fridge or cellar. Summer is very hot where I live, so I buy smaller amounts of these foods during this season. During the rest of the year, I store them in glass containers in my pantry.

I keep all fats and oils in the fridge during the hotter weather; during the cooler months I keep the **coconut** and **olive oils** out at room temperature.

Legumes bought in bulk go into glass jars in the pantry. **Sugars** most often come in their packets, and these I group together in a plastic storage container. **Dried fruits** are kept in glass jars, and in summer moved to the fridge — this is to avoid any problems with weevils, which love organic dried fruits.

IN THE PANTRY

To save space, I keep food groups together, and pack items such as flours and grains in their own containers. Here are the basic items I like to have on hand.

Tins
Tomatoes, fire-roasted tomatoes, coconut cream. Kidney, borlotti (cranberry) and black (turtle) beans.

Dairy substitutes
Rice milk, coconut milk.

Dried foods
Dried shiitake and porcini mushrooms.

Flours and baking needs
White and wholemeal spelt, oat flour and oatmeal, barley flour, buckwheat flour, yellow corn/maize flour, masa harina. Baking powder, desiccated coconut. Vanilla beans, natural vanilla extract, vanilla paste.

Grains and pasta
Buckwheat groats, brown long- and short-grain rice, brown arborio rice, wild rice, white basmati rice, quinoa (white and red), oat kernels, rolled (porridge) oats, hulled millet, barley (pearled and natural), polenta. Soba (100% buckwheat) noodles, wholegrain couscous, wholegrain pasta, my daughter's home-made pasta, ramen noodles, rice noodles, rice paper.

Legumes
Dried beans: black (turtle), pinto, borlotti (cranberry), cannellini, butter (lima), great northern. Chickpeas, black-eyed peas, mung dal, yellow and green split peas. Lentils: brown, green, split red lentils, whole red lentils.

Oils
Extra virgin olive oil, unrefined coconut oil, deodorized/flavourless coconut oil, roasted sesame oil.

Sauces
Wheat-free tamari, soy sauce, mirin, fish sauce, sweet chilli, kelpamare, whey concentrate.

Sea vegetables
Agar powder and flakes, arame, nori paper, kombu, wakame.

Spices
Cinnamon (ground and sticks), whole nutmeg (and grater), whole cloves, whole cardamom, cumin (seeds and ground), coriander (seeds and ground), chilli (chipotle powder and New Mexico powder), yellow and red mustard seeds, fennel seeds, juniper seeds, peppercorns, turmeric, paprika, ground ginger, ground mustard, dried herbs (thyme, basil, oregano, sage), asafoetida.

Sweeteners
Raw sugar, raw caster (superfine) sugar, unrefined icing (confectioners') sugar, rapadura sugar, palm sugar (jaggery), maple syrup, rice syrup (malt), barley malt, agave nectar. Honey, apple and pear juice concentrate.

Thickeners
Arrowroot, kudzu (kuzu), cornflour (cornstarch).

Vinegars
Apple cider, brown rice, umeboshi, balsamic.

IN THE FRIDGE

The following staples stay in my fridge year-round: flax oil, hazelnut oil, almond oil, unrefined sesame oil, tahini, nuts, linseeds (flax seeds), sesame seeds, pepitas (pumpkin seeds), sunflower seeds, nut butters, mustards, quince paste, curry pastes, white (shiro) miso and brown rice (genmai) miso (both unpasteurized and/or pasteurized).

When summer comes I move as many of my grains, flours and dried fruits as possible to the fridge.

Cooking up magic

There is a lot more to cooking than simply following a recipe, and although some might say it's not rocket science, it is a skill nonetheless. Give two or three people the same recipe and the results will generally be very different! For the best results, the most important elements to always bear in mind are the actual ingredients themselves, and the method and process of heat transfer.

START WITH THE BEST INGREDIENTS

Firstly to the quality of the ingredients used. I know this seems like a 'no-brainer', but surprisingly it is so often overlooked. I find that organic or biodynamically raised animals (preferably grass-fed), animal products (milk, eggs, yoghurt, cheese etc), fruit, vegetables and grains have a consistently better flavour.

Equally important is the issue of how fresh the ingredients are. Meat and grain products do have a longer 'shelf life', but fruit and vegetables begin to lose their 'life force' (their flavour and goodness) the minute they are pulled from the ground, tree or bush. Even the most luscious organic apple will be a sad and sorry shadow of its former self, both in flavour and nutritional content, after a few months of cold storage. Thus I am a firm believer in seasonal products — a fruit or vegetable is best when it is fresh, and this will mean in season. The closer to picking you eat or cook it, the better it will taste. This taste will reflect in your finished dish. Fruit and vegies that have been in cold storage for months will not give you a good end result, and tastewise you might even be better off with a freshly pulled conventionally grown product. However, I would choose to give that recipe a miss altogether and cook with what I could get that was fresh and organic.

The general rule of thumb is this: the simpler a dish is — especially when vegetarian — the more important it is that the initial ingredients are fresh, and to my mind, organic.

TURN UP THE HEAT

Now to the second important point: how you choose to transfer heat during cooking is critical, and some cooking vessels do this better than others. This particular aspect of cooking is most relevant to stews, braises and gratins.

The best piece of cooking advice I can give in this area is to go out and buy yourself some enamel-coated (or not) cast iron. Don't bother about the smaller saucepans here, I mean the French ovens (of all sizes, but generally 24 cm/ 9½ inches upwards), casseroles and baking dishes. If you want a very high heat, they will retain and reflect that heat; if you want a low heat they will hold and warmly bathe the entire contents. They behave so differently to stainless steel, as even the best stainless steel cannot hold heat in the way that cast iron does. They will make the difference between an ordinary and stunning end result.

China and glass do not hold, transfer or reflect heat well, and I'm not a fan of these when you are trying to develop flavour. They're fine for mixing something up and then putting it into a dish to brown or cook through, but not when you are depending on the cooking process to work its alchemy.

This is also true for pastry — make sure the tinware you use for baking is good quality, not the flimsy, cheap stuff, as proper tinware will allow a quick transfer of heat, resulting in lovely, crisp pastry.

For roasting, cast iron is fabulous, but a simple, cheap enamel dish (think camping equipment) will also give you a great end result.

Heat transfer also involves *your oven*. Every oven is different, so forget about what the manufacturer says, get to know yours. Buy yourself an oven thermometer and check how true your thermostat is. *The oven temperatures specified for the recipes in this book are for a conventional oven.*

If your oven is fan forced, you'll need to lower your oven temperature by about 10–15°C (50–60°F) from the specified conventional temperature. A moderate oven is generally 180°C (350°F/Gas 4); for a fan-forced one this will be anywhere from 150°C to 165°C (300–320°F/Gas 2–3). Also, check if it is a high fan or a low fan — higher ones will cook food in about two-thirds of the time, even set at the same temperature. Conventional ovens will take longer still, and food will need to be positioned higher in the oven, as heat rises.

Remembering these simple basics will help you gain the cooking results you are looking for. Enjoy!

breakfast

A good breakfast is essential and needn't take long to put together. Breakfast can be anything (good) you like — it doesn't have to be cereal or eggs. In fact, it could be soup or stew from the night before.

There are three main breakfast categories: wholegrains, protein and fruit. Of these, protein breakfasts (see 'The breakfast cook-up', page 53), are the most sustaining. ✳

Wholegrain breakfasts

Wholegrain porridges for breakfast are wonderful sources of slow-release energy, provide excellent fibre and are inexpensive. It's far cheaper to make your own muesli (such as the muesli mix in the Muesli Bars on page 49) and porridge mixes than to buy them — and the results are far more delicious. Wholegrain flours can be used to make delicious breakfast pancakes, waffles and muffins.

The 'down' side with wholegrain porridges is that they can take a long time to cook. I get around this to some extent by soaking the grain overnight. This can reduce the cooking time by 10–15 minutes for the longer-cooking grains; however, it won't reduce the time for the quicker-cooking grains such as oats, hulled millet, quinoa, buckwheat and polenta (I often don't even bother to soak hulled millet or buckwheat). I get up, prepare the porridge and put it on the stove. While it comes to the boil, I usually make my morning cup of tea. Once it comes to the boil, I place a heat diffuser underneath, then set the timer for the allotted cooking time. Really, by the time I have had my tea and done what I have needed to do, the grain is ready.

For the longer-cooking grains — wheat, spelt, rye, kamut, barley and sometimes oats — I either grind them in the blender before soaking (so that they cook more quickly), or plan these porridges for a day when I don't have to scream out of the house. I usually make more than I need and put the extra in the fridge for the next day. ❧

Time saver

MAKE EXTRA PORRIDGE AND STORE IT IN THE FRIDGE. IT WILL SET TO AN ALMOST CAKE-LIKE CONSISTENCY — BUT PLACE IT IN A SAUCEPAN OVER LOW HEAT WITH A LITTLE MORE LIQUID AND IN 5 MINUTES YOU HAVE BREAKFAST

A real oat porridge with cinnamon stewed apples

WHEAT FREE

SERVES 3 - 4

Rather than cooking the oat groats whole, save time by roughly grinding them in the blender — it also gives a creamier result. Adding a delicious cooked fruit to the basic porridge changes the entire dynamic. You could either prepare the apples while the porridge is cooking — making extra for tonight's dessert — or save some from dessert the night before.

200 g (7 oz/1 cup) oat groats/kernels (see Kitchen notes)
1 tablespoon yoghurt, or 2 teaspoons whey or lemon juice, for soaking

For serving

6–8 tablespoons good-quality, full-cream yoghurt or coconut milk
brown rice syrup, honey or maple syrup, to taste
2 tablespoons combined ground pepitas (pumpkin seeds), sunflower seeds
   and linseeds (flax seeds)

Cinnamon stewed apples

3 large apples (550 g/1 lb 4 oz in total), peeled, cored and fairly thickly sliced
1 tablespoon maple syrup or rapadura sugar
90 ml (3 fl oz) apple or pear juice
¼ teaspoon ground cinnamon
½ teaspoon natural vanilla extract
1 teaspoon kudzu (kuzu) or cornflour (cornstarch)

Place the oat groats in the blender and roughly grind — a couple of pulses should do the trick. Tip into a bowl.

If possible, soak the groats overnight in 500 ml (17 fl oz/2 cups) water with the yoghurt, whey or lemon juice. (This mixture can sit at room temperature, even in summer. You can reserve the soaking water for cooking the porridge, or discard and use fresh water.) Pour the mixture into a sieve, then place the drained oats in a saucepan with 750 ml (26 fl oz/3 cups) water.

If the groats are unsoaked, rinse them well and place in a saucepan with 875 ml (30 fl oz/3½ cups) water.

Place over a gentle heat and bring to the boil, then reduce to a slow simmer. Cook for 20–25 minutes if soaked, and 30 minutes if unsoaked, or until the oats are tender. If the porridge is too thin, increase the heat and bring to a rapid boil to encourage evaporation, stirring frequently until thick enough.

While the porridge is cooking, prepare the apples. In a saucepan, combine the apples, maple syrup, 60 ml (2 fl oz/¼ cup) of the fruit juice, the cinnamon and vanilla. Cover and cook over a gentle heat, stirring occasionally, for 8 minutes, or until the apples are *just* tender. In a cup, combine the kudzu and remaining fruit juice, then add to the apples and cook, stirring constantly, until thickened.

Time saver

LEFTOVER APPLES ARE DELICIOUS FOR AFTERNOON TEA WITH PIKELETS (GRIDDLE CAKES), OR IN A PIE WITH CUSTARD, OR IN A CRUMBLE (YOU COULD USE THE CRUMBLE TOPPING FROM THE PEACH ANZACS RECIPE ON PAGE 171)

Spoon the porridge into serving bowls. Top each bowl with the stewed apples, 2 tablespoons yoghurt or coconut milk, sweetener to taste, and a sprinkle of the ground seeds.

KITCHEN NOTES: *If you cannot find oat groats/kernels, buy 'steel-cut' oats (also called Scottish oats). These are simply the oat groats cut into smaller pieces.*

ଓ

Black sticky rice with coconut milk and mango

GLUTEN FREE

SERVES 6

I was introduced to black sticky rice in my Byron Bay days and I still think it's one of the best summer breakfasts around. Black sticky rice is a sweet rice variety, with a black bran and endosperm. Thai black sticky rice is long grain; Chinese is short grain. They both become sticky and glutinous when cooked. Black sticky rice is a brilliant 'take with you' snack. Put the cooked rice in a container, pour over some coconut milk or cream and you have a wonderful morning tea after a protein or vegetable breakfast.

200 g (7 oz/1 cup) black sticky (glutinous) rice
1 tablespoon yoghurt, or 2 teaspoons whey or lemon juice, for soaking
4 fresh dates, pitted and roughly chopped

For serving
2 mangoes, sliced
500 ml (17 fl oz/2 cups) coconut milk, approximately
40 g (1½ oz/¼ cup) sesame seeds, lightly toasted (optional)
shaved palm sugar (jaggery) or maple syrup

Time saver

MAKE MORE THAN YOU NEED OF THIS. LEFTOVER BLACK STICKY RICE WILL SET TO AN ALMOST CAKE-LIKE CONSISTENCY. IT CAN BE STORED IN THE FRIDGE AND USED AGAIN THE NEXT MORNING — JUST ADD SOME EXTRA LIQUID

Put the rice in a glass or stainless steel bowl. If possible, soak overnight in 750 ml (26 fl oz/3 cups) water with the yoghurt, whey or lemon juice. (This mixture can sit at room temperature, even in summer.) Pour the mixture into a sieve, then place the drained rice in a saucepan with 2 litres (70 fl oz/8 cups) water, and the dates.

If the grain is unsoaked, simply rinse well and place in a saucepan with 2.25 litres (79 fl oz/9 cups) water.

Place the rice over a gentle heat, bring to the boil, then reduce to a slow simmer, stirring from time to time. If you are worried the pan will boil dry, place a heat diffuser underneath, but make sure there is still a slow simmer. Cook for 50 minutes if soaked, and 70 minutes if unsoaked, or until the rice is tender. If the 'porridge' is too thin, increase the heat and bring to a rapid boil to encourage evaporation, stirring frequently until thick enough.

Spoon the rice into bowls, top each with mango slices and drizzle with coconut milk. Sprinkle with sesame seeds if using, and palm sugar or maple syrup to taste.

VARIATIONS

There are so many versions of black sticky rice. Other flavourings you could add to the rice during cooking are:

3 – 4 pandanus leaves
zest of 1 lemon or lime
seeds from 4 cardamom pods
palm sugar (jaggery) as desired

߷

Buckwheat and quinoa waffles or pancakes
with a cinnamon orange sauce

GLUTEN FREE

ANY MILK CAN BE USED IN THIS RECIPE, BUT IF USING A VERY LOW-FAT MILK SUCH AS OAT, SOY, ALMOND OR RICE, I WOULD SUGGEST USING ONLY 375 ML (13 FL OZ/ 1½ CUPS) AND ADDING 125 ML (4 FL OZ/½ CUP) COCONUT MILK TO MOISTEN IT

Take a whole grain and soak it overnight. The next morning add yummy things to it, blend it up and in a couple of minutes you have the best possible mixture for waffles or pancakes, with all the goodness intact. This is a great way to enjoy wholegrain breakfasts in summer. The delicious orange sauce ensures a lovely soft mouthfeel, but these waffles or pancakes are also delicious with the Honey and Cinnamon Yoghurt Cream (page 196). They are best eaten warm on the day they are made, but will freeze well. To heat frozen ones, wrap them in baking paper, then a layer of foil so they don't dry out, and place in a warm oven. Any leftover uncooked batter will keep for a day, covered, in the fridge.

200 g (7 oz/1 cup) buckwheat groats
200 g (7 oz/1 cup) quinoa
500 ml (17 fl oz/2 cups) milk
1 tablespoon yoghurt, or 1 teaspoon whey or lemon juice
1 egg
60 ml (2 fl oz/¼ cup) coconut milk
2 tablespoons melted coconut oil, butter or ghee
1 tablespoon (or less) rapadura sugar or raw sugar
45 g (1½ oz/½ cup) desiccated coconut
½ teaspoon baking powder
½ teaspoon cinnamon
¼ teaspoon ground cardamom
finely grated zest of 1 orange
maple syrup, brown rice syrup or honey, to taste
coconut oil or ghee, for frying

Orange sauce
1 tablespoon kudzu (kuzu)
500 ml (17 fl oz/2 cups) orange juice
1 cinnamon stick
2 tablespoons maple syrup

For serving
good-quality, full-cream yoghurt or coconut milk
ground pepitas (pumpkin seeds), sunflower seeds and linseeds (flax seeds)
stewed or poached seasonal fruit as desired (see 'Cooked fruit desserts',
    pages 197–202)

Put the buckwheat in a frying pan. Lightly toast over a gentle heat, shaking the pan frequently for even toasting. Tip into a bowl and add the quinoa, milk, and the whey, yoghurt or lemon juice. Refrigerate overnight.

Next morning, put the buckwheat mixture in a blender with the egg, coconut milk, melted coconut oil, sugar, coconut, baking powder, cinnamon, cardamom and orange zest. Give it a good blend (quinoa can be a bit stubborn) — the batter should be smooth, but will still be heavily textured.

To make the orange sauce, put the kudzu in a saucepan and mix in a small amount of the orange juice to make a slurry. Add the remaining orange juice and the cinnamon stick. Cook over medium heat, stirring continually until boiled. Allow to boil for a few seconds, then remove from the heat. Taste and adjust the sweetness with maple syrup, then set aside. Leave the cinnamon stick in until ready to serve.

To make pancakes, heat the oil or ghee in a frying pan, using enough to just coat the base. When a small amount of batter dropped into the pan sizzles, the oil is ready — it should not be smoking. (To indicate a good temperature, the oil should be gently sizzling around the batter. If the pan is too hot, the pancakes will burn before the inside is cooked.) Drop 2–3 tablespoons of the batter into the pan to form a pancake about 9–10 cm (3½–4 inches) in diameter. Cook for 2–3 minutes on each side, or until lightly golden. Remove from the pan and keep warm while cooking the remaining pancakes.

To make waffles, brush a heated waffle iron lightly with either coconut oil or ghee and cook until ready — this will be about 5 minutes for an electric waffle iron. Cook the waffles in batches, keeping them warm in a low oven.

Serve with the orange sauce, some yoghurt or coconut milk, and a sprinkle of ground seeds. Stewed seasonal fruit is a delicious addition.

ଓଃ

LEFTOVER PANCAKES MAKE AN EXCELLENT GLUTEN-FREE FLATBREAD TO SERVE WITH SOUP IN WINTER — YOU CAN OMIT THE SUGAR. IF SERVING THEM IN THIS WAY THEY ARE BEST USED THE SAME DAY THEY ARE MADE, OR KEPT FROZEN AND THEN WARMED

Christmas morning scones

WHEAT FREE

MAKES 16

So called because we get up early to see what Santa has brought, unwrap presents and generally go crazy, and it's all a bit early for a big breakfast, given we have a huge lunch. These scones take no time to prepare and are divine with a cup of tea or coffee. Dried blueberries are expensive, hence their appearance for this special Christmas morning treat. At other times, you could easily use grated orange zest and currants. The scones freeze brilliantly and are easily warmed in the oven.

375 g (13 oz/3 cups) plain (all-purpose) white spelt flour
85 g (3 oz/½ cup) rapadura or raw sugar
1½ tablespoons baking powder
1 teaspoon apple cider vinegar
250 ml (9 fl oz/1 cup) full-cream, non-homogenized milk or buttermilk
150 g (5½ oz) chilled butter, cut into small pieces
90 g (3¼ oz/½ cup) dried blueberries
zest of 1 lemon
butter, to serve (optional)

Preheat the oven to 200°C (400°F/Gas 6). Line a baking tray with baking paper. Put the flour, sugar and baking powder in a bowl and mix well to thoroughly combine. Add the vinegar to the milk and set aside.

Using your fingertips, rub the butter into the dry ingredients until the mixture resembles breadcrumbs. Mix the blueberries and lemon zest through. Pour in the soured milk and mix to just combine — take care not to overmix.

Divide the dough in half and place on a lightly floured surface. Gently press (don't knead) to form each into a circle 10–12 cm (4–4½ inches) in diameter and about 2.5 cm (1 inch) thick. Using a sharp, floured knife, cut each circle into eight wedges and place on the lined tray. Repeat with the other dough. Bake for 20 minutes, or until lightly browned and just cooked in the middle (break one open to check). Remove and serve as they are, or with butter.

℃

Muesli bars

WHEAT FREE / DAIRY FREE / VEGAN

MAKES 12 LARGE OR 18 MEDIUM MUESLI BARS

Even when made entirely with organic ingredients, these are still far cheaper to make than to buy. They're quick too — so it's a win all round. These muesli bars are sweetened with body-compatible brown rice syrup.

    200 g (7 oz/2 cups) rolled (porridge) oats
    40 g (1½ oz/¼ cup) sesame seeds
    30 g (1 oz/¼ cup) pepitas (pumpkin seeds)
    30 g (1 oz/¼ cup) sunflower seeds
    60 g (2¼ oz/½ cup) sultanas (golden raisins)
    25 g (1 oz/¼ cup) desiccated coconut
    45 g (1½ oz/¼ cup) of your favourite dried fruit, finely diced
    90 ml (3 fl oz) flavourless coconut oil, measured in liquid state
        (see Kitchen notes)
    45 ml (1½ fl oz) brown rice syrup
    45 ml (1½ fl oz) maple syrup

Preheat the oven to 180°C (350°F/Gas 4). Line a 28 x 18 cm (11¼ x 7 inch), 3.5 cm (1½ inch) deep biscuit (cookie) tray with baking paper. Do not trim the corners of the baking paper to fit neatly into the tray — this will allow some of the syrup from the muesli bar to leak through and stick, making it difficult to lift out later.

Put all the dry ingredients in a bowl and mix through to get rid of any clumps.

Measure the coconut oil into a small bowl, then the syrups (the oily spoon will make it easier to measure the brown rice syrup). Mix together, then pour over the dry ingredients and mix through well. Tip the mixture into the biscuit tray and press down well using the back of a spoon. Bake for 25–30 minutes, or until golden and ever so slightly crisp on the edges. Remove from the oven and allow to cool completely.

When the muesli bar has cooled, lift the longer sides of the baking paper and swiftly remove to a chopping board. Cut into bars using a good, sharp knife. (The brown rice syrup can sometimes make things a little sticky — especially with bars that are not fully cooked.) If the bars tear apart as you are cutting, just leave them to cool a little longer.

Time savers

INDIVIDUALLY WRAP THE MUESLI BARS IN WAXED PAPER AND STORE IN AN AIRTIGHT CONTAINER. THEY MAKE AN EXCELLENT TAKE-ANYWHERE SNACK

FOR A QUICK BREAKFAST OR AFTERNOON TEA, CRUMBLE A MUESLI BAR INTO A BOWL AND SERVE WITH YOGHURT (THE YOGHURT WILL ENHANCE DIGESTION)

KITCHEN NOTES: *If the coconut oil is solid (when the weather is cooler, or it has been in the fridge), place a small amount in a small pot and gently melt it. Any leftover oil can be poured straight back into the jar.*

◆

Keep the uncooked muesli mixture in an airtight container (glass is best) in a cool, dark spot to protect the valuable oils and you will have muesli mix on hand for a quick breakfast, or for making muesli bars or breakfast muffins. Feel free to include nuts — I have left them out as so many schools ban them nowadays.

ॐ

Breakfast muffins
WHEAT FREE

MAKES 10 – 12 MUFFINS

Look in any café and you'll see something posing as a muffin — white, enormous, no flavour, sweet and tasteless. Muffins are not nutrient dense or sustaining enough to make a good breakfast but, if you have to do it, these are the sort I recommend. Muesli and wholemeal flour are soaked overnight to make for a quick job the next morning, but more importantly, the soaking breaks down the phytic acid and anti-nutrients, making them more digestible. These muffins freeze beautifully.

140 g (5 oz/1 cup) muesli
125 g (4½ oz/1 cup) plain (all-purpose) wholemeal spelt flour
60 g (2¼ oz/¼ cup) yoghurt
2½ teaspoons baking powder
1 egg
90 g (3¼ oz/½ cup) rapadura sugar, or 115 g (4 oz/⅓ cup) honey
60 g (2¼ oz) butter, melted and cooled a little
a 250 ml (9 fl oz/1 cup) measure of fresh fruit, peeled if necessary, and
    chopped into 1–1.5 cm (½–⅝ inch) dice if large

Topping
40 g (1½ oz / ¼ cup) almonds or 30 g (1 oz / ¼ cup) walnuts, roughly chopped
2 tablespoons rapadura or light brown sugar
2 tablespoons desiccated coconut
½ teaspoon ground cinnamon

The night before, put the muesli and flour in a small bowl. Mix the yoghurt with 350 ml (12 fl oz) water, then stir through the muesli mixture. Refrigerate overnight.

The next morning, heat the oven to 180°C (350°F/Gas 4). Stir the baking powder through the muesli — the mixture will be thick.

In a separate bowl, mix together the egg and sugar. Add to the muesli with the butter and stir through. Gently fold in the fruit, then spoon into a 12-hole muffin tin.

Toss the topping ingredients in a bowl and spoon over the muffins. Bake for 30–35 minutes, or until the muffins are lightly golden, slightly cracked in the centre, and don't look wet. Serve warm.

VARIATIONS

Use plain (all-purpose) white spelt flour instead of wholemeal, and reduce the soaking water by 40 ml (1¼ fl oz).

Berries are lovely in these muffins — especially blueberries (frozen is fine) — as are apricot, apple, pear and banana. For slightly drier fruits such as apple, pear or banana, you can add a little more than specified if you like. I tend to avoid the wetter fruits such as fresh peaches, plums and mangoes.

C3

THESE MUFFINS ARE MOIST AND NEED TO BE KEPT IN THE FRIDGE WHEN THE WEATHER IS HOT. THEY ARE BEST ENJOYED WARM ON THE DAY THEY ARE MADE. ALLOW ANY UNEATEN MUFFINS TO COOL, THEN FREEZE FOR FUTURE USE

TO REHEAT THE FROZEN MUFFINS, SIMPLY PLACE IN A MODERATE OVEN FOR 15 MINUTES, OR UNTIL THAWED AND WARM

Flapjacks

GLUTEN FREE / DAIRY FREE

MAKES 6

SERVED WITH EGGS, FLAPJACKS ARE A GREAT ALTERNATIVE TO BREAD. THEY ARE ALSO DELICIOUS IN A BREAKFAST COOK-UP, MAKE A LOVELY LUNCH SERVED WITH STEAMED VEGIES OR THE BIG GREEN (PAGE 108), OR A PERFECT SUNDAY NIGHT DINNER

Great for breakfast, lunch or dinner and quick to put together, these flapjacks are well received by children and adults alike. I think it's because of the crispy, golden taste of potatoes — a healthy version of hash browns. Leftovers are fine cold, or you can quickly reheat them for a snack on the run.

2 celery stalks, finely chopped
3–4 basil leaves, finely sliced
2 tablespoons finely chopped fresh parsley
2 eggs
1 large potato (300 g/10½ oz), skin on, scrubbed well
ghee or olive oil (or a mixture of both), for frying

Put the celery, basil, parsley and eggs in a bowl and whisk well. Grate the potato — peel and all — into the bowl and mix through. Season with sea salt and freshly ground black pepper.

Heat 1 tablespoon of ghee in a frying pan over medium heat. When the ghee is hot, but not at all smoking, add 2 tablespoons of the mixture to the pan — it should sizzle a little. Spread into a rough pattie about 8 cm (3¼ inches) across. Cook over a gently sizzling heat for 6–8 minutes, or until golden. The key to success is a nice, moderate heat that allows the potato to cook through without burning the outside, but allowing enough time and heat to make the outside golden and crispy.

Turn and cook the other side for 5 minutes, or until golden. Remove and keep warm while cooking the remaining flapjacks.

ognizable

The breakfast cook-up: beyond bacon and eggs

Eggs are commonly served with bacon or ham for breakfast — and there's no problem with that when the meat is organic and nitrate free. And while bacon and eggs are of course delicious, here are some other extremely tasty options when you want to vary it a little. 🅒🅢

Breakfast hash

GLUTEN FREE

SERVES 4

Such an old-fashioned but entirely brilliant kind of thing. My recipe doesn't use ham or sausage, but adding them to the hash will make them just as delicious and boost the nutrient density — simply cook them up in a separate pan, then add to the cooked hash before cooking the eggs. If you don't want to use meat, the cooked Tempeh Patties on page 55 are also fabulous in this hash. This hearty breakfast is also a great alternative for those who are gluten intolerant as it isn't grain-based. Some people even like to give it a dash of Green Tabasco sauce!

500 g (1 lb 2 oz/1 bunch) English spinach, or 5 small stems of
    silverbeet (Swiss chard)
1 very large or 2 small potatoes (400 g/14 oz in total), skins on,
    scrubbed well and cut into 1.5 cm ($^5/_8$ inch) dice
1 tablespoon ghee
150 g ($5^1/_2$ oz) mushrooms (Swiss browns are best), sliced
    1 cm ($^1/_2$ inch) thick
1 tablespoon olive oil (or omit the ghee above and use
    2 tablespoons olive oil)
1 brown onion, cut into 5 mm ($^1/_4$ inch) slices
1 red capsicum (pepper), finely sliced
a good handful of roughly chopped fresh mixed herbs, such as marjoram,
    thyme, oregano, basil and parsley, plus extra, for sprinkling
chopped ham, cooked sausages or cooked tempeh sausages (optional)
4 eggs

If using spinach, trim away the roots, then wash the leaves well, making sure all traces of sand are removed. Set aside. (If using silverbeet, trim the stems to 5 cm/2 inches beneath the leaf. Wash the leaves well and bring a large pot of water to the boil. Cook the silverbeet leaves, a couple at a time, for 1–2 minutes. Remove, drain in a colander, then roughly slice.)

Steam the potatoes for 10 minutes, or until almost tender. Drain and set aside.

Heat 2 teaspoons of the ghee in a large frying pan and sauté the mushrooms over medium–high heat for 8 minutes, or until the mushrooms are lightly golden and no juices remain. Remove from the pan and set aside.

Add the remaining ghee and the olive oil to the pan and heat a little, stirring any remaining mushroom solids into the oil. Add the onion and sauté over medium–high heat for 5 minutes — the onion should be sizzling. Add the potato cubes and cook for 5–8 minutes, or until they start to turn golden, turning and moving them about from time to time.

Add the capsicum, herbs, mushrooms and a generous pinch of sea salt and freshly ground black pepper. Mix through, then immediately reduce the heat a little and cook for a further 5 minutes.

If using spinach leaves, add them to the pan and cook for 3 minutes, stirring until wilted, or add the cooked silverbeet leaves and stir through. Add the ham, sausage or tempeh sausages, if using, and stir through to heat.

Move the hash around and make four egg-sized holes in the mixture. Crack the eggs into these holes and cook for 3 minutes, then cover the pan for a few minutes to set the eggs on top. Sprinkle with extra herbs and serve.

ര

Tempeh patties

WHEAT FREE / DAIRY FREE / VEGAN

MAKES 10–12 PATTIES

WILL ONLY BE GLUTEN FREE IF THE TAMARI DOES NOT CONTAIN WHEAT

If you're not into meat, try these tempeh 'sausage patties' — they're delicious, easy to make and freeze well (cooked or uncooked). Rather than shape the mixture into flattened patties, you could roll it into sausage shapes — or try rolling the mixture into walnut-sized balls, then frying and using as meatballs.

1 tablespoon olive oil, plus extra, for pan-frying
1 small onion, finely chopped
1 garlic clove, finely chopped
250 g (9 oz) tempeh
2 tablespoons tamari
generous ½ teaspoon fresh sage
generous ½ teaspoon fresh marjoram
generous ½ teaspoon fresh thyme
generous ½ teaspoon fresh oregano
¼ teaspoon paprika
½ teaspoon fennel seeds
1½ tablespoons oat flour
maize flour (the light golden yellow type), for dredging

Heat the olive oil in a frying pan and gently sauté the onion for 3–4 minutes. Add the garlic and cook gently for another minute or so until the onion is soft. Tip the onion into a food processor, add the remaining ingredients (except the maize flour) and some freshly ground black pepper. Process until well combined.

TO SPICE UP THE PATTIES, TRY ADDING A PINCH OF CHIPOTLE CHILLI POWDER

Shape the mixture into small golf balls, then press into patties 5 cm (2 inches) across and 5 mm (¼ inch) thick. Dredge in the maize flour.

Add enough olive oil to a frying pan to cover the base and heat — do not allow to smoke. When hot, add the patties in batches — they should sizzle when they touch the oil, but not burn. Fry over medium heat for 3 minutes, or until golden, then turn and cook the other side for about 2 minutes. Remove from the pan and drain on paper towels while cooking the remaining patties.

☙

Summer harvest frittata

GLUTEN FREE

SERVES 3 – 4

This is the kind of recipe that's easy to adjust for one person, and it's what I reach for when I need a quick, sustaining breakfast. A frittata is a great way to include vegies in a dish that even kids will love. This recipe calls for zucchini (courgette) — an incredibly cheap and nourishing vegetable when in season and prolific in the home garden, paired with that other great summer vegetable, corn. Use organic zucchini (especially small ones), corn, tomatoes and basil for a full-flavoured result.

> 6 eggs
> 50 g (1¾ oz/½ cup) finely grated parmesan or pecorino cheese (optional)
> 1 tablespoon olive oil, ghee or butter
> 2 zucchini (courgettes), about 200 g (7 oz) in total, sliced 1 cm (½ inch) thick (see Kitchen notes)
> 2 corn cobs, kernels cut off — you need about 200 g (7 oz/1 cup) kernels (you can keep the cobs for a stock)
> 125 g (4½ oz) lush, ripe cherry tomatoes, cut in half
> 1 spring onion (scallion), finely sliced
> 1–2 tablespoons finely sliced chives
> 10 basil leaves, roughly chopped
> 2 flat-leaf (Italian) parsley stalks, leaves picked and roughly chopped

Preheat the grill (broiler) to low–medium heat.

Crack the eggs into a bowl. Add the grated cheese, if using, then season with a little sea salt and freshly ground black pepper and whisk well. Set aside.

Heat 2 teaspoons of the olive oil in a 26 cm (10½ inch) frying pan over medium heat. Add the zucchini slices and fry for 3 minutes, or until lightly golden. Turn the zucchini, scatter the corn kernels over the top and cook for another minute.

Add the remaining oil, tilting the pan to distribute it evenly. Leave for a few seconds to make sure the oil is hot, then add the tomatoes, spring onion, chives, basil and parsley. Pour the eggs over, lightly shaking the pan to distribute the eggs. Cook over gentle heat for 6–10 minutes, until the base of the frittata is just set (not rock hard) and the top is still just a little runny. Run a spatula around the edges and underneath to loosen the frittata.

Place the frying pan under the grill for 1–2 minutes, or until the frittata is just set — take care not to burn the top or overcook it. Alternatively, simply place a lid on the frying pan halfway through cooking to set both the top and bottom of the frittata at the same time.

Serve the frittata directly from the frying pan, or run a spatula around the edges and underneath and slide it onto a platter.

KITCHEN NOTES: *Zucchini has a lot of moisture. To remove any excess moisture it can be grated, placed in a colander (sitting over a bowl to catch the drips), then sprinkled with salt. Allow to sit for about 20 minutes, then rinse and squeeze dry in a tea towel (dish towel). However, this takes time, so I simply slice the zucchini and fry it, before adding the other vegies; I've never had any trouble cooking it this way.*

VARIATIONS

This frittata is a very flexible dish and a wonderful way to use up those bits and pieces in the fridge: ham, bacon, caramelized onion or leek, or leftover cooked vegetables such as diced or sliced pumpkin (winter squash), sweet potato and roasted red capsicum (pepper). Fresh asparagus and mushrooms can be cooked quickly in the pan before adding the eggs — generally, though, the vegetables will need to be already cooked before adding the eggs, and any cooking liquid reduced.

The cheese adds extra deliciousness, but can be omitted if you prefer. Instead of the parmesan or pecorino, you could use some crumbled goat's cheese or feta and add some pitted olives to the frittata, and serve with a green salad.

ɔȝ

Individual summer harvest frittatas

GLUTEN FREE

MAKES 12 MUFFIN-SIZED FRITTATAS

These muffin-sized frittatas are great for the lunchbox, served with a salad.

230 g (8 oz/1½ cups) mixture of finely diced zucchini (courgette) and
   corn kernels
1 spring onion (scallion), finely sliced
1 tablespoon finely sliced chives
10 small basil leaves, roughly chopped
1 flat-leaf (Italian) parsley stalk, leaves picked and roughly chopped
12 small-medium eggs
1–2 tablespoons finely grated parmesan or pecorino cheese (optional)
12 cherry tomatoes, cut in half

Preheat the oven to 180°C (350°F/Gas 4). Line the holes of a 12-hole muffin tin with baking paper — the paper will fold a little to fit the shape, and will probably pop out, but can be fixed up later.

Toss the zucchini, corn, spring onion, chives, basil and parsley together in a bowl.

Crack the eggs into a small bowl. Add the grated cheese, if using, and season with sea salt and freshly ground black pepper. Whisk well.

Divide the vegetable mixture between the muffin holes — as you do this, the baking paper will stay in place. Top each with two cherry tomato halves, then carefully pour in the egg mixture. Bake for 15 minutes, or until softly set and ever so lightly golden.

ఇ

Bacon and egg toasties

SERVES 6

These toasties are really a kind of tartlet, except they are made using bread rather than pastry — which is great for people who are allergic to wheat or spelt as they can use any non-wheat or spelt bread that suits them. Toasties are also portable, and very quick to put together.

> 6 slices of good-quality bread, no thicker than 1 cm (½ inch)
> (see Kitchen notes)
> 20–30 g (¾–1 oz) butter, softened
> 6 small eggs (see Kitchen notes)
> 3 slices of organic, nitrate-free bacon or ham, finely sliced

Preheat the oven to 190°C (375°F/Gas 5). Remove the crusts from each slice of bread. If your bread is more free-form and oval in shape, trim the slices into a square shape, or the closest thing to it. Flatten each piece of bread slightly using a rolling pin or bottle.

Use the butter to grease six holes of a 12-hole muffin tin and to butter each slice of bread. Gently press each slice, buttered side up, into the muffin holes — some corners might poke up a bit. Break an egg into each bread cup, then sprinkle the bacon or ham on top.

Bake for 15–20 minutes, or until the egg yolk is set but not overcooked. Sprinkle with a little sea salt and freshly ground black pepper if desired. Allow to sit in the tin for a minute before removing.

> KITCHEN NOTES: *You need a fairly wide piece of square or rectangular bread for this recipe and the Beanie Toasties (see next page) — it's good for the bread to poke up above the muffin cups as it will help hold the filling.*
>
> ◆
>
> *Take care to use small eggs, as they will overflow the muffin cups otherwise.*

套

Beanie toasties

> 6 slices of good-quality bread, no thicker than 1 cm (½ inch)
>   (see Kitchen notes, previous page)
> 20–30 g (¾–1 oz) softened butter, ghee or olive oil
> 230 g (8 oz/1 heaped cup) Quick Beanie Mix (see page 113)
> ½ large or 1 small avocado, finely diced

Preheat the oven to 190°C (375°F/Gas 5). Remove the crusts from each slice of bread. If your bread is more free-form and oval in shape, trim the slices into a square shape, or the closest thing to it. Flatten each piece of bread slightly using a rolling pin or bottle.

Grease six holes of a 12-hole muffin tin with the butter, ghee or olive oil, then either butter the bread or brush it with the oil. Gently press each slice, buttered side up, into the muffin holes — some corners might poke up a bit.

Spoon 2 tablespoons of the beanie mix into each bread cup. Bake for 15 minutes, or until the bread is lightly toasted. Allow to sit in the tin for a minute before removing. Serve topped with avocado.

ᚼ

Fresh fruit for breakfast

On really hot mornings, a big bowl of delicious summer fruit is just the thing —
except it doesn't keep you going for very long. The following recipes offer more
sustained energy from nutrient-dense fats, nuts, seeds and agar sea vegetable. ❧

Fruit salad with coconut and pineapple agar jelly

GLUTEN FREE / DAIRY FREE / VEGAN

SERVES 4

You could make the jelly from any juice — I have chosen pineapple because it's so
lovely and fresh, and added coconut for the good-quality fat. You could also enjoy
this for dessert on a hot summer night — serve the jelly cut into large triangles,
with fresh fruit and a fruit coulis.

Coconut and pineapple agar jelly
250 ml (9 fl oz/1 cup) coconut milk
250 ml (9 fl oz/1 cup) pineapple juice
1 teaspoon agar powder, or 2 tablespoons agar flakes

180 g (6 oz/1⅓ cups) fresh mixed berries
300 g (10½ oz) watermelon, cut into 2 cm (¾ inch) cubes
300 g (10½ oz) rockmelon or other orange-fleshed melon,
    cut into 2 cm (¾ inch) cubes
3 nectarines
3 plums

Put all the agar jelly ingredients in a saucepan and whisk to distribute the agar.
Gently bring to the boil, then reduce the heat to a simmer. If using agar powder,
cook for 10 minutes; if using agar flakes, cook for 20 minutes, or until the flakes
have dissolved. Stir frequently with a whisk or spoon to stop the mixture sticking to
the base of the pan, and boiling too hard and reducing.

Pour into a 14 cm (5½ inch) square dish about 5 cm (2 inches) deep. Set aside at room
temperature for 1–2 hours to set, or in the fridge for about 1 hour to set.

Gently wash the berries, if needed, and place on a tea towel (dish towel) to dry. Put the diced melon in a wide, shallow serving bowl. Using a small knife, cut the nectarines and plums into wedges directly into the salad bowl — the juices will drip directly into the bowl and help moisten the salad. Add the berries.

Cut the jelly into 2 cm (¾ inch) cubes (the bottom of the jelly will be clear, and the top more milky). Add to the salad, gently mix through with the berries and serve.

VARIATIONS

Keeping price in mind, I have opted for a small quantity of berries mixed in with cheaper fruit — but feel free to use any other choice of fruit.

ଔ

Summer fruit and nut cream

GLUTEN FREE

MAKES ABOUT 350 ML (12 FL OZ)

Grab yourself a big bowl of fruit and top with this fabulous and easy 'cream'. It's a powerhouse of nutrients — all of them bio-available, as the nuts and seeds are soaked.

80 g (2¾ oz/½ cup) raw whole almonds, soaked overnight with
   1 teaspoon yoghurt, or ½ teaspoon lemon juice, vinegar or whey
1 teaspoon linseeds (flax seeds), soaked overnight with ½ teaspoon yoghurt,
   or ¼ teaspoon lemon juice, vinegar or whey
2 ripe peaches
60 ml (2 fl oz/¼ cup) coconut milk
1 tablespoon maple syrup, honey, brown rice syrup or agave nectar
maple syrup, extra, for serving (optional)

YOU CAN KEEP THE SKIN ON THE ALMONDS IF YOU PREFER, BUT THE NUT CREAM WILL HAVE LITTLE FLECKS OF SKIN, WHICH MAY FEEL A BIT GRITTY. I PREFER TO PEEL THE SOAKED ALMONDS

Drain the almonds, then peel and discard the skins. Put the almonds in a blender. Turn the linseeds into a sieve to drain, then add to the blender.

Peel the peaches over a bowl to catch the juices, then roughly slice the peaches into the bowl. Discard the skin and stones. Add the peaches to the blender with the coconut milk and your choice of sweetener. Blend until well combined (the linseeds can take a while). I prefer the cream to retain some texture rather than be perfectly smooth, but keep blending if you prefer a smooth consistency.

Serve over summer fruits with extra maple syrup, if desired.

VARIATIONS

Add more liquid — fruit juice is lovely! — to the nut cream if you'd like a more 'custard' consistency.

CB

lunch

During the day, we use a vast amount of nutrients; what to eat for lunch is the eternal question. It generally comes down to time — not having enough of it — but we often overlook the direct relationship between the time set aside to organize and prepare good food, and the worrying and stressing time this saves each day. It's also easy to overlook how much better we feel when we eat a healthy lunch: more grounded, well fuelled, emotionally stable and less stressed. We work better, live better, feel better and love better.

Your lunch choices will have a lot to do with what you had for breakfast and what you will be having for dinner — this is why it helps to have a game plan. Porridge for breakfast, then bread or grain as a base for lunch, and a pasta or risotto for dinner is a good example of an unbalanced menu with a reliance on carbohydrate. Even the best complex carbohydrate in the world will lose its goodness when we have it for breakfast, lunch and dinner.

You'll find a variety of lunches in this chapter — some are carbohydrate based (lovely complex whole grains), some are protein based, some are vegetable based, and most have built-in alternatives to make the recipe dairy free or vegan if that is what you prefer. There are bits and pieces such as spreads, dips and soups that you can set out on the table for a weekend lunch, and more substantial meals for when you have more time. There's something for everyone to have at home, or to pack up and take out. ❧

Soups, dips and spreads

Some of the best and easiest lunches fall under this category — they store and keep well, and supply a wealth of options from which to build a lunch. Take a piece of good bread, top it with a dip or spread, maybe some gorgeous goat's cheese and a few greens, and you won't find yourself hungry — while a big bowl of soup enriched with a whole grain will keep you going on a cold winter's day. Leftovers are easily portioned up and frozen, ready for another lunch or quick evening meal. ❧

Time saver

SLOW COOKERS OR CROCKPOTS ARE PERFECT FOR COOKING SOUPS OVERNIGHT. THE NEXT MORNING, A HEARTY LUNCH AWAITS

Shiitake mushroom, vegetable and barley soup

GLUTEN FREE / DAIRY FREE / VEGAN

SERVES 4 - 6

A hearty and satisfying soup — perfect for a cold-weather lunch to keep you going. Leftovers freeze brilliantly, though you might need to thin the soup with a little liquid.

WILL ONLY BE GLUTEN FREE IF THE TAMARI DOES NOT CONTAIN WHEAT

8 dried shiitake mushrooms

110 g (3¾ oz/½ cup) pearled or naked barley, soaked overnight in 750 ml (26 fl oz/3 cups) water with 1 tablespoon yoghurt, or 2 teaspoons whey or lemon juice

a 5 cm (2 inch) piece of kombu

3 teaspoons tamari

¼ teaspoon dried thyme

1.75–2 litres (61–70 fl oz/7–8 cups) vegetable stock or water

2 tablespoons extra virgin olive oil

1 onion, finely diced

2 garlic cloves, finely diced or crushed

2–3 fresh thyme sprigs, leaves picked

a pinch of dried basil

2 unpeeled carrots, finely diced

½ orange sweet potato, peeled and finely diced

1 small-medium swede (rutabaga), peeled and finely diced

1 medium or 2 small parsnips, peeled, the woody centre removed if very large or old, then finely diced

SHIITAKE MUSHROOMS STRENGTHEN, DETOXIFY AND RESTORE THE BODY AND ARE RENOWNED IMMUNE BOOSTERS, WITH ANTI-VIRAL AND ANTI-TUMOUR PROPERTIES. THEY ARE RICH IN VITAMINS D, B12 AND PROTEIN

1 celery stalk, finely diced
1–2 teaspoons mirin (optional)
a handful of parsley, finely chopped

Crumble or roughly break the mushrooms into a large pot. Add the drained barley, kombu, tamari, dried thyme and 1.75 litres (61 fl oz/7 cups) stock or water. Partly cover and cook at a gentle simmer for 20 minutes.

Put the olive oil, onion, garlic, fresh thyme and dried basil in a frying pan with a pinch of sea salt and freshly ground black pepper. Sauté over a gentle heat for 5–8 minutes, or until slightly blushed with colour.

Add the onion mixture to the soup with all the vegetables. Partly cover and gently simmer for 45 minutes. Add more stock or water if needed, then cook for a further 15 minutes, or until the barley is soft. Check for taste — you may need a touch of mirin (especially if you have no parsnip in the soup). Add the parsley and serve.

VARIATIONS

MAKING THIS SOUP WITH LAMB/MUTTON SHANKS

Soups such as this are an all-round winner. Firstly they extend high-cost items such as meat, and secondly, they deliver all the goodness from the bone. Mutton is far cheaper than lamb, but even if it weren't, I prefer it for its deeper flavour.

Replace the shiitake mushrooms with 2 lamb or mutton shanks, and omit the kombu and tamari. Add the shanks to a large soup pot and cook over a very, very gentle heat for about 15 minutes to render some of the fat from the shanks. Add the onion, garlic, fresh thyme and dried basil with a pinch of sea salt and freshly ground black pepper, then cook over a very gentle heat for 10 minutes, or until very lightly coloured. Add 1.75 litres (61 fl oz/7 cups) of water or stock and 1 teaspoon white wine or apple cider vinegar. Cook, partly covered, over low–medium heat for 1 hour. Skim off any scum, then add the drained barley, vegetables and a pinch of sea salt and freshly ground black pepper. Gently simmer, partly covered, for a further 45 minutes. Add the remaining stock or water if needed, then cook for 15 minutes more, or until the barley is soft. Remove the shanks and cut the meat from the bones. Add the meat to the soup, stir in the parsley and serve.

℃ℬ

BARLEY CONTAINS A WONDERFULLY SOLUBLE FIBRE AND IS RICH IN MINERALS SUCH AS MAGNESIUM. IT STRENGTHENS THE INTESTINES AND BLOOD, AND BENEFITS THE GALL BLADDER AND NERVES

BOTH BARLEY AND LAMB ARE SAID TO ENHANCE 'QI' — WHAT EASTERN MEDICINE CALLS THE LIFE FORCE AND INITIATOR OF ALL MOTION AND HEAT. LAMB IS ALSO HIGH IN B VITAMINS SUCH AS NIACIN, RIBOFLAVIN AND B12 — ALL ESSENTIAL FOR GOOD HEALTH

Labneh

GLUTEN FREE

MAKES 8 SMALL LABNEH

Drained for 12 hours or more, plain yoghurt is transformed into a light and tangy cheese called labneh — a welcome and delicious addition to salads, or spread it on bruschetta with tapenade. Yoghurts that do not contain milk solids are preferable and will take longer to firm up.

    a pinch of sea salt, if desired
    600 ml (21 fl oz) plain, full-cream, non-homogenized yoghurt
    a handful of fresh herbs, such as chives, thyme (lemon thyme is
        especially good), basil, oregano or marjoram

Line a sieve with four layers of muslin (cheesecloth) — don't worry if the corners hang over the edge of the sieve. Set the sieve over a bowl to catch the whey.

If using salt, mix it into the yoghurt, then spoon the yoghurt into the muslin-lined sieve and leave in the refrigerator for about 24 hours. The cheese will be soft, but still quite dense. If you want a firmer cheese, fold the muslin corners over the yoghurt and weigh it down with something heavy before refrigerating it — I generally place a small plate on the muslin, and a tin of tomatoes on the plate.

When the cheese is the desired consistency, finely chop the herbs and place in a shallow bowl or on a plate. Roll the labneh mixture into small balls, then gently roll in the herb mix to coat. Gently place in a dish and serve immediately.

KITCHEN NOTES: *The labneh can be made ahead of time and kept in the fridge for up to 2 weeks. After rolling the labneh in the fresh herbs, place in a clean jar or bowl with 1–2 finely sliced garlic cloves and a good grind of black pepper. Add enough extra virgin olive oil to cover the labneh, then cover and refrigerate. The oil will be beautifully fragrant and can be used for dressings.*

ఇ

Kalamata olive tapènade

GLUTEN FREE / DAIRY FREE / VEGAN

MAKES ABOUT 165 G (5¾ OZ / ¾ CUP)

Quick to make, this tapenade keeps very well in the fridge, and is absolutely delicious spread on a summer sandwich, bruschetta or even pizza.

155 g (5½ oz / 1 cup) pitted kalamata olives
1-2 garlic cloves
7-8 oregano leaves
1 small rosemary sprig, leaves picked
80 ml (2½ fl oz / ⅓ cup) extra virgin olive oil, approximately
olive oil, for coating

Put the olives, garlic, oregano, rosemary sprigs and extra virgin olive oil in a food processor with some freshly ground black pepper and blend to the desired consistency — I like my tapenade fairly coarse. Check for taste and add more black pepper, garlic or oregano as needed.

Spoon into clean jars and top with a thin layer of olive oil to prevent discolouring.

ଓଷ

Roast pumpkin, red lentil and pepita hummus

GLUTEN FREE / DAIRY FREE / VEGAN

MAKES ABOUT 580 G (1 LB 5 OZ / 1½ CUPS)

A variation on the classic chickpea hummus, using quicker-cooking split red lentils as well as pepitas (pumpkin seeds), which are rich in omega-3 fats. A lovely hummus for a sandwich or wrap.

½ butternut pumpkin (squash), about 500 g (1 lb 2 oz) in total, skin on, washed well, then cut in half lengthways
2 teaspoons olive oil
¼ teaspoon ground cumin

WILL ONLY BE GLUTEN FREE IF THE TAMARI DOES NOT CONTAIN WHEAT

TAKE CARE NOT
TO USE WHOLE RED
LENTILS HERE AS
THEY WILL TASTE
ASTRINGENT DUE
TO THEIR SKINS

UNRIPE PUMPKINS
CAN TASTE QUITE
BLAND, SO TAKE
CARE TO CHOOSE A
DEEPLY COLOURED,
RIPE ONE. ORGANIC
PUMPKINS HAVE
THE BEST FLAVOUR

125 g (4½ oz / ½ cup) split red lentils
70 g (2½ oz / ½ cup) pepitas (pumpkin seeds)
1 teaspoon tamari, plus extra, to taste
1 small garlic clove
½ teaspoon ground coriander
1 teaspoon brown rice (genmai) miso
2 teaspoons lemon juice

Preheat the oven to 200°C (400°F/Gas 6). Place the pumpkin on a baking tray, drizzle with the olive oil and sprinkle with the cumin. Bake for 40–50 minutes, or until the pumpkin is tender, with some lovely golden, caramelized bits. Remove from the oven and allow to cool.

Sort through the lentils, discarding any stones, and place in a small pot with 250 ml (9 fl oz/1 cup) water. Cook for about 30 minutes over a gentle heat, stirring often, adding a little more water if necessary — when cooked, the lentils will have lost their opaque orange centre. Set aside and allow to cool (the lentils will solidify a bit).

Put the pepitas in a frying pan and toast for 1–2 minutes over a gentle heat, shaking the pan often so the seeds don't burn. When they are just lightly coloured, turn off the heat and stir in the teaspoon of tamari. Tip the seeds into a bowl.

When the seeds are cool, place in a food processor and pulse until ground. Add the garlic and pulse again. Scoop the cooled pumpkin flesh from its skin into the processor. Add the remaining ingredients with some sea salt and freshly ground black pepper to taste and blend until well combined. Check for taste and add some more tamari if you think it needs it.

KITCHEN NOTES: *You can make this dip while the pumpkin and lentils are still hot, but the mixture will be more liquid — it will set and thicken as the lentils cool.*

ଔ

Black bean dip

GLUTEN FREE / DAIRY FREE / VEGAN

MAKES ABOUT 280 G (10 OZ/1½ CUPS)

You can make delicious spreads from any cooked bean, using spices and flavours that complement the bean. Here, cumin and chipotle chilli are a beautiful match for black (turtle), pinto or borlotti (cranberry) beans. This dip is delicious with avocado, tomatoes and sour cream.

250 g (9 oz/1½ cups) cooked black (turtle) beans, plus
    2 tablespoons cooking liquid from the beans
1 garlic clove
1–1½ tablespoons lemon juice
1–2 tablespoons tahini (hulled or unhulled)
½ teaspoon ground cumin
¼ teaspoon sea salt, or to taste
⅛ teaspoon cayenne pepper, or chipotle chilli powder (optional)
1–2 tablespoons chopped coriander (cilantro)

Put the beans in a food processor with the cooking liquid, garlic, 1 tablespoon of the lemon juice, 1 tablespoon of the tahini, ¼ teaspoon of the cumin, the sea salt and the cayenne or chilli powder, if using.

Blend until smooth, then add extra lemon juice, tahini and seasonings to taste. Stir in the coriander, leaving a little to scatter over the top.

☙

Caponata

GLUTEN FREE / DAIRY FREE / VEGAN

MAKES ABOUT 380 G (13½ OZ/2 CUPS)

Serve this classic eggplant (aubergine) dish with some good bread and Labneh (page 68) for a fabulous lunch. It will keep in the fridge for a couple of days, but you might decide to use leftovers in a frittata, or heat it up and serve over some polenta or grain, or with fish for dinner. You could even fry up some tempeh, pour the caponata over it and bake it. All options are very good.

IF YOUR EGGPLANT HAS A LOT OF SEEDS, IT WILL NEED SALTING. SPRINKLE SOME SALT ONTO THE DRAINING AREA OF YOUR SINK. PLACE THE EGGPLANT SLICES ON THE SALT, THEN SPRINKLE WITH MORE SALT. LEAVE FOR 30 MINUTES, RINSE WELL AND PAT DRY

1 eggplant (aubergine)
2 tablespoons olive oil, approximately
1 small onion, finely diced
1 celery stalk, finely diced
185 g (6½ oz/¾ cup) tinned or fresh diced tomatoes, with juice
40 g (1½ oz/¼ cup) pitted kalamata olives, roughly diced
1 tablespoon balsamic vinegar
1 teaspoon apple juice concentrate
10 basil leaves, roughly chopped

Preheat a cast-iron chargrill pan (see Kitchen notes). Slice the eggplant about 1 cm (½ inch) thick. When the grill is hot, brush the eggplant on one side with some of the olive oil, place oiled side down on the grill and cook for about 1 minute, or until nicely scored underneath. Repeat on the other side. Set aside.

Heat the remaining olive oil in a frying pan. Add the onion and sauté over a gentle heat for 5 minutes, then add the celery and sauté for a further 5 minutes, or until soft.

Add the tomatoes and olives and cook gently for 10 minutes. (If using fresh tomatoes, cover and very gently cook for 20 minutes, or until they have sweated out their juices, then remove the lid and cook for 5 minutes more.) Add the remaining ingredients and roughly chopped grilled eggplant. Cook for a further 5–10 minutes, or until the liquid has reduced by half. The caponata should be lovely and thick.

KITCHEN NOTES: *You could roast the eggplant instead. Slice as instructed, sprinkle with 1 teaspoon dried basil, rub with olive oil and place on a baking tray. Roast in a moderate oven for 20 minutes, or until very lightly browned.*

ൈ

Wraps, breads and rolls

Sandwiches with lots of bread can really slow you down in the afternoon, but they are popular because they are a great way to hold a filling, and the bread does a good job of filling you up. The recipes here provide a lighter approach to the traditional sandwich — less carbohydrate, and a larger reliance on filling it with good things to nourish you. ☙

Rice paper spring rolls with a sesame lime dipping sauce

GLUTEN FREE / DAIRY FREE / VEGAN

MAKES 12 – 16 ROLLS

Once made, these rolls will keep for a few hours in an airtight container, and make a great lunch. I have used smoked tofu here, but cooked prawns are an excellent replacement if you prefer. The dipping sauce will keep in the fridge for about 4 days and is also lovely served with fish. When put out on a platter for lunch, cover the rolls with a damp cloth until ready to use.

Sesame lime dipping sauce

1 lime
1 garlic clove
2 teaspoons grated fresh ginger
1–2 tablespoons palm sugar (jaggery)
5–6 coriander (cilantro) stems, including leaves
6–8 mint leaves
1 tablespoon white (shiro) miso
1 makrut (kaffir lime) leaf, roughly chopped
80 g (2¾ oz/½ cup) sesame seeds
1 teaspoon sweet chilli sauce

Filling

1 carrot, peeled and sliced into julienne strips

30 g (1 oz) rice or mung bean vermicelli

¼ – ½ red capsicum (pepper), sliced into julienne strips

10 – 12 snow peas (mangetout), sliced very finely on the diagonal

a handful of sunflower sprouts

135 g (4¾ oz/1½ cups) bean sprouts

25 – 50 g (1 – 1¾ oz) smoked tofu (or to taste), cut into very small pieces

1 – 2 drops of roasted sesame oil (the darker-coloured one)

a small handful of mint and coriander (cilantro) leaves — an equal amount of
    each, or more as desired

rice paper wrappers (see Kitchen notes)

Zest the lime into a blender. Using a sharp knife, cut away and discard the white pith from the lime. Roughly chop the lime and place in the blender with the remaining dipping sauce ingredients and 125 ml (4 fl oz/½ cup) water. Blend for 5 minutes, or until smooth — the sauce will not be velvety smooth, but quite thick and textured from the sesame seeds. If you feel it is too thick, add a little more water. Set aside.

Place a colander in the sink. Bring a pot of water to the boil and add the carrots. After 30 seconds reduce the heat to low, scoop the carrots into the colander and immediately refresh under cold water to cool. Remove and place in a bowl lined with a paper towel or tea towel (dish towel).

Bring the water back to the boil, add the vermicelli and gently boil for 2 minutes. With the colander still in the sink, turn the vermicelli out into the colander and allow it to drain and cool. When cool, roughly chop into shorter lengths using kitchen scissors.

Put the cooled carrots and vermicelli in a bowl, together with all the remaining filling ingredients. Using your hands, toss until well combined.

Lay a clean tea towel on a work surface, with half of it hanging off the work surface. Have a large bowl of very warm water at your side. Gently put a rice paper wrapper into the water and allow to soak for 30 seconds to 1 minute, or until softened and pliable. The hotter the water, the shorter the soaking time. Take care not to soak the wrappers too long or they will be too soft and will tear when you try to roll them.

Remove the wrapper from the water and place on the tea towel, bringing the bottom of the tea towel up to pat it dry. Place a small portion of the filling along the centre of the wrapper. Fold the bottom of the wrapper over the filling, then fold in the two sides. Gently roll up, ensuring the filling is tightly enclosed, and place on a serving plate. Repeat with more wrappers until the filling is used up.

Once you get the hang of it, it's easy to soak two wrappers at a time — roll one, then the next. Replace the tea towel if it becomes too wet.

> KITCHEN NOTES: *The quality of rice paper varies enormously, so find one you like and stick with it. I prefer the 15 cm (6 inch) square — you end up with less 'paper' to chew through and more filling. This recipe will make about 16 rolls, 9 cm (3½ inches) in length. Using the more common 21 cm (8¼ inch) round, it will make about 12.*

ᔕ

Vegetarian sausage rolls

WHEAT FREE IF SPELT PUFF PASTRY USED

MAKES 15

If you want to notch up brownie points with your family, hot sausage rolls on a cold day will do it. The following recipe has a vegetarian filling, but for a quick meat version, simply remove the skins from six of your favourite organic sausages and use the sausage meat as a filling. Uncooked, both versions of these rolls will freeze fabulously well.

1½ sheets of ready-rolled puff pastry, about 20–24 cm (8–9½ inches) wide and 24 cm (9½ inches) long (see Basics, page 247)

FOR A GLUTEN-FREE VERSION OF THE VEGETARIAN FILLING, MAKE SURE THE TAMARI YOU USE IS WHEAT FREE, AND CHECK THAT THE TEMPEH IS MADE WITHOUT WHEAT-BASED SOY SAUCE. IF YOU BUY A SEASONED TEMPEH, OMIT THE TAMARI FROM THE RECIPE

Filling

1 tablespoon olive oil
1 small onion, finely chopped
1 garlic clove, finely chopped
200-250 g (7-9 oz) tempeh
2 tablespoons tamari
generous ½ teaspoon fresh sage
generous ½ teaspoon fresh marjoram
generous ½ teaspoon fresh thyme
generous ½ teaspoon fresh oregano
¼ teaspoon paprika
½ teaspoon fennel seeds
a pinch of freshly ground black pepper
1½ tablespoons oat flour

Preheat the oven to 200°C (400°F/Gas 6). Cut the whole pastry sheet in half down the middle—you should now have three sheets, each about 10–12 cm (4–4½ inches) wide and 24 cm (9½ inches) long. Place the pastry on a baking tray lined with baking paper, or two baking trays if needed to fit. Keep the pastry well chilled until ready to use.

To make the filling, heat the olive oil in a frying pan and gently sauté the onion for 3–4 minutes, then add the garlic. Cook gently for another minute or so until the onion has softened. Tip the onion into a food processor, add the remaining filling ingredients and pulse until just combined, taking care not to overmix.

IF YOU WANT TO INCREASE THE VEGETABLES YOUR CHILDREN EAT, MIX ½ GRATED CARROT (IF IT'S ORGANIC, LEAVE THE SKIN ON) INTO THE FILLING BEFORE SHAPING THE ROLLS

Divide the filling into three portions. Mould each portion into a sausage shape and lay one down the middle of each pastry half. Gently fold the pastry over, making a nice tight roll. If you feel there is too much pastry at the join, just trim a bit off using a sharp knife.

Cut each log into five smaller rolls and spread them slightly apart on the baking trays. Bake for 20–25 minutes, or until the pastry is puffed and golden. Serve hot.

☙

Roasted vegetable wrap

DAIRY FREE / VEGAN

SERVES 4

This wrap is a great balance of complex carbohydrate (the bread and beans), vegetables and good-quality fat from avocado, and will release fuel over a lengthy period. It's great for breakfast, morning tea or lunch. It takes about 5 minutes to chop and throw these vegetables into the oven, but feel free to use other vegies as well. The zucchini (courgette) strips could also be chargrilled to add an extra dimension of flavour. A pinwheel version for kids follows.

1 zucchini (courgette) cut lengthways into 4 strips
1 red capsicum (pepper), cut into quarters
½ orange sweet potato (about 150 g/5½ oz), peeled and cut into
    long strips about 4–5 cm (1½–2 inches) wide
olive oil, for coating
4 tortillas, chapatti or thin, unleavened flatbreads such as lavash
    or mountain bread (see Kitchen notes)
8 lettuce leaves, washed and dried
85 g (3 oz/ ½ cup) cooked beans such as pinto or black (turtle) beans,
    well drained
1 avocado

Quick salsa
½ – ¾ cup ready-made salsa (choose a good-quality one)
½ ripe tomato, finely chopped
2–3 coriander (cilantro) stalks, finely chopped

Preheat the oven to 200°C (400°F/Gas 6). Toss all the vegetables in a little olive oil and place on a baking tray, ensuring the capsicum skin is exposed. Bake for 20–30 minutes, or until the vegetables are soft. The capsicum skin should be blistered and may even have a few black spots; the zucchini and sweet potato should be soft, but not collapsed.

Allow the vegetables to cool a little, then peel the skin from the capsicum. If not using them immediately, place the vegetables in an airtight container and refrigerate. They will keep for several days.

THOUGH I AM NOT A GREAT FAN OF THE MICROWAVE, YOU CAN USE IT TO BRIEFLY HEAT THE FILLED WRAPS TO ENJOY WARM

Time savers
USING A GOOD-QUALITY COMMERCIAL SALSA AND TINNED BEANS SAVES HEAPS OF TIME

ROAST SOME EXTRA VEGETABLES TO USE IN A SOUP, PIE (SEE THE PUFF PASTRY TART ON PAGE 87), STEW OR EVEN A FRITTATA

ANY LEFTOVER
SALSA WILL KEEP
IN THE FRIDGE
FOR A FEW DAYS.
USE AS A DIP WITH
FRESH VEGIES,
OR ADD TO RED
LENTILS TO MAKE
A QUICK DAL

Put all the salsa ingredients in a small bowl and mix together.

To assemble, lay out the flatbreads. Lay two lettuce leaves down the middle of each, then a zucchini strip, two sweet potato strips and a roasted capsicum quarter, torn in two. Divide the beans and salsa among the wraps, then slice one-quarter of the avocado over each. Roll up tightly and serve, or wrap in baking paper and store.

KITCHEN NOTES: *Mountain bread is quite fragile, so if you're using it for these rolls, wrap the filling just before eating so it doesn't weep into the bread and break it. Tortillas or chapatti are thicker and can be filled well ahead of time, then wrapped in baking paper and refrigerated, ready to eat — just make sure you can find a good-quality tortilla or chapatti made with good-quality fat, rather than refined vegetable oil.*

VARIATIONS

PINWHEELS FOR CHILDREN

Spread a sheet of lavash or mountain bread with avocado and either some mashed-up beans, or a bean spread such as Black Bean Dip (page 71) or Roast Pumpkin, Red Lentil and Pepita Hummus (page 69). Sprinkle with grated carrot, salad leaves and roasted capsicum (pepper) strips, or leftovers such as cooked mushrooms and Pesto (see Basics, pages 255–256).

Roll up the flatbread as you would a nori roll, wrap tightly in baking paper and twist the ends. Let sit for 1 hour or overnight.

Cut into slices as you would a nori roll — that is, sawing with a sharp knife. Don't use a serrated knife, and don't press too hard.

Ꮵ

Terrines and tarts

Back in my wholefood café days, a quiche or tart was a guaranteed seller. They are such a fabulous meal — how sad that most of those that are commercially available today are a sorry replica of their original selves. A slice of tart with salad leaves you feeling nourished and sustained, without the heaviness of bread. Tarts freeze fabulously. Terrines are the original brilliant nutrient-dense addition to some salad and a piece of good bread — really a French version of the English ploughman's lunch. They keep well, are absolutely delicious and not at all difficult to make. ☙

Shiitake mushroom, walnut and lentil terrine

GLUTEN FREE / DAIRY FREE / VEGAN

SERVES 6 AS PART OF A LUNCH

One of the most memorable lunches I have ever had was at Alice Water's Café in Berkeley, California. Sitting under the pergola, I ate a simple meal — the best organic sourdough bread with eggplant (aubergine), tapenade, roasted red capsicum (pepper) and greens. My friends, though, had the terrine — a stunning pork and pistachio number with an excellent bread. Given I don't eat a lot of meat, I wanted to create a vegetarian version that had the same rustic, country wholesomeness. A hefty slice of this with a piece of good bread and some salad bits will provide a sustaining, well-balanced and delicious lunch. A good slab on bread with avocado will also deliver a powerful, slow-release breakfast. This terrine will keep covered in the fridge for 3 days and is absolutely delicious with the Orange and Date Chutney on page 225.

8 small dried shiitake mushrooms (about 16 g/½ oz in total)
125 g (4½ oz/⅔ cup) green or brown lentils, stones removed
1 bay leaf
2–3 small thyme sprigs
½ orange sweet potato (about 200 g/7 oz), cut into 1 cm (½ inch) dice
100 g (3½ oz/1 cup) walnut halves
1 tablespoon plus 1 teaspoon olive oil
1 shallot, finely diced

WILL ONLY BE GLUTEN FREE IF THE TAMARI DOES NOT CONTAIN WHEAT

1 carrot, finely diced
1 small celery stalk, finely diced
½ teaspoon dried basil
¼ teaspoon dried oregano
¼ – ½ teaspoon fresh thyme
3 garlic cloves, crushed
1 teaspoon white (shiro) miso
1 teaspoon tamari
1 teaspoon mirin

Preheat the oven to 180°C (350°F/Gas 4). Place the mushrooms in a small pot with 250 ml (9 fl oz/1 cup) water, cover and bring to the boil. Turn off the heat and leave until cool.

Put the lentils, bay leaf and thyme sprigs in a saucepan with enough water to cover the lentils by about 5 cm (2 inches). Put the sweet potato in a steamer pot or heatproof sieve and place it over the saucepan. Put the saucepan over a gentle heat and simmer for 10 minutes, or until the sweet potato is tender, but not overcooked. Remove the steamer or sieve and set the sweet potato aside.

Simmer the lentils for a further 35 minutes, or until cooked. Increase the heat and boil off any remaining liquid, then remove the bay leaf and thyme sprigs. Set the lentils aside.

While the lentils are cooking, place the walnuts on a baking tray and toast them in the oven for 8 minutes, or until ever so lightly golden — be careful not to burn them. Set aside to cool, then finely chop.

Remove the mushrooms from their soaking liquid, reserving the soaking liquid. Cut off and discard any tough stems and cut the mushrooms into small pieces. Set aside.

Put 1 tablespoon of olive oil in a frying pan and add the shallot, carrot, celery, basil, oregano and thyme. Sauté over a gentle heat, taking care not to burn, for 5–8 minutes. Stir in the garlic and mushroom soaking liquid and simmer over medium heat for 15 minutes, or until the liquid has entirely evaporated and the vegetables are cooked. Add the extra teaspoon of olive oil and cook for a further 5 minutes, or until the vegetables are slightly coloured.

Put the lentils in a mixing bowl with the sweet potato. Using a spoon, roughly mash the sweet potato into the lentils. Add the mushrooms, walnuts, cooked vegetables, miso, tamari and mirin. Mix together well, pressing on the lentils so some of their inner starch will help bind the mixture. Taste and add sea salt and freshly ground black pepper if desired.

Spoon into an oiled loaf (bar) dish (see Kitchen notes), press down well, and smooth over. Bake for 30 minutes, or until ever so slightly dry on top — the edges will have shrunk from the sides a little. Leave to cool, then cover and refrigerate.

When the terrine is fully cooled, run a sharp knife around the edges, invert a plate over the dish and unmould. Cover with plastic wrap and refrigerate until needed.

KITCHEN NOTES: *I prefer to use a glass rather than metal loaf dish, to avoid a 'tin' taste as the terrine cools. My loaf dish is narrower at the base than the top. The base is about 18 cm (7 inches) long and 8 cm (3¹/₄ inches) wide; the top is about 21 cm long (8¹/₄ inches) and 11 cm (4¹/₄ inches) wide.*

 CB

Little savoury chicken cakes

GLUTEN FREE / DAIRY FREE

MAKES 10 MUFFIN SIZE OR 24 – 30 MINI-MUFFIN CAKES

This recipe was developed for children of all ages — a nutrient-dense little something that's essentially a scaled-down terrine. It's an excellent way to extend expensive organic chicken, and at the same time incorporate a large number of vegies into children's diets. The chicken cakes can also be made in a mini muffin tin. They should be chilled before being packed in a picnic hamper or lunchbox.

2 teaspoons olive oil
½ small red onion, very finely diced
1 small carrot, very finely diced
1 small–medium corn cob, kernels cut off to give about 125 g
    (4½ oz / ⅔ cup)

WILL ONLY BE
GLUTEN FREE IF
THE TAMARI DOES
NOT CONTAIN
WHEAT

1 celery stalk, very finely diced
¼ red capsicum (pepper), very finely diced
2 garlic cloves, crushed or finely diced
1 tablespoon coconut milk
6 small sage leaves, finely chopped
6 basil leaves, finely chopped
2 parsley stalks, leaves picked and finely chopped
1 generous teaspoon thyme leaves
500 g (1 lb 2 oz) minced (ground) chicken (see Kitchen notes)
2 teaspoons tamari

Preheat the oven to 190°C (375°F/Gas 5). Line 10 holes of a 12-hole muffin tin with squares of baking paper — the paper will fold a little to fit the shape. Don't cut the paper to fit the holes, otherwise the juices from the chicken will seep through.

Heat the olive oil in a frying pan. Add the onion, carrot, corn, celery, capsicum, garlic and a pinch of sea salt. Sauté over a gentle heat with just a little sizzle for 5 minutes. Stir in the coconut milk and herbs and continue to cook at a gentle sizzle until the milk has evaporated.

Put the chicken mince in a bowl, together with the cooked vegetables, tamari and some sea salt and freshly ground black pepper. Mix through well, pressing the chicken to help break it up and incorporate the vegetable mixture.

Divide the mixture among the lined muffin holes and bake for 15 minutes, or until the chicken is cooked, taking care not to overcook it or it will become dry. (The mini-muffins will cook in 8–10 minutes.)

Allow the cakes to cool a little, then carefully remove from the tray, keeping all the lovely juices contained within the baking paper cup. Serve warm, or refrigerate until needed.

KITCHEN NOTES: *If you can't find minced (ground) chicken, use thighs instead. Remove any gristle, roughly chop the meat, then place in a food processor and process into mince, or very finely chop using a sharp knife.*

℃ઝ

Little confetti tarts

WHEAT FREE

MAKES 12 TARTS

Universally loved, little tarts (or quiches) are the perfect lunchbox or afternoon tea fare. Once cooked, they freeze brilliantly. Even if you make them from scratch, they don't take long, and if you have a tray of pastry shells in the freezer, they will take even less time — about 10 minutes to put together.

butter, for greasing
90 g (3¼ oz/¾ cup) plain (all-purpose) wholemeal spelt flour
90 g (3¼ oz/¾ cup) plain (all-purpose) white spelt flour
100 g (3½ oz) chilled butter, chopped
50-60 ml (1½-2 fl oz) ice-cold water
1 small corn cob, kernels cut off to give about 70 g (2½ oz/⅓ cup)
½ zucchini (courgette), finely diced
¼ red capsicum (pepper), finely diced
5 basil leaves, finely sliced
1 spring onion (scallion), greens only, finely sliced
185 ml (6 fl oz/¾ cup) full-cream, non-homogenized organic milk
2 eggs
60 g (2¼ oz/½ cup) grated cheddar cheese, or other good melting cheese
    (optional)

Preheat the oven to 190°C (375°F/Gas 5). Grease twelve 6 x 2 cm (2½ x ¾ inch) tartlet tins with a little butter. Cut out 24 strips of baking paper, each measuring about 11 x 1 cm (4¼ x ½ inch), and lay two strips, in a cross, in each tartlet tin — these will help you pull the baked tart shells out. (Alternatively, use loose-based tins and you won't need the baking paper.)

Put all the flour in a bowl. Using your fingertips, rub the butter into the flour until incorporated — the mixture should look like small (but not too fine) breadcrumbs. Alternatively, put the flour and butter in a food processor, pulse once or twice until just combined, then turn out into a bowl. (It's important not to overwork the pastry or it will become tough.)

Using a bread and butter knife, begin to gradually 'cut' the iced water into the flour mixture. Use only as much water as you need — some flours will absorb more

I PREFER MAKING MY OWN PASTRY AS IT GIVES ME THE OPPORTUNITY TO USE SPELT FLOUR. TO SAVE TIME, READY-ROLLED PUFF PASTRY (SEE BASICS, PAGE 247) IS GREAT, AS ARE TART TINS WHICH HAVE BEEN PRE-LINED USING THE SHORTCRUST IN THIS RECIPE AND FROZEN. EVEN USING A GOOD COMMERCIAL PASTRY IS FINE, BUT THE BETTER ONES (MADE USING BUTTER OR LARD) ARE GENERALLY EXPENSIVE

liquid than others. Once the mixture looks evenly moist, bring it together into a ball (but don't knead or work it too much). Flatten slightly, then cover with plastic wrap (or place in a plastic bag) and chill for 20 minutes, or until cold to the touch. The pastry is now ready to use.

To roll out the pastry, use as little flour as possible, but enough to make sure the rolling surface is covered. Lightly flour a heavy, decent-sized rolling pin. Roll the pastry once or twice, then run a palette knife underneath, move the pastry firmly and quickly, lightly dust the rolling area with more flour and turn the dough over. Lightly sprinkle the surface of the pastry with flour and swiftly rub over. Continue to repeat this process, folding the dough, if necessary, to move it.

Roll the pastry out to a diameter of about 38 cm (15 inches). Using an 8 cm (3¼ inch) cutter, cut the pastry into 12 circles. Use a palette knife to lift the pastry circles and line each tart tin. Place in the freezer to chill for about 10 minutes.

Toss the corn, zucchini, capsicum, basil and spring onion together in a bowl. Place the milk and eggs in a bowl, season with sea salt and freshly ground black pepper and whisk together. Transfer to a small jug.

Divide the vegetable mixture among the pastry shells. Pour about 1 tablespoon of the egg mixture into each tart, taking care that it does not overfill the pastry.

Bake for 25–30 minutes, or until the pastry is golden and the egg is set. If using cheese, sprinkle it on the tarts 10 minutes before the end of cooking time.

VARIATIONS

Just about anything works in a tart — most vegetables will need to be pre-cooked though. Leftover roast vegies are fabulous. Try sautéed mushrooms and cooked sweet potato, or lightly cooked asparagus with sautéed leek and thyme.

☙

Quiche lorraine

WHEAT FREE

SERVES 4 – 6

A good lorraine (named after a region in France) is the king of all tarts, and makes a wonderful brunch or lunch. Organic nitrate-free ham is a treat and in this tart a little goes a long way. I would serve this with a hearty green salad for a sustaining and nourishing lunch.

90 g (3¼ oz / ¾ cup) plain (all-purpose) wholemeal spelt flour
90 g (3¼ oz / ¾ cup) plain (all-purpose) white spelt flour
100 g (3½ oz) chilled butter, chopped
80–100 ml (2½ – 3½ fl oz) ice-cold water
butter, for greasing
2 eggs
2 egg yolks
560 ml (19¼ fl oz / 2¼ cups) full-cream, non-homogenized organic milk
80 g (2¾ oz / ⅔ cup) grated cheddar cheese
175 g (6 oz) organic, nitrate-free ham, finely diced
2 tablespoons finely sliced chives

Put all the flour in a bowl. Using your fingertips, rub the butter into the flour until incorporated — the mixture should look like small (but not too fine) breadcrumbs. Alternatively, put the flour and butter in a food processor, pulse once or twice until just combined, then turn out into a bowl. (It's important not to overwork the pastry or it will become tough.)

Using a bread and butter knife, begin to gradually 'cut' the iced water into the flour mixture. Use only as much water as you need — some flours will absorb more liquid than others. Once the mixture looks evenly moist, bring it together into a ball (but don't knead or work it too much). Flatten slightly, then cover with plastic wrap (or place in a plastic bag) and chill for 20 minutes, or until cold to the touch.

To roll out the pastry, use as little flour as possible, but enough to make sure the rolling surface is covered. Lightly flour a heavy, decent-sized rolling pin. Roll the pastry once or twice, then run a palette knife underneath, move the pastry firmly and quickly, lightly redust the rolling area with flour and turn the dough over. Lightly sprinkle the surface of the pastry with flour and swiftly rub over. Continue

TRADITIONALLY MADE WITH CREAM, I PREFER TO MAKE THIS QUICHE USING FULL-CREAM, ORGANIC NON-HOMOGENIZED MILK. IT IS NOT AS RICH BUT STILL TASTES FABULOUS. YOU WON'T GET THE SAME RESULT USING SOY OR CONVENTIONAL MILK, AND I WOULDN'T RECOMMEND THEM HERE

to repeat this process, folding the dough if necessary to move it, until it is abut 33 cm (13 inches) in diameter.

Preheat the oven to 200°C (400°F/Gas 6) and place a baking tray in the oven to warm.

Grease a loose-based tart tin measuring 24 cm (9½ inch) across and 3 cm (1¼ inches) deep with softened butter. To line the tart tin, swiftly fold the pastry into four (so it looks like a triangle) and place the pointy end of the triangle in the centre of the tin.

Unfold the triangle and fit the pastry into the tin. Trim the edges to fit, then place the tart tin in the freezer for 10 minutes, or until the pastry is very firm and cold to the touch. Form the trimmings into a small ball and place in the fridge.

Remove and place a sheet of baking paper (never plastic wrap) over the pastry-lined tart tin. Fill with dried beans or pastry weights and place in the hot oven, on the hot baking tray. Bake for 10 minutes, then remove the baking paper and beans, reduce the oven temperature to 180°C (350°F/Gas 4) and bake for a further 9 minutes.

While the pastry is blind-baking, put the eggs, egg yolks and milk in a bowl, season with sea salt and freshly ground black pepper and whisk well. Set aside.

Remove the blind-baked tart shell from the oven and increase the temperature to 200°C (400°F/Gas 6). Carefully check there are no cracks in the pastry where the filling will seep through, patching up any cracks with the reserved pastry if necessary. Sprinkle half the cheese over the base of the tart, then the ham and chives.

Carefully pour half the egg mixture into the tart. Place it on the baking tray, then carefully pour in the remaining egg mixture. Bake for 15 minutes, then reduce the oven temperature to 180°C (350°F/Gas 4) and bake for a further 35–45 minutes, or until the filling is lightly puffed and the centre is just set. The top should be lightly golden, not a harsh brown. Sprinkle the remaining cheese over the top 20 minutes before the end of cooking time. Serve warm.

ଔ

Puff pastry tart with roasted vegetables and pesto

WHEAT FREE IF SPELT PUFF PASTRY USED

SERVES 4 – 6

This is a perfect weekend lunch dish, and takes about 15 minutes of your time to prepare. It is equally good the next day. Serve with a large green salad — a rocket (arugula) salad would be excellent.

- 3 young eggplants (aubergines), about 180 g (6 oz) in total
  (see Kitchen notes)
- 2 zucchini (courgettes), about 280 g (10 oz) in total
- 150 g (5½ oz) butternut pumpkin (squash), cut into 2 cm
  (¾ inch) cubes (about 1¾ cups)
- ½ red capsicum (pepper), cut in half
- 150 g (5½ oz) cherry tomatoes
- 2 tablespoons olive oil
- ½ teaspoon dried basil
- 1 piece of puff pastry, rolled to a 24 cm (9½ inch) square sheet,
  2-3 mm (¹⁄₁₆ - ⅛ inch) thick
- 60-70 g (2¼ - 2½ oz) feta or soft goat's cheese
- 2 tablespoons Pesto (see Basics, pages 255-256)
- 35 g (1¼ oz / ¼ cup) pitted kalamata olives, roughly torn
- 2-3 flat-leaf (Italian) parsley stems, leaves picked and roughly torn

Preheat the oven to 200°C (400°F/Gas 6). Roughly chop the eggplant and zucchini into 2 cm (¾ inch) pieces (if your zucchini are small, cut them slightly smaller). Toss in a bowl with the pumpkin, capsicum, cherry tomatoes, olive oil and basil, season with sea salt and freshly ground black pepper and mix well.

Spread the vegetables out on a baking tray, making sure the capsicum pieces are sitting skin side up. Bake for 20 minutes.

Meanwhile, line a baking tray with baking paper. Place the pastry on the baking tray and freeze for 5 minutes.

Cut a 19 cm (7½ inch) square from a sheet of baking paper. Remove the pastry from the freezer and place the baking paper over it, leaving a pastry border. Top the paper with baking weights or dried beans, making sure they come right to the edge.

Bake for 15 minutes (the vegetables will still be roasting), then remove the pastry from the oven. Lift off the baking paper and tip the weights into a bowl to cool.

Reduce the oven temperature to 190°C (375°F/Gas 5). Prick the pastry all over with a fork and bake for a further 10 minutes.

Remove the vegetables and pastry from the oven. Put the capsicum aside, allow to cool a little, then peel off the skin and cut the flesh into strips. Spread the eggplant, caspicum and zucchini over the pastry case. Arrange the tomatoes and capsicum strips over the top. Crumble the cheese over the tart, dot with the pesto and olives, sprinkle with parsley and serve.

KITCHEN NOTES: *Try to find fresh, young eggplants (aubergines) — these have little seed development and don't require salting. If your eggplant has a lot of seeds, you will need to salt it. Sprinkle a small amount of salt onto the draining area of your sink. Place the eggplant pieces on this, then sprinkle again with salt (1 medium-sized eggplant will need about 2 teaspoons salt). Leave to sit for 30 minutes, then rinse well and pat dry.*

☙

Salads

Salads are a fabulously healthy lunch, but they don't sustain you very long. The following salads all include some protein or complex carbohydrate to anchor the vegetables, and will thus fuel the body over a greater length of time. ☙

Barley salad with Greek flavours

WHEAT FREE

SERVES 4

Barley is a big grain — big in nutrients (especially folic acid), big in size and big in flavour — so it needs a big salad with robust flavours to match. This salad improves in flavour the next day. If you are gluten sensitive, you could use any other suitable cooked grain in place of the barley. In a perfect world, I would pair a bowl of this salad with grilled vegies.

165 g (5¾ oz/¾ cup) pearled or natural barley, soaked overnight if desired
    in 500 ml (17 fl oz/2 cups) water with 1 tablespoon yoghurt,
      or 2 teaspoons whey or lemon juice
2 teaspoons olive oil
1 zucchini (courgette) or yellow squash, sliced 1 cm (½ inch) thick
2 generous tablespoons roughly chopped flat-leaf (Italian) parsley
3 mint leaves, finely sliced
2 small Lebanese (short) cucumbers, cut into 1 cm (½ inch) cubes
2 tomatoes, seeded and cut into 1 cm (½ inch) cubes
2 tablespoons finely sliced spring onion (scallion) greens
40-50 g (1½ - 1¾ oz/⅓ - ¼ cup) pitted kalamata olives
3 tablespoons extra virgin olive oil
2 tablespoons freshly squeezed lemon juice
2 teaspoons red wine vinegar

Drain the barley and rinse well. Place in a saucepan with 1.25 litres (44 fl oz/5 cups) water and cook, uncovered, at a gentle simmer for 50–70 minutes if soaked, or 60–80 minutes if unsoaked, or until the barley is tender. (If using naked barley, you may need to cook it a little longer — simply add extra water if you see it running low.) Tip the barley into a colander and allow to cool. Squeeze out any excess liquid (it shouldn't be too wet when added to the salad).

GOOD ORGANIC OR BIODYNAMIC PEARLED BARLEY HAS HAD THE OUTER INEDIBLE HUSKS REMOVED, WITH MUCH OF THE GERM AND BRAN LEFT INTACT AND IS BROWNISH IN APPEARANCE. SUPERMARKET-BOUGHT PEARLED BARLEY HAS ALL THE GERM AND BRAN REMOVED, LEAVING THE WHITE INNER STARCH EXPOSED, AND I DON'T ADVOCATE USING IT. 'NATURAL' OR NAKED BARLEY HAS HAD ONLY THE HUSK REMOVED, WITH ALL THE GERM AND BRAN LEFT INTACT. I PREFER ORGANIC OR BIODYNAMIC PEARLED BARLEY — STILL FULL OF GOODNESS, BUT NOT QUITE AS CHEWY

IN THIS RECIPE
THE BARLEY IS
COOKED BY A
FREE-BOIL
METHOD RATHER
THAN ABSORPTION.
THIS ALLOWS SOME
OF ITS STARCH TO
RELEASE INTO THE
WATER, MAKING IT
LESS STICKY FOR
A SALAD

Heat the olive oil in a frying pan. Add the zucchini and fry over medium–high heat for 1 minute, or until coloured underneath. Turn and cook for another minute or so, or until nicely coloured, then remove and allow to cool.

Put the zucchini in a salad bowl with the parsley, mint, cucumber, tomato, spring onion and olives. Add a good grind of black pepper and a pinch of sea salt, then add the drained barley.

Put the olive oil, lemon juice and vinegar in a small bowl and whisk together. Pour over the salad and gently stir to combine.

ଔ

Poached chicken salad with Asian flavours

GLUTEN FREE / DAIRY FREE

SERVES 4

A lovely dish for lunch or a hot summer night's dinner. Containing both broccoli sprouts and arame sea vegetable, this is a salad brimming with minerals, vitamins and more goodness in general than you could poke a stick at. If you've poached your chicken the night before, it's very quick to prepare. While some might think a lovely glazed tofu would work here in place of the chicken as a vegetarian option, I find cold tofu rather rubbery, and not a good option for a cold salad.

BROCCOLI
SPROUTS ARE LESS
BITTER AND MORE
BODY-COMPATIBLE
THAN ALFALFA
SPROUTS. THEY
ALSO CONTAIN
ISOTHIOCYANATES
— POTENT
ANTI-CANCER
COMPOUNDS

5 g (⅛ oz/¼ cup) arame
1 boneless chicken breast (about 250 g/9 oz), skin on or off
125 ml (4 fl oz/½ cup) coconut milk
1 makrut (kaffir lime) leaf
2 slices of fresh, unpeeled ginger, about 3 mm (⅛ inch) thick
50 g (1¾ oz/⅓ cup) roasted cashews, roughly chopped
10-12 snow peas (mangetout), cut lengthways into julienne strips
2 spring onions (scallions), greens only, finely sliced on the diagonal
75 g (2½ oz/1 cup) broccoli or other sprouts (but not alfalfa)
1 small mango or ½ large mango, flesh cut into thick julienne strips
a handful of coriander (cilantro) leaves

Dressing

2 tablespoons coconut milk

2 teaspoons brown rice vinegar (or another mellow rice vinegar)

2 teaspoons umeboshi vinegar

1 tablespoon mirin

1 tablespoon unrefined sesame oil

1 teaspoon roasted sesame oil

2 teaspoons finely grated fresh ginger

Put the arame in a small bowl with 250 ml (9 fl oz/1 cup) water. Leave for about 15 minutes to reconstitute.

Meanwhile, put the chicken breast in a saucepan with the coconut milk, lime leaf, ginger and enough water to cover the chicken well. Cover, place over medium heat and bring to a gentle simmer. Simmer for 10–15 minutes, or until the chicken is just cooked, taking care not to overcook it. Remove the chicken, place in a bowl and drizzle with a little poaching liquid to keep it moist. Cover and refrigerate while preparing the salad.

Put the dressing ingredients in a small bowl and whisk together. Set aside.

Put the remaining salad ingredients in a bowl and gently toss together. Shred the chicken into the bowl (remove the skin if it is still attached), letting any juices run into the bowl. Add the drained arame and the dressing. Gently toss together with your hands to mix through well, then serve.

ଔ

Chicken and bread salad

DAIRY FREE

SERVES 3

No crumb of good bread should go to waste — there's always a good way to put them to use. This is the perfect weekend lunch, and quick to throw together, especially if you have poached the chicken the night before. Piled onto a plate, it's the sort of salad you can pick at, rather than a knife-and-fork kind of meal.

2 boneless chicken breasts (about 500 g/1 lb 2 oz), skin on or off
2 bay leaves
2 thyme sprigs
1 carrot, roughly chopped
1 tablespoon currants
2 garlic cloves
a handful of lemon thyme, stems removed
2 tablespoons olive oil
180 g (6 oz) organic sourdough bread (day-old bread is fine)
1 tablespoon pine nuts
100 g (3½ oz) mixed salad greens — I prefer rocket (arugula),
    cos (romaine) lettuce and mizuna

Dressing
3 tablespoons olive oil
1 garlic clove, crushed
1 teaspoon lemon juice
2 teaspoons apple cider vinegar
tiniest pinch of raw sugar

IF YOU ARE USING CHICKEN YOU HAVE POACHED THE NIGHT BEFORE (SEE BASICS, PAGE 252), THERE SHOULD BE LOVELY BITS OF JELLED JUICES STUCK TO THE CHICKEN — DO INCLUDE THOSE IN THIS SALAD, AS THEY WILL ADD FLAVOUR AND AID DIGESTION

Put the chicken breasts in a saucepan and add enough water to cover the chicken well. Add a pinch of sea salt, a good grind of black pepper, the bay leaves, thyme sprigs and carrot. Cover, place over medium heat and bring to a gentle simmer. Simmer for 10–15 minutes, or until the chicken is just cooked, taking care not to overcook it. Remove the chicken, place in a bowl and drizzle with a little poaching liquid to keep it moist. Cover and refrigerate while preparing the salad.

Preheat the oven to 170°C (325°F/Gas 3). Place the currants in a small dish and pour a little boiling water over. Set aside.

Put the garlic cloves and lemon thyme in a mortar and give them a good grind. Add the olive oil and continue to mix, making sure the garlic and thyme are well broken down into the oil.

Cut the bread into rough 2 cm (3/4 inch) dice. Tip the flavoured oil from the mortar onto a baking tray, using a piece of the bread to help scrape out every last bit. Add the bread to the tray and mix it through the oil using your hands, making sure the oil is evenly distributed. Bake for 15–20 minutes, or until the croutons are just crisp on the outside, but soft to press. Remove from the oven and set aside.

Spread the pine nuts on a baking tray or baking dish and bake for 6 minutes, or until ever so lightly golden. Set aside.

Put the dressing ingredients in a screw-top jar with a pinch of sea salt and some freshly ground black pepper. Add the pine nuts and drained currants. Shake well, taste and adjust the seasoning if necessary.

Shred the chicken into a salad bowl (remove the skin if it is still attached), letting any juices run into the bowl. Add the salad leaves, croutons and dressing, then gently toss together using your fingers. Sprinkle with sea salt and freshly ground black pepper and serve.

ᙡ

Roast vegetable, quinoa and chickpea salad with a Moroccan dressing

GLUTEN FREE / DAIRY FREE

SERVES 4 – 6

WILL ONLY BE
GLUTEN FREE IF
THE TAMARI DOES
NOT CONTAIN
WHEAT

This is a sustaining, robust and delicious salad. When you can, make it with red quinoa — the colour looks fabulous. Any vegetable can be used for roasting. In winter, try using orange sweet potato, carrots, and even steamed kale.

- 240 g (8½ oz) butternut pumpkin (squash), cut into 2 cm (¾ inch) dice (about 1¾ cups)
- 2 eggplant (aubergines), about 150 g (5½ oz) in total, cut into 2 cm (¾ inch) dice
- 2 small or 1 large zucchini (courgettes), about 150 g (5½ oz) in total, sliced 1 cm (½ inch) thick
- 4–5 yellow squash, sliced 1 cm (½ inch) thick
- 8–10 cherry tomatoes
- 1 red capsicum (pepper), cut into quarters, core and seeds removed
- 1 tablespoon olive oil
- ¼ teaspoon ground coriander
- ¼ teaspoon ground cumin
- 200 g (7 oz/1 cup) quinoa, soaked overnight if desired, with 2 teaspoons whey or yoghurt, or 1 teaspoon lemon juice
- 240 g (8½ oz/1½ cups) cooked or tinned chickpeas
- 2 tablespoons roughly chopped coriander (cilantro) leaves

Time saver

THE CHICKPEAS
WILL HAPPILY
MARINATE IN THE
DRESSING FOR UP
TO I WEEK IN THE
FRIDGE, TAKING
ON EXTRA
FLAVOUR

Dressing
- 60 ml (2 fl oz/¼ cup) extra virgin olive oil
- 2 teaspoons balsamic vinegar
- 3 teaspoons lemon juice
- 1 teaspoon tamari
- 2 teaspoons apple juice concentrate
- 1 teaspoon honey
- ½ teaspoon ground cumin
- ¼ teaspoon ground coriander
- 2 garlic cloves, crushed
- 1 teaspoon finely grated fresh ginger

Preheat the oven to 200°C (400°F/Gas 6). Put the vegetables in a mixing bowl together with the olive oil, ground coriander and cumin. Add some sea salt and freshly ground black pepper and toss through well.

Spread the pumpkin and eggplant on one baking tray, and the zucchini, squash, tomatoes and capsicum on another, making sure the capsicum is skin side up. Bake for 20–25 minutes, then remove the zucchini, squash, tomatoes and capsicum from the oven. Continue roasting the pumpkin and eggplant for a further 10–15 minutes, or until lightly golden. Take care not to overcook and dry them out. When the capsicum is cool, peel off and discard the skin, then shred the flesh into pieces.

Turn the quinoa and soaking water into a strainer and rinse. Drain well, pat the quinoa dry with a tea towel (dish towel), then place in a saucepan. Add 435 ml (15¼ fl oz/1¾ cups) water if soaked, and 500 ml (17 fl oz/2 cups) if unsoaked. Cover and bring to the boil, then immediately turn the heat down low and simmer for 15–20 minutes. About 5 minutes before the end of cooking time, check if there is any water left by tipping the pan on an angle — if there is, continue to cook until there is no water left. When the quinoa is ready, small steam holes should appear on the surface.

Remove from the heat, place a clean tea towel or paper towel over the grain, put the lid back on and leave to cool.

Put the dressing ingredients in a screw-top jar with a pinch of sea salt and some freshly ground black pepper. Shake well.

Put the quinoa in a salad bowl, breaking up the grains with a fork. Add the chickpeas, roast vegetables and dressing. Gently toss together, sprinkle with coriander and serve.

VARIATIONS

Cold lamb is also a great addition to this salad. If you would like a more robust flavour, try adding the following spices while cooking the quinoa.

½ teaspoon cumin, extra
¼ teaspoon each ground cinnamon, ginger and coriander
⅛ teaspoon ground turmeric

છ

dinner

In our busy days, dinner is often the only event that allows us to slow down, sit down at a table with friends or family and eat together. May I make a plea for the evening meal, and even suggest to you Sunday dinner at lunchtime. Over dinner, we strengthen family and community bonds — talking, laughing and sometimes even yelling. We interact as social beings. It's no coincidence that our most sacred acts of worship involve food and that celebrations involve family, community and food shared at the table.

We live in an increasingly disconnected world; this makes it even more important to come back to the table whenever we can to share a meal. Give yourself and those you love the opportunity to smell the aromas of delicious food cooking and to know that true sustenance is at hand — good food is powerful medicine. Bring back or unearth your table, set it with a beautiful cloth and lay out a bounty of good food. Stop, take a deep breath, give thanks for the meal and enjoy. In this space, your food will be taken in and understood, your heart will be lighter, and you will be renewed.

Soups

Rather than thickening a soup if it is too thin, I prefer to reduce it. When you reduce a soup, you concentrate flavour — a powerful tool. If you find that a soup (or stew for that matter) is too thin, simply remove the lid from your pot and increase the heat until you have a robust boil. Continue to boil until the soup reaches the desired thickness. Make sure you keep an eye on it, and stir from time to time, as it can stick — this is because a lot of the solids sink to the bottom, and the thinner watery liquid rises. You should notice that reducing brings the flavour together, so wait until later in the reduction process to adjust the flavours by adding seasonings such as salt, freshly ground black pepper or tamari. ଔ

Creamy corn chowder

GLUTEN FREE

SERVES 6 - 8

THIS IS A SOUP TO MAKE WHEN CORN IS IN SEASON, FRESHLY PICKED AND CHEAP. OUT-OF-SEASON CORN WILL NEVER HAVE THE SAME DELICIOUS FLAVOUR

A luscious late summer or early autumn meal. The key to this soup is a good stock; the rest is simple. This is a very flexible soup — you may like to add fresh coriander (cilantro) and finely sliced lemon grass to the onion base, or fold finely chopped jalapeno chilli or red capsicum (pepper) to the soup after it has been puréed — all are delicious.

1 tablespoon olive oil, ghee or butter
1 onion, roughly chopped
1 garlic clove, finely diced
2 celery stalks, finely diced
1–2 teaspoons finely grated fresh ginger (optional)
4–6 corn cobs (6 if the cobs are small)
1 potato, skin on, washed and roughly diced
1.75 litres (61 fl oz/7 cups) vegetable or chicken stock
2–3 tablespoons chopped coriander (cilantro)
crème fraîche, to serve (optional)

Put the oil or ghee in a good-sized pot — I use a 24 or 26 cm (9½ or 10½ inch) enamel-coated French oven. Add the onion, garlic, celery and ginger if using, and a sprinkle of sea salt and freshly ground black pepper. Cook over a gentle heat for 5–6 minutes, or until ever so slightly blushed with colour.

Cut the kernels from the corn and add to the pot, along with the leftover cobs, potato and 1.5 litres (52 fl oz/6 cups) of the stock. Cover, leaving the lid slightly ajar, and simmer for 20 minutes, or until the vegetables are cooked.

Remove the cobs and discard. Process half the soup very well, either in a blender, or using a stick blender, then stir back into the soup.

If the soup is too thin, cook over medium heat at a generous simmer until reduced to the desired consistency. If it is too thick, add the remaining stock. Check for taste and season with sea salt and freshly ground black pepper as desired. Serve sprinkled with coriander, with some crème fraîche stirred through if desired.

∝ঙ

Warmly spiced pumpkin and adzuki bean soup

GLUTEN FREE

SERVES 6 – 8

A warmly spiced soup for a cold day, and very sustaining thanks to the adzuki beans. This soup is best served with a little yoghurt and coriander (cilantro) to break up what is otherwise a fairly dull brown colour.

> 1.3 kg (3 lb) very ripe pumpkin (winter squash), such as butternut,
>   jap or kent
> 2 tablespoons olive oil
> 1 brown onion, finely diced
> 3 garlic cloves, finely chopped
> 1 tablespoon finely diced fresh ginger
> a pinch of freshly ground nutmeg
> 1 teaspoon ground cumin
> 1 teaspoon ground coriander

WILL ONLY BE
GLUTEN FREE IF
THE TAMARI DOES
NOT CONTAIN
WHEAT

a handful of coriander (cilantro), roughly chopped
220 g (7¾ oz/1 cup) adzuki beans, soaked overnight in plenty of water
a 5 cm (2 inch) piece of kombu
1.75 litres (61 fl oz/7 cups) vegetable stock
2 teaspoons tamari
2 tablespoons yoghurt (optional)

Preheat the oven to 200°C (400°F/Gas 6). If using a butternut pumpkin, cut it in half lengthways and scoop out the seeds. If using jap or kent, cut it into very large sections and remove the seeds. Rub the flesh with 1 tablespoon of the olive oil. Place on a baking tray and bake for 60–70 minutes, or until soft. Remove from the oven and leave until cool enough to handle.

Once the pumpkin is cooked, put the remaining olive oil in a large saucepan — I use a 24 cm (9½ inch) French oven. Add the onion, garlic and ginger and sauté over a gentle heat for 5–6 minutes, or until the onion has softened and is lightly coloured. Add the nutmeg, cumin, ground coriander and half the fresh coriander, stir through and cook for about 1 minute.

Scoop the flesh from the roasted pumpkin and add to the pot with the drained beans and kombu. Pour in the stock, partly cover and cook at a gentle simmer for 1 hour.

Blend the soup well using a stick blender, or use a blender and return the soup to the pot. If the soup is too thin, cook over medium heat at a generous simmer until reduced to the desired consistency, stirring frequently. Check for taste and add the tamari if required.

Spoon into warm bowls, swirl 1 teaspoon or so of yoghurt through each bowl if desired and sprinkle with the remaining fresh coriander.

ঙ

Lightly spiced parsnip soup

GLUTEN FREE

SERVES 4 - 6

WILL ONLY BE
GLUTEN FREE IF
THE TAMARI DOES
NOT CONTAIN
WHEAT

Parsnip is an excellent source of slow-release energy. Here, apple is used to counterbalance its slight astringency, and helps to make a well-flavoured soup. You will achieve the best flavour using butter or ghee.

    1 tablespoon butter, ghee or olive oil (or a mixture)
    1 large onion, finely diced
    1 teaspoon curry powder
    4 small–medium parsnips, about 600 g (1 lb 5 oz) in total,
        peeled, woody core removed, then roughly diced
    1 potato, cut into 3–5 cm (1¼–2 inch) dice
    1 granny smith apple, peeled and roughly diced
    1 litre (35 fl oz/4 cups) vegetable stock
    2 teaspoons mirin, or to taste
    1 teaspoon tamari, or to taste
    plain yoghurt, to serve (optional)
    chopped chives, to serve (optional)

Put the butter and onion in a large pot and cook over a gentle heat for 5–6 minutes. Add the curry powder and cook for 1 minute.

Add the parsnip, potato, apple, stock and a pinch of sea salt. Partly cover with a lid and slowly simmer for 35–40 minutes, or until the vegetables are well cooked.

Blend well using a stick blender, or use a blender and return the soup to the pot. Check for taste and adjust with mirin, freshly ground black pepper and tamari. If the soup is too thin, cook over medium heat until reduced; if it's too thick, stir in a little more stock.

Serve in warm bowls, with a little yoghurt swirled through and sprinkled with chives, if desired.

 C3

Split pea and ham shank soup

GLUTEN FREE / DAIRY FREE

WILL ONLY BE GLUTEN FREE IF THE TAMARI DOES NOT CONTAIN WHEAT

SERVES 6 - 8

This is the most wonderful soup to have on a cold winter's day, for lunch or dinner. It's a thrifty way to use organic ham, and using the bone ensures maximum nutrients, especially minerals, in the soup. If it jells when cold, you know you have a powerful soup.

800 g (1 lb 12 oz) organic, nitrate-free ham shanks
2 brown onions
2 garlic cloves
3 carrots, skin on
2 large celery stalks
5 thyme sprigs
110 g (3¾ oz/½ cup) green split peas, picked through for stones, then rinsed
330 g (11½ oz/1½ cups) yellow split peas, picked through for stones,
    then rinsed
a big handful of parsley, stalks and all, finely chopped
2 teaspoons apple cider vinegar
2 tablespoons chopped mint, or to taste
tamari, to taste

Carefully cut the skin from the shanks and discard. Put the shanks in a large pot over a gentle heat — this will begin to render the fat from the shanks.

Meanwhile, roughly chop the onions, garlic, carrots and celery, adding each to the pot as you cut them. Pull some of the leaves from the thyme sprigs and add them to the pot with the stems. Add all the split peas, half the parsley, the vinegar, a good grind of black pepper and 2.5 litres (87 fl oz/10 cups) water. Partly cover and gently simmer, stirring often, for 1½–1¾ hours, or until the peas are well broken down.

Remove the shanks to a plate and cut the meat from the bones. Return the meat to the pot, together with half the mint. Test for flavour and add more mint if necessary, and tamari as desired. If the soup is too thin, cook over high heat until reduced to the desired consistency, stirring often as the peas will sink and stick to the bottom. Just before serving, add the remaining parsley and stir through.

☙

Sides and salads

When vegetables are very fresh — straight from the garden or grower — there is really very little else that needs to be done. One of my favourite meals came from a handful of asparagus, potato and spinach from the San Francisco Farmers Market, taken home and simply cooked. By adding fat in the form of dressings, butter, oils or bacon and ham to the vegetables you maximize their flavour, but critically, you also ensure optimum absorption of vitamins. ❧

Garlic runner beans

GLUTEN FREE

SERVES 4 - 6

I far prefer green runner beans to stringless beans — they have so much more flavour and body. Allow 50–100 g (1¾–3½ oz) beans per person, depending on how many other vegies you'll be serving with the meal.

400 g (14 oz) runner beans
½ tablespoon butter or ghee
1–2 garlic cloves, crushed

Add a pinch of sea salt to a large pot of water and bring to the boil. Top and tail the beans, then run a vegetable peeler along both sides to remove the strings. Depending on their length, either leave the beans whole or cut in half, then cut the beans in half lengthways into long, thin strips.

Add the beans to the boiling water and cook for 1–2 minutes — taste after 1 minute to check if they are just cooked. Tip the beans and water into a colander, drain well, then return the beans to the pot.

Add the butter and garlic and cook over medium–high heat for 30 seconds, or just long enough to take the 'sting' out of the garlic. Add sea salt and freshly ground black pepper to taste, then serve.

❧

Baked heirloom carrots with flavoured salt

GLUTEN FREE / DAIRY FREE / VEGAN

SERVES 4 - 6

Roasting carrots concentrates their delicious sweetness and everyone will love them. I prefer the glorious colours of the 'heirloom' varieties — yellow, white and purple — but the generic orange carrot is also fine for this dish. Oranges are a beautiful match with carrots, and any citrus zest would be a lovely addition.

    1 teaspoon sea salt
    a pinch of celery salt or celery seed
    1/8 – 1/4 teaspoon freshly ground black pepper
    1 teaspoon thyme
    1 teaspoon oregano
    600 g (1 lb 5 oz) young, small carrots, tops trimmed and scrubbed
    2 teaspoons olive oil

Preheat the oven to 200°C (400°F/Gas 6). Put the salt, celery salt, pepper, thyme and oregano in a mortar and pound until finely ground. Alternatively, grind them in a mini food processor.

Place the carrots, olive oil and half the herb salt on a baking tray and rub through. Spread the carrots out so they roast — rather than steam — in the oven.

Bake for 20–30 minutes, or until just tender and lightly coloured. Taste and add more herb salt if desired.

∞

Braised garlic kale

GLUTEN FREE

SERVES 4 - 6

Kale is cheap and highly nutritious — it's an especially rich source of calcium, as are all dark leafy greens. It comes in two varieties: curly and the very dark Tuscan, which has a more compact and flat leaf. I prefer it with butter, but olive oil is fine also — you are best to serve some fat with it, as this will ensure optimum uptake of the nutrients. Kale reduces hugely, so be game with the amount you cook. If serving this dish with Pirates Pie (page 147), squeeze the juice from half a lemon into the remaining liquids before reducing.

750 g (1 lb 10 oz) curly or Tuscan kale
30 g (1 oz) butter, or 1 tablespoon olive oil or ghee
3 garlic cloves, roughly chopped
185 ml (6 fl oz/¾ cup) vegetable stock or water, approximately

Cut the stems from the kale and discard. Wash the leaves well and shake dry. Roughly chop the leaves — but not too finely, especially if using Tuscan kale.

Heat the butter and garlic in a wok or large frying pan over medium heat. Add the kale — it should lightly sizzle — and cook for 5 minutes, stirring or turning frequently. Add the stock and a pinch of sea salt and freshly ground black pepper, bring to the boil, then reduce the heat to a simmer. Cover and cook for a further 10–15 minutes, or until the kale is tender.

Remove the kale and keep warm. Increase the heat and simmer the remaining liquid until reduced by about half, then pour over the kale and serve.

VARIATIONS

Rather than pouring the reduced cooking liquid over the kale, try serving it with the Pine Nut and Currant Dressing from the Beetroot and Goat's Cheese Salad on page 110.

ༀ

KALE IS ALSO WONDERFUL COOKED IN SOME KIND OF BROTH. ADD IT TO A CHICKEN OR VEGETABLE SOUP, MINESTRONE, OR THE FRAGRANT COCONUT FISH AND VEGETABLE CURRY ON PAGE 154 10 MINUTES BEFORE SERVING

Time saver
BRAISE SOME EXTRA KALE AND FOLD ANY LEFTOVERS INTO PASTA FOR A QUICK MEAL, OR USE IN SANDWICHES, A FRITTATA, OR ON A PIZZA

Zucchini coins with pesto

GLUTEN FREE / DAIRY FREE OR VEGAN DEPENDING ON PESTO USED

SERVES 4

This side dish is an incredibly quick and wonderful thing to put together. It can sit until you're ready for it, and is delicious at room temperature.

2 zucchini (courgettes), about 400 g (14 oz) in total
1 tablespoon olive oil
pesto (see Basics, pages 255–256), to taste

Cut the zucchini into 1 cm (½ inch) 'coins', or if the zucchini are very narrow, into 1.5 cm (⅝ inch) coins.

Put half the olive oil in a frying pan over medium heat. When the oil is hot, but not at all rippling or smoking, add half the zucchini and cook without turning for 1–2 minutes, or until speckled with brown underneath. Turn and cook on the other side, then turn out into a serving dish.

Add the remaining oil to the pan and cook the rest of the zucchini.

When all the zucchini is in the serving dish, toss with sea salt and freshly ground black pepper to taste, and as much pesto as desired.

ଔ

Calabacitas (summer harvest stew)

GLUTEN FREE

SERVES 2 - 3

Come high summer, every farmers market will have corn, zucchini (courgettes) and tomatoes — with maybe a few beans thrown in. Every corn-growing nation has some variation of this stew — I know it by the name of Calabacitas, Maque Choux or Succotash, but it's basically a quick stovetop stew of seasonal vegetables.

The butter really is a must — it provides depth to the dish, and makes the difference between boring vegetables and something you can't stop eating. It also requires fresh, vital vegetables and herbs — it's a true fresh-from-the-garden-to-the-table kind of dish. It's lovely by itself, or as a side to some fish or grilled meat.

1 corn cob
1 ripe tomato, or 150 g (5½ oz) ripe cherry tomatoes
30 g (1 oz) butter
2 green or yellow zucchini (courgettes), or one of each,
    sliced 1 cm (½ inch) thick
5 chives, finely chopped
2 tablespoons finely chopped coriander (cilantro) leaves
4–5 basil leaves, finely chopped

Using a sharp knife, cut the kernels from the corn cob and place in a bowl. Run the blunt side of the knife along the cob to remove any remaining milk and germ, and add to the kernels. Discard the cob.

If you're using a large tomato and it is still quite firm, peel off the skin using a vegetable peeler. If it is very squishy-ripe, score a cross in the base, place in a heatproof bowl and cover with boiling water. Leave for 30 seconds, then plunge in cold water. Peel the skin away from the cross, then cut the tomato into 1 cm (½ inch) slices, or into large dice. If using cherry tomatoes, leave them unpeeled and whole.

Heat the butter in a frying pan or skillet over medium–high heat. When the butter is hot, add the zucchini and cook for 2 minutes, or until lightly browned underneath — it's important this happens fairly quickly, so the zucchini doesn't 'stew'. Turn and brown the other side for 1 minute.

Stir in the corn and some sea salt and freshly ground black pepper to taste — smell that corn! Reduce the heat to medium and cook for 2 minutes, then stir in the tomato and herbs. Cook for 5 minutes, or until the corn is tender. Serve.

VARIATIONS

For extra body, add some cooked white beans, such as butterbeans (lima beans) or cannellini. If you love a bit of heat, fresh or roasted chilli is a great addition.

ↂ

THIS DISH IS REALLY BEST MADE WHEN TOMATOES, CORN AND ZUCCHINI ARE IN SEASON

Time saver
LEFTOVER CALABACITAS MAKES FOR A GREAT FRITTATA THE NEXT DAY. GENTLY HEAT THE STEW IN A FRYING PAN, WHISK UP SOME EGGS AND POUR OVER. SEE THE FRITTATA RECIPES ON PAGES 56–58 AND PAGE 112

The big green

GLUTEN FREE / DAIRY FREE / VEGAN

SERVES 4 – 6

Time saver

MAKE EXTRA
TAMARI PEPITAS.
THEY KEEP FOR
ABOUT 1 WEEK
IN AN AIRTIGHT
CONTAINER, AND
WILL ADD TASTE
AND NUTRIENTS
TO A QUICK
LUNCH SALAD

An all-purpose green salad, absolutely brimming with nutrients and enzymes. Use whatever greens take your fancy, but include broccoli sprouts if you can — they have more disease-fighting nutrients than you can credit. Avocado provides the important fats required to assimilate all the vitamins and minerals, and the tamari pepitas … well they just make all that goodness delicious — even kids love them.

Dressing
60 ml (2 fl oz/ $\frac{1}{4}$ cup) best-quality extra virgin olive oil or
    linseed (flax seed) oil
1 tablespoon balsamic vinegar
$\frac{1}{2}$ teaspoon wholegrain mustard
2 garlic cloves, crushed
$\frac{1}{2}$–1 teaspoon apple juice concentrate

70 g (2$\frac{1}{2}$ oz/ $\frac{1}{2}$ cup) pepitas (pumpkin seeds)
1 tablespoon tamari
1 small head of lettuce — any variety is fine
75 g (2$\frac{1}{2}$ oz/1 cup) broccoli sprouts
1 avocado, sliced

Put all the dressing ingredients in a small bowl and whisk together. Check for taste, adjust as desired and set aside.

Put the pepitas in a frying pan and cook over medium heat for 4–5 minutes, or until lightly coloured and beginning to pop — take care not to overcook. Immediately turn off the heat, stir in the tamari and tip the seeds into a small bowl — they will crisp up as they cool.

Separate the leaves from the lettuce, wash well and dry. Tear any large leaves, then arrange on a serving platter with the sprouts and avocado slices. Sprinkle with the cooled tamari pepitas and the dressing, then gently toss through with your fingers.

CB

Salad of orange, fennel and olives with a cumin and honey vinaigrette

GLUTEN FREE / DAIRY FREE

SERVES 4 – 6

The most flexible of salads, with the lovely sweetness from oranges and honey adding gorgeous flavour hues — delicious with just about everything. This salad is particularly fine with the Spanish Capsicum, Chickpea and Fennel Pie on page 136. You could also drizzle the vinaigrette over any green salad.

Cumin and honey vinaigrette
1 teaspoon honey
1 tablespoon lemon juice
3 – 4 mint leaves, finely chopped
½ teaspoon ground cumin
2 tablespoons extra virgin olive oil
a pinch of sea salt

2 generous handfuls of lettuce leaves (mizuna is a lovely choice)
1 small fennel bulb, washed, dried and sliced wafer-thin
1 – 2 oranges
10 – 12 pitted kalamata olives, torn apart
3 – 4 flat-leaf (Italian) parsley sprigs, leaves picked

Put all the vinaigrette ingredients in a small bowl and whisk together.

Wash the lettuce leaves and dry them well. Break off any stems, then arrange the lettuce on a platter with the fennel.

Peel the oranges, making sure the white pith is removed. Holding the orange in your other hand, use a small sharp knife to cut the segments from each orange, so that the skin on both sides of each segment is removed but the flesh remains intact. Arrange the orange segments over the salad, scatter with the olives and parsley and drizzle with the vinaigrette.

ଓଃ

WHEN IN SEASON, BLOOD ORANGES ARE BEAUTIFUL IN THIS SALAD

Beetroot and goat's cheese salad with a pine nut and currant dressing

GLUTEN FREE

SERVES 4 – 6

Currently my most favourite salad. It's a perfect marriage, where the sweetness of beetroot is cut with the delicious tartness of the goat's cheese. Again, the dressing is wonderful for other uses, and is superb over Braised Garlic Kale (page 105). This salad makes a beautiful first course or wonderful light dinner.

Pine nut and currant dressing
125 ml (4 fl oz/½ cup) good-quality, fruity extra virgin olive oil
1½–2 tablespoons apple cider or white wine vinegar, to taste
1–2 garlic cloves, crushed
¼ teaspoon apple juice concentrate or sugar, or to taste
1–2 tablespoons pine nuts
1–2 tablespoons currants

4 small–medium beetroot (or 6 if very small), skins on and washed
a great big handful of salad leaves, such as mizuna, rocket (arugula)
    or baby English spinach
6 slices of organic sourdough bread
200–300 g (7–10½ oz) young goat's cheese — allow 50 g (1¾ oz)
    per person

The vinaigrette is best prepared the night before to allow the pine nuts and currants to absorb the flavours. Simply put all the ingredients in a screw-top jar with a pinch of sea salt and shake well. Check for taste, then adjust with more vinegar and sweetener if needed, remembering that the beetroot in the salad will be quite sweet. Refrigerate until required.

Preheat the oven to 180°C (350°F/Gas 4). Place the beetroot in a baking dish and add 1½ tablespoons water. Cover with foil and bake for about 1 hour, or until soft (the actual time will depend on the size of the beetroot).

Remove the beetroot from the oven and allow to cool a little. While they are still warm, slip off the skins, wearing gloves to stop your hands staining. Cut the beetroot into quarters or halves, depending on their size.

Toss the salad leaves with a small amount of the vinaigrette and arrange on a platter. Arrange the beetroot over the greens.

Grill or toast the sourdough bread and serve separately on a board with the goat's cheese. Serve the remaining vinaigrette in a small jug for pouring over.

VARIATIONS

Roast the pine nuts for extra flavour before adding to the dressing.

ↂ

Mains

What to eat for dinner is the perennial question, but I believe it's not the cooking that does you in, but the thinking about what on earth you are going to cook that does. I hope the following recipes give you some inspiration. I've included my 'haven't gone shopping and the cupboards are pretty bare' options, the 'I'm feeling pretty confident tonight and able to put together something a little more complex' options, my quick and simple alternatives, and all the scenarios in between.

Most of the following recipes are vegetarian, but have built-in alternatives to make the recipe dairy free or vegan if that is what you desire. For example, the Quick Beanie Mix with Arepas (opposite) will be vegan and dairy free if olive oil and avocado are used, but vegetarian if butter and sour cream are used. ⁓

Cupboard love frittata

GLUTEN FREE / DAIRY FREE

SERVES 4 – 6

This is the kind of meal to put together when the cupboards are a little bare: simple food that tastes great and fills a hungry stomach. Generally, there are potatoes around, some eggs, and if you're lucky, some herbs in the garden. The frittata is excellent served hot or warm with a generous salad (olives are a perfect match here), or cold as part of an antipasto platter or lunch the next day.

1 garlic bulb, broken into cloves
1 tablespoon olive oil, plus extra, for drizzling
480 g (1 lb 1 oz) potatoes, skin on, scrubbed, and cut into
   2 cm (¾ inch) chunks
2 small–medium onions, finely sliced
1 teaspoon mirin
2 teaspoons finely chopped rosemary
1 tablespoon finely chopped chives
1 tablespoon finely chopped parsley
6 eggs

A WAXY POTATO
SUCH AS A KIPFLER
(FINGERLING),
PINK EYE OR
PATRONE IS BEST IN
THIS FRITTATA,
THOUGH I HAVE
USED PRETTY WELL
ANY TYPE WITH
GOOD RESULTS

Preheat the oven to 180°C (350°F/Gas 4). Place the garlic in a square of baking paper, drizzle with a little olive oil and twist the paper up to form a little parcel. Bake for 15–20 minutes, or until the garlic is soft and squishy to the touch. Remove from the oven, open the paper and allow to cool a little.

Meanwhile, place the potato chunks in a steamer and cook until just tender.

Heat the olive oil in a frying pan. Add the onion and sauté for 20 minutes over a gentle heat until very soft and lightly coloured. Add the mirin and herbs and cook for a further 10 minutes. Turn off the heat and add the potato.

Squeeze the roasted garlic cloves from their skins over the potato mixture and gently mix the garlic purée through. Transfer the potato mixture to a baking dish.

Crack the eggs into a bowl, season with sea salt and freshly ground black pepper and whisk well. Pour over the potato mixture and gently shake the dish from side to side to distribute the egg.

Bake for 35 minutes, or until the centre is just cooked — the frittata will cook and puff slightly from the outside in. I prefer it when the outer edges are puffed and lightly browned, with a softer centre.

ೞ

Quick beanie mix with arepas
GLUTEN FREE

SERVES 4

I always have some basics on hand — generally tinned beans and tomatoes. With that I can put together a quick bean mix that forms the basis of many a meal — on toast for breakfast, on nachos topped with avocado, olives, sour cream and salsa for dinner, into some puff pastry or bread cup for a pie, or simply heated in a bowl with avocado for a sustaining lunch. I've included a recipe here for an arepa — really it's a corn tortilla, only softened with a little fat. It's definitely worth making yourself when you consider that it only takes about 5 minutes, tastes awesome, and any commercial tortilla will generally contain loads of damaged fat. These arepas are also a brilliant gluten-free option.

2 tablespoons olive oil

½ onion, finely diced

2 carrots, cut into 1 cm (½ inch) dice

½ celery stalk, finely diced

¼ teaspoon ground cumin

¼ – ½ teaspoon good-quality chilli powder, or to taste

½ small orange sweet potato, about 115 g (4 oz), peeled and cut into 1 cm (½ inch) dice

2 garlic cloves, finely chopped

1 x 400 g (14 oz) tin pinto, borlotti (cranberry) or red kidney beans, rinsed and drained

1 x 400 g (14 oz) tin tomatoes

1 zucchini (courgette), cut into 1 cm (½ inch) dice

1 avocado, roughly chopped (optional)

yoghurt or sour cream, to serve (optional)

2 tablespoons chopped coriander (cilantro) leaves

Arepas (cornmeal flatbreads)

125 g (4½ oz/1 cup) masa harina (white, blue or yellow) (see Kitchen notes)

30 g (1 oz) melted butter, or 3 teaspoons olive oil or ghee

To make the beanie mix, heat the olive oil in a frying pan and add the onion, carrot and celery. Sauté over a gentle heat for 5 minutes, or until the onion is translucent. Add the cumin, chilli powder, sweet potato and garlic, stir well, then cook for a further 2–3 minutes.

Stir in the beans, tomatoes and 250 ml (9 fl oz/1 cup) water, then cover and gently simmer for 20 minutes, or until the vegetables are nearly cooked. Remove the lid and add the zucchini. Stirring frequently, cook at a hearty simmer for 10 minutes, or until the mixture is thick but still saucy.

Meanwhile, make the arepas. Put the flour in a bowl and have 250 ml (9 fl oz/1 cup) warm (not hot) water at the ready. Add the melted butter to the flour, with 125 ml (4 fl oz/ ½ cup) of the water. I have found I need to add more water for yellow masa than blue masa, using about 210 ml (7½ fl oz) for yellow masa, and about 170 ml (5½ fl oz/⅔ cup) for blue masa. Using a wooden spoon, mix vigorously until the dough comes together and starts to form a ball — it will firm up as you mix, and should be moist but not wet. Continue to give it a good mix, then cover with a tea towel (dish towel) and leave to cool. It will firm up during this time — the resulting dough should be malleable and easy to roll, but not at all stiff or dry looking.

When cool, divide the dough into four. Roll the dough out between two sheets of baking paper to an 18 cm (7 inch) diameter. The paper will stick to the dough, so you will need to pick up the paper and peel it off, replace it, turn the whole thing over and release and replace the bottom sheet of paper. After another couple of rolls, the dough will begin to stick again, so release and replace the paper again until you are able to roll the dough to the desired size.

Heat a frying pan (cast iron is best) over high heat — do not add any fat to the pan. Peel the top sheet of paper from the arepa, and invert into the frypan. Gently peel the paper off and and cook for 2–3 minutes, or until lightly speckled underneath with colour — this colour is harder to see when using the blue masa, so take care not to overcook. Turn and cook for a further 2–3 minutes. Cook the remaining arepas in the same way.

To serve, pile the beanie mix in the middle of the arepa, add some avocado if desired, drizzle with a little yoghurt or sour cream if desired, sprinkle with the chopped coriander and simply fold over to eat!

KITCHEN NOTES: *Masa harina, a ground cornmeal flour, is probably one of the handiest things to have in your store cupboard. However it is really only available from specialized stores and may also be called 'maseca'. The corn is unique in the sense it has been cooked in a lime (alkaline) solution, and then dried. This releases the bound vitamin B3 and balances the protein, which is especially important if you eat a lot of corn products. When you add liquid to masa it forms a dough that is very malleable and smells and tastes very corny — entirely delicious. Any unused mixture will keep in an airtight container in the fridge for a day or so. This great gluten-free flatbread is equally good hot or cold.*

08

DIFFERENT BRANDS AND DIFFERENT COLOURED MASAS VARY IN THE AMOUNT OF WATER THEY ABSORB. IF, AFTER COOKING, YOUR AREPA IS CRISP AND DRY, YOU HAVE NOT ADDED ENOUGH WATER

Black-eyed pea and summertime vegetable stew

GLUTEN FREE / DAIRY FREE AND VEGAN DEPENDING ON PESTO USED

SERVES 4 – 6

WILL ONLY BE
GLUTEN FREE IF
THE TAMARI IS
WHEAT FREE

Black-eyed peas are one of my favourite legumes — they don't require pre-soaking and take only 45 minutes or so to cook. This is a simple and delicious stew to make, but it is seasonal, and depends heavily on the quality of the ingredients. Fresh, organic vegetables will give you the flavour you are after, and the addition of pesto completes it. (If you do make this dish out of season, try frying up some chopped bacon or pancetta before adding the onion.) The stew easily extends to feed up to eight, by serving it with pasta.

BLACK-EYED PEAS
ARE ALSO CALLED
BLACK-EYED
BEANS IN SOME
COUNTRIES. DON'T
CONFUSE THEM
WITH THE BLACK
(TURTLE) BEAN
— THEY ARE A
LOVELY BEIGE OR
CREAM COLOUR,
WITH A MARKED
BLACK 'EYE'
WHERE THE BEAN
WAS JOINED TO
THE POD

1 generous tablespoon olive oil
1 small onion or well-washed leek (white part only), finely sliced
2–3 garlic cloves, finely sliced or crushed
¼ teaspoon dried oregano
1 teaspoon fresh oregano
10–15 basil leaves, roughly chopped
¼–½ teaspoon ground fennel (organic is much stronger in flavour)
100 g (3½ oz/¾ cup) dried black-eyed peas
4–5 small carrots, scrubbed and cut into quarters lengthways
15 green beans, cut into 6 cm (2½ inch) lengths
½ small orange sweet potato, cut into batons about 3–4 cm
    (1¼–1½ inch) long and 2 cm (¾ inch) wide
3 large ripe tomatoes, cut into thin wedges, or 400 g (14 oz) tin
    chopped tomatoes
2 small zucchini (courgettes) or yellow squash, sliced if small,
    or cut into 2 cm (¾ inch) dice if large
1 teaspoon tamari, or to taste
pesto, to serve (see Basics, pages 255–256)

I make this stew in a 24 cm (9½ inch) cast-iron, enamel-coated French oven, but a large saucepan or pot will do.

Warm the pot over gentle heat. Add the olive oil and start adding the onion, garlic, dried and fresh oregano and basil as you chop them.

Add the ground fennel and gently sauté for 10 minutes, allowing the flavours to come together. Stir every now and then, cooking until very soft — the mixture should be very lightly coloured.

Add the black-eyed peas, some freshly ground black pepper and enough water to cover by about 2 cm (³/₄ inch). Partly cover and simmer for 30 minutes, checking after 15 minutes that there is still enough water.

Add the carrot, beans, sweet potato and tomatoes, with a little more water if necessary to come about two-thirds up the side of the vegetables — they should not be covered, as too much liquid will dilute the flavour of the stew. Stir well, then cover and simmer for 20 minutes, or until the vegetables are just soft, stirring every now and then.

Remove the lid, add the zucchini and simmer for 8 minutes, or until the zucchini is just cooked. Check for taste, adding sea salt and freshly ground black pepper, then adding tamari if needed (this will depend a lot on the sweetness of your vegetables). Serve with pesto.

VARIATIONS

If you come across a handful of fresh broad (fava) or borlotti (cranberry) beans, you could use those instead for this recipe, or mix them in with the black-eyed peas. Fresh borlotti beans will need to be cooked as per the recipe, while fresh broad beans (double-peel them if old) should be added with the zucchini (courgette).

You can also simmer the black-eyed peas in vegetable stock instead of water.

CB

Red beans with brown speckled rice

GLUTEN FREE

SERVES 4 - 6

Such a plain name that does no justice to one of the best comfort meals of all time — Michael Franti even has a song named after this most loved of meals. This dish can easily be enriched by adding celery, carrot, red wine and tomato paste (concentrated purée) — those bastions of the casserole or ragout. This is a great dish for the slow cooker — sautéeing the flavourings in a pan as described, then adding all the ingredients to the slow cooker. Served with Brown Speckled Rice (see Basics, page 246), this is a deeply satisfying meal for a cold winter's night.

USING BUTTER OR GHEE IN THIS RECIPE WILL GIVE A BETTER RESULT THAN USING OIL

½ –1 tablespoon butter, ghee or olive oil
1 onion, finely diced
a generous pinch of dried basil
a generous pinch of dried oregano
¼ teaspoon dried thyme
2 bay leaves
2 garlic cloves, crushed or finely diced
finely sliced red or green chilli, to taste
¼ – ½ teaspoon freshly ground black pepper, to taste
210 g (7½ oz/1 cup) dried red kidney beans, sorted through and soaked overnight in 2.5 litres (87 fl oz/10 cups) water
a 5 cm (2 inch) strip of kombu
1–2 tablespoons finely chopped flat-leaf (Italian) parsley
1 quantity Brown Speckled Rice, to serve (see Basics, page 246)

TRADITIONAL INGREDIENTS FOR THIS DISH INCLUDE RED AND GREEN CAPSICUMS (PEPPERS), SPRING ONIONS (SCALLIONS) — INCLUDING THE GREEN BITS — AND HAM BONES. THE ONIONS, SPRING ONIONS, CAPSICUMS, GARLIC AND SPICES WOULD BE SAUTÉED IN BACON DRIPPINGS

Melt the butter or heat the oil over a gentle heat in a large flameproof casserole dish. Add the onion, dried herbs and bay leaves and very gently sauté for 5 minutes, or until the onion is softened but not browned. Add the garlic, chilli and black pepper and sauté for a further 3 minutes.

Drain the beans and rinse well. Add to the pot with 1 litre (35 fl oz/4 cups) water and the kombu. Partly cover and increase the heat to a gentle boil. Cook for 1½–2 hours, making sure the beans remain covered with water.

Remove the lid and increase the boil, then cook the beans for a further 5 minutes, or until reduced to a thick, saucy consistency, stirring often. Check for taste, adjusting the pepper if necessary. Stir in the parsley and serve with the speckled rice.

ભ

Black bean cakes with crunchy green salsa

GLUTEN FREE / DAIRY FREE / VEGAN

MAKES 6 PATTIES

A little bit spicy and very delicious. Hearty and sustaining, quick to throw together, these bean cakes make a satisfying dinner or lunch any time of year. Lime is a must: if you are not serving these with the Crunchy Green Salsa, which is really more of a salad, make sure you squeeze a bit over before eating. The simple lime-based salsa complements the black bean cakes and the Market Vegetable Enchiladas on page 121 perfectly — it's not a stand-alone salad. It provides great colour, texture, nutrition and flavour. Without the dressing the salsa will keep, covered, in the fridge for a day or so.

½ orange sweet potato, about 200 g (7 oz), peeled and cut into 2 cm
  (¾ inch) dice
1 tablespoon olive oil
1 small brown onion, finely chopped
2 garlic cloves, crushed or finely chopped
1 teaspoon ground cumin
½ teaspoon ground coriander
1 tablespoon roughly chopped fresh coriander (cilantro)
⅛ – ¼ teaspoon chipotle chilli powder, to taste
425 g (15 oz) tin or 250 g (9 oz/1½ cups) cooked black (turtle) beans
95 g (3¼ oz/½ cup) cooked brown rice, hulled millet or quinoa
maize flour, for dusting (see Kitchen notes)
olive oil or flavourless coconut oil, for pan-frying

THESE BEAN CAKES ARE A GREAT WAY TO USE UP SMALL AMOUNTS OF LEFTOVER COOKED GRAIN

Crunchy green salsa
½ savoy or Chinese cabbage
a large handful of snow pea (mangetout) shoots
10–12 snow peas (mangetout), cut lengthways into julienne strips
1 avocado, thinly sliced
a large handful of coriander (cilantro) leaves
seeded and finely sliced red or green chilli, to taste (optional)
2 tablespoons lime juice
1 teaspoon finely grated fresh ginger
1 garlic clove, crushed

Time saver

ANY LEFTOVER
CRUNCHY GREEN
SALSA IS A GREAT
ADDITION TO
THE FRAGRANT
COCONUT FISH
AND VEGETABLE
CURRY ON
PAGE 154

Boil the sweet potato for 7 minutes, or until soft. Drain well and set aside.

Put the olive oil in a frying pan and gently heat. Add the onion, garlic, cumin, dried and fresh coriander, and some sea salt and freshly ground black pepper. Gently sauté for 5 minutes, stirring every now and then. Add the chilli powder and cook for a further 2 minutes, or until the onion is translucent and cooked through.

Put the beans in a bowl with the rice and sweet potato. Mix together well, taking care to mash a good percentage of the beans, until the mixture holds together. Add the sautéed onion and mix well, then form the mixture into six patties. Dust in the maize flour, making sure they are evenly coated. Refrigerate for 30 minutes.

Meanwhile, make the salsa. Cut the cabbage in half and remove the core. Slice the cabbage finely and place in a bowl. Cut the lovely green leafy ends from the snow pea shoots and add to the bowl, discarding the stems. Add the snow peas, avocado, coriander and chilli, if using. In a small bowl, combine the lime juice, ginger and garlic. Pour over the greens, and gently toss through with your hands. Refrigerate until required.

Pour enough oil into a frying pan to cover the base well and heat to medium–high. When the oil is hot (but not smoking), add all the patties and cook for 2 minutes, or until browned underneath. The patties should sizzle lightly. Turn and cook for a further 2 minutes. Drain on paper towels and serve with the salsa.

KITCHEN NOTES: *Maize flour is a fine golden-yellow flour, not to be confused with white cornflour (cornstarch).*

രു

Market vegetable enchiladas

GLUTEN FREE

SERVES 4

Enchiladas make a great family meal, and are a wonderful way to sneak vegetables into the diet. Look for good-quality corn tortillas — this means you don't want to see the words 'vegetable oil' or 'vegetable shortening' on the ingredient list. Serve with the Crunchy Green Salsa opposite, or for a quicker option, with shredded lettuce, coriander (cilantro) and avocado with a bit of lime drizzled over. Sour cream or crème fraîche is also a lovely addition and will aid the digestion.

Tomato sauce
1 tablespoon olive oil
1 small–medium brown onion, finely diced
3 garlic cloves, crushed or finely diced
1/4 teaspoon ground cumin
1/4 teaspoon dried oregano
2 tablespoons roughly chopped coriander (cilantro)
1/4 teaspoon chipotle chilli powder
1/8–1/4 teaspoon good-quality mellow-flavoured chilli powder, to taste
185 ml (6 fl oz/3/4 cup) vegetable or chicken stock
2 x 400 g (14 oz) tins chopped tomatoes

Filling
2 tablespoons olive oil
200 g (7 oz) zucchini (courgette) or yellow squash, cut into 1 cm
    (1/2 inch) dice
1/2 teaspoon ground cumin
1 corn cob, kernels sliced off
1 blackened red capsicum (pepper), cut into strips (see Basics, page 255)
chopped fresh jalapeno chilli, to taste (optional)
2 tablespoons roughly chopped coriander (cilantro)

8 corn tortillas, 15–16 cm (6 inches) in diameter
100 g (3½ oz/heaped 3/4 cup) grated melting cheese, such as cheddar
1 quantity of Crunchy Green Salsa (see opposite)

I USE A MELLOW, GOOD-QUALITY CHILLI POWDER MADE FROM THE NEW MEXICO CHILLI, WHICH HAS A SWEET, LIGHT, SMOKY FLAVOUR

To make the tomato sauce, heat the olive oil in a frying pan, add the onion, garlic, cumin, oregano and coriander and stir through. Cook over a gentle heat for 5 minutes, or until the onion is translucent and soft. Add the chipotle powder, chilli powder, stock and tomatoes, stir through and simmer for a further 20–30 minutes, or until the sauce has reduced by one-third. Season with sea salt and freshly ground black pepper and set aside.

Preheat the oven to 180°C (350°F/Gas 4).

To make the filling, put 1 tablespoon of the olive oil in a frying pan or skillet and heat to medium–high. Add the zucchini pieces — they should sizzle slightly — and cook for 1–2 minutes, allowing them to colour a little. Stir a couple of times, then add the cumin, corn, capsicum strips and chilli, if using. Sauté for 5 minutes, or until the vegetables are just cooked. Turn off the heat and stir in the coriander and 2 tablespoons of the tomato sauce.

LIGHTLY COATING
THE TORTILLAS
WITH OIL AND
WARMING THEM
IS IMPORTANT —
IT SEALS THEM
AND STOPS THEM
BECOMING
TOO SPONGY

Spread the tortillas on two baking trays and brush each side lightly with the remaining oil. Heat in the oven for about 1 minute. Spread about 3 tablespoons of the tomato sauce in a 31 x 20 cm (12½ x 8 inch) baking dish (glass, enamel or cast iron is best). Spoon the filling down the centre of each tortilla, then roll them up and lay them in the baking dish, seam side down. Spoon the sauce over, making sure it covers the entire length of the tortillas, then sprinkle with the cheese. Cover and bake for 40–50 minutes, or until the cheese and sauce are bubbling around the edges, and the sauce is no longer watery.

To serve, top with some of the salsa, and serve the remaining salsa on each plate.

VARIATIONS

Add a finely shredded poached chicken breast or a small quantity of cooked black (turtle) beans to the hot vegetables.

For a smokier flavour, use tinned fire-roasted tomatoes in the sauce.

03

Orange pan-glazed tofu or tempeh

GLUTEN FREE / DAIRY FREE / VEGAN

SERVES 4

WILL ONLY BE
GLUTEN FREE IF
THE TAMARI IS
WHEAT FREE

A totally delicious vegetarian meal! Braising and frying is an extremely quick and easy way to add great flavour to tofu and tempeh. Any leftovers would be great added to some left-over grain and salad for lunch the next day.

> 250 ml (9 fl oz/1 cup) freshly squeezed orange juice
> 1 tablespoon finely grated fresh ginger
> 2 teaspoons tamari
> 1½ tablespoons mirin
> 2 teaspoons maple syrup
> ½ teaspoon ground coriander
> 2 small garlic cloves, crushed
> 300 g (10½ oz) firm tofu
> 2 tablespoons olive oil
> ½ lime
> a handful of coriander (cilantro) leaves

BE SURE TO USE A
FIRM TOFU HERE,
AS SOFTER/SILKEN
TOFU WILL NOT
HOLD UP

Put the orange juice in a small bowl. Squeeze the grated ginger over the bowl to extract the juices, then discard the pulp. Add the tamari, mirin, maple syrup, ground coriander and garlic. Mix together and set aside.

Cut the tofu in half diagonally, then cut each half into three slices and pat dry with a paper towel.

Put the olive oil in a frying pan over medium–high heat. When the oil is hot but not smoking, add the tofu and fry for 5 minutes, or until golden underneath. Turn and cook the other side for 5 minutes, or until golden. Pour the orange juice mixture into the pan and simmer for 10 minutes, or until the sauce has reduced to a lovely thick glaze. Turn the tofu once more during this time and spoon the sauce over the tofu from time to time.

Serve the tofu drizzled with any remaining sauce and a squeeze of lime, with the coriander scattered over the top.

CЗ

Sweet spiced potato and vegetable patties

GLUTEN FREE / DAIRY FREE / VEGAN

MAKES 12

WILL ONLY BE
GLUTEN FREE IF
THE TAMARI IS
WHEAT FREE

These are a fabulous alternative to tuna or salmon patties, and a great way to include cauliflower and broccoli in the diet. They are equally good the next day heated for lunch. Serve with mango chutney and steamed vegies or a salad.

DUTCH CREAM OR
NICOLA POTATOES
ARE GOOD CHOICES
FOR THESE PATTIES

600 g (1 lb 5 oz) potatoes, skin on, scrubbed and cut into 2.5 cm (1 inch) dice
230 g (8 oz) cauliflower
1 carrot, skin on, washed
100 g (3½ oz) broccoli (including the stalk)
¾ teaspoon ground cumin, or ½ teaspoon if using organic
¾ teaspoon garam masala, or ½ teaspoon if using organic
2 tablespoons finely chopped coriander (cilantro)
1 tablespoon lime or lemon juice
1 teaspoon tamari
maize flour, for dusting
ghee, flavourless coconut oil or olive oil, for pan-frying

THE MAIZE
FLOUR IS A FINE
GOLDEN-YELLOW
FLOUR, NOT TO
BE CONFUSED
WITH WHITE
CORNFLOUR
(CORNSTARCH)

Steam the potatoes for 10–13 minutes, or until soft, then turn into a bowl and mash. While the potatoes are steaming, cut the cauliflower into 1 cm (½ inch) dice. Cut the carrot and broccoli stalk the same size, and the broccoli florets a little bigger. Steam the cauliflower and carrot together for 4 minutes, then add the broccoli and steam for 3–4 minutes, or until all the vegetables are just soft.

Add the steamed vegetables to the potatoes and mash them in a little, still keeping their shape. Add the cumin, garam masala, coriander, lime juice, tamari and some freshly ground black pepper, then mix together well using a spoon. Taste and add some sea salt if needed. Form into 12 patties (or make them larger if desired). Lightly dust with the maize flour and place on a board.

Put enough ghee or oil in a frying pan to cover the base well and heat. Add the patties in batches and cook over medium heat (they should sizzle lightly) for 5–7 minutes, or until golden underneath, then turn and cook the other side until golden. Drain on paper towels before serving.

ჹ

Mushroom and white bean cacciatore

GLUTEN FREE

SERVES 4 – 6

A robust stew to serve on a cold winter's night over polenta (see Basics, page 245) or mash. Alternatively you might like to reduce it to a thicker consistency, place it in a baking dish and top with mashed potatoes for a delicious pie.

100 g (3½ oz/½ cup) dried butterbeans (lima beans), cannellini or great northern beans, soaked overnight in 2 litres (70 fl oz/8 cups) water, or a 410 g (14½ oz) tin butterbeans (lima beans), drained
a 5 cm (2 inch) piece of kombu (if using dried beans)
30 g (1 oz) butter
1 tablespoon olive oil
1 large or 2 small brown onions, cut in half and finely sliced
200 g (7 oz) small Swiss brown mushrooms or button mushrooms
3 garlic cloves
2 teaspoons rosemary
2 bay leaves
1 tablespoon balsamic vinegar
60 ml (2 fl oz/¼ cup) red wine
2 carrots, skin on, scrubbed and cut into 5 mm (¼ inch) slices
2 celery stalks, finely sliced
3 teaspoons dark brown sugar
375 ml (13 fl oz/1½ cups) vegetable stock
400 g (14 oz) tin chopped tomatoes
10 kalamata olives, pitted and roughly chopped
a handful of flat-leaf (Italian) parsley, finely chopped

If using dried beans, drain and rinse well. Place in a good-sized pot with the kombu and enough water to cover by 10 cm (4 inches). Bring to the boil, then reduce the heat and cook at a gentle simmer for 1½ hours, or until soft. Drain the beans, discarding the kombu. Set aside.

Put the butter and olive oil in a large saucepan over low–medium heat. When the butter has melted, add the onion with a pinch of sea salt and sauté for 10 minutes, or until the onion is lightly coloured. Add the mushrooms and cook for a further 5–6 minutes, or until lightly coloured.

Finely chop the garlic and rosemary together, then add to the saucepan with the bay leaves. Stir through, increase the heat to high, splash in the vinegar and let it sizzle and reduce. After 1 minute, stir in the wine, carrot, celery, sugar, stock, tomatoes and some sea salt and freshly ground black pepper. Reduce the heat, cover and cook at a gentle simmer for 10 minutes.

Remove the lid, add the beans and gently simmer for 10 minutes, or until the carrots are just cooked. Add the olives, increase the heat to a gentle boil and cook, stirring often, for a further 10–15 minutes, or until you have a nice, thick sauce. The flavour should adjust and balance out during this phase. Stir in the parsley and serve.

VARIATIONS

This is a very flexible base recipe. You could add 6 boneless chicken thighs, cut into 2 cm (¾ inch) pieces, or a small chicken, cut into legs, thighs, wings and breast (you can freeze the carcass for stock). If using chicken, you'll need another 125 ml (4 fl oz/½ cup) stock.

ლ

Roasted eggplant with a salsa of chickpeas, black olives and blackened capsicum

GLUTEN FREE

WILL ONLY BE
GLUTEN FREE IF
THE TAMARI IS
WHEAT FREE

SERVES 4

A robust example of how easy it is to put together a quick and delicious meal after a visit to a farmers market. Don't be afraid to experiment a little with this recipe… you might like to include tomatoes in the salsa as well.

Balsamic baste
1 tablespoon balsamic vinegar
1 tablespoon tamari
2-3 garlic cloves, crushed
6 large basil leaves, finely sliced
2 tablespoons olive oil

2 small eggplants (aubergines), or 4 slender eggplants
olive oil, for pan-frying

Chickpea, black olive and capsicum salsa

1 blackened red capsicum (pepper), finely diced (see Basics, page 255)
80 g (2¾ oz/½ cup) pitted kalamata olives, roughly chopped
160 g (5½ oz/1 cup) cooked chickpeas
2 large basil leaves, finely sliced
3 tablespoons finely chopped flat-leaf (Italian) parsley
1 tablespoon finely chopped mint
100 g (3½ oz) feta cheese, cut into small dice

Preheat the oven to 170°C (325°F/Gas 3). Put all the balsamic baste ingredients in a small bowl. Add freshly ground black pepper to taste, mix well and set aside.

Cut each eggplant in half lengthways, then lightly cut into the exposed flesh in a crisscross pattern. Heat enough olive oil in a frying pan to lightly cover the base, then add the eggplant, cut side down. Fry, in batches if necessary, over medium heat for 5 minutes, or until lightly golden underneath — make sure the oil does not smoke; if it does, the temperature is too high.

Transfer the eggplant to a baking dish, cut side up. Paint or spoon half the balsamic baste onto and into the eggplant — squeezing each piece a little to open the flesh and take in the flavours. Bake for 20–30 minutes, or until the flesh is soft.

Combine all the salsa ingredients in a small bowl. Add the remaining balsamic baste, mix together, then season to taste with sea salt and freshly ground black pepper. Serve spooned over the roasted eggplant.

VARIATIONS

Skinned, seeded and finely diced fresh, ripe tomatoes are wonderful added to the salsa instead of the capsicum. And instead of the chickpeas, use some fresh cannellini or fresh broad (fava) beans in the salsa.

Pesto (see Basics, pages 255–256) can be brushed onto and into the eggplants instead of (or as well as) the balsamic baste.

CB

YOUNG, FRESHLY PICKED EGGPLANTS ARE BEST HERE. IF THEY HAVE A LOT OF SEED DEVELOPMENT, THEY WILL NEED TO BE SALTED. SPRINKLE SOME SALT ONTO THE DRAINING AREA OF YOUR SINK. PLACE THE EGGPLANT SLICES ON THE SALT, THEN SPRINKLE WITH MORE SALT. LEAVE FOR 30 MINUTES, RINSE WELL AND PAT DRY

LEFTOVERS OF THIS DISH WILL NEVER GO ASTRAY AND WILL BE GREAT AS A SALAD FOR LUNCH THE NEXT DAY — YOU COULD ADD EXTRA VEGIES, AND EVEN SOME LEFTOVER GRAIN

Cannelloni

When silverbeet (Swiss chard) is in season and abundant, cannelloni is always on the menu. Make sure to use young, fresh leaves that are not too large, as these have the best flavour and texture. The tofu option is also fabulous, but I think it still needs cheese on top for the best result.

2 tablespoons olive oil, or 40 g (1½ oz) butter
1 red onion, finely diced
5 garlic cloves
a large handful of basil
2 x 400 g (14 oz) tins chopped tomatoes, or 800 g (1 lb 12 oz)
    finely chopped fresh, ripe tomatoes
1–2 teaspoons apple juice concentrate or rapadura sugar
16–18 small-medium silverbeet (Swiss chard) stalks
200 g (7 oz) mushrooms, sliced 1 cm (½ inch) thick
250 g (9 oz/1 cup) ricotta cheese, young goat's cheese or silken tofu
40 g (1½ oz/¼ cup) pine nuts
16 cannelloni shells
1–2 tablespoons finely grated parmesan, romano or manchego cheese

BECAUSE OF ITS OXALIC ACID, SILVERBEET IS ALWAYS BEST TEAMED WITH DAIRY OF SOME SORT TO PROVIDE A RICH SOURCE OF CALCIUM, AS OXALIC ACID BINDS TO CALCIUM, MAKING IT LESS BIOAVAILABLE — HENCE THE RICOTTA OR GOAT'S CHEESE USED HERE

Gently heat half the olive oil or butter in a saucepan, add the onion and cook for 5 minutes. While the onion is cooking, finely chop 3 garlic cloves and 10 large basil leaves, then add to the pan and stir. Cook for another 5 minutes or so.

Stir in the tomatoes and 1 teaspoon of your chosen sweetener and gently simmer for 30 minutes. (If using fresh tomatoes, cover and cook at a very low temperature for about 20 minutes for the tomatoes to release their juices, then remove the lid and cook for 10 minutes.) The sauce should be quite watery, as the cannelloni will absorb moisture as it cooks. Check for taste, adding more sweetener as desired.

Meanwhile, preheat the oven to 180°C (350°F/Gas 4) and bring a large pot of water to the boil.

Trim the silverbeet stalks to 10 cm (4 inches) below the leaf line, then rinse well. Submerge the silverbeet, in batches if necessary, in the boiling water for 2 minutes, or until the stems are tender. Drain into a colander and allow to cool.

Put the remaining oil or butter in a frying pan and heat until the butter is lightly bubbling or the oil is warm. Add the mushrooms and cook over medium–high heat for 5 minutes, stirring frequently.

Place the ricotta and pine nuts in a food processor or blender with the remaining garlic and basil. Blend until just smooth, then tip into a mixing bowl.

Squeeze the cooled silverbeet to remove most of the liquid, then finely chop and add to the ricotta mixture with the mushrooms, and sea salt and freshly ground black pepper to taste.

Lightly smear the base of a baking dish (see Kitchen notes) with the tomato sauce. Fill each cannelloni shell with the silverbeet mixture and arrange in the baking dish. Pour the remaining sauce over and sprinkle with the grated cheese. Cover with a sheet of foil or baking paper and bake for 40–50 minutes, then remove the sheet and bake for a further 10 minutes.

KITCHEN NOTES: *You'll need a baking dish in which the 16 cannelloni shells will fit easily, without being squashed together or too far apart — 30 x 20 cm (12 x 8 inches) should be about right.*

CB

Wild rice and autumn vegetable harvest gratin

CAN BE GLUTEN FREE DEPENDING ON THE BREAD USED

WILL ONLY BE
GLUTEN FREE IF
THE BREAD AND
TAMARI ARE
WHEAT FREE

SERVES 4

A complex and hearty dish to welcome autumn. I've used wild rice as it's such a treat, with a deep nutty flavour and rich in B vitamins. Any hearty grain can be used instead with great results, only their cooking times will differ — barley, about 70 minutes; roasted buckwheat (kasha), 20 minutes; spelt or rye berry, 60–80 minutes. I like to serve this with Garlic Runner Beans (see page 103). Any leftovers can be stuffed into a capsicum (pepper) for a delicious, quick meal the following evening (see Variations).

50 g (1¾ oz/¼ cup) wild rice
20 g (¾ oz) butter
1½ tablespoons roughly sliced sage
750 g (1 lb 10 oz) butternut pumpkin (squash), peeled, seeded and
    cut into 2 cm (¾ inch) dice
2 teaspoons olive oil
1 small–medium brown onion, cut into 1 cm (½ inch) dice
1 celery stalk, cut into 1 cm (½ inch) dice
½ fennel bulb, woody tips removed, then cut into 1 cm (½ inch) dice
1 carrot, skin on, and cut into 5 mm (¼ inch) dice
2 garlic cloves, finely diced
2 teaspoons thyme
1 apple, peeled, cored and cut into 1 cm (½ inch) dice
1 teaspoon tamari
2 tablespoons roughly chopped flat-leaf (Italian) parsley
125 ml (4 fl oz/½ cup) vegetable stock

Topping
20 g (¾ oz) butter
2–3 slices of good sourdough bread, torn into small pieces — you'll need
    about 90 g (3¼ oz/1½ cups)
30 g (1 oz/¼ cup) pecans, pistachios or walnuts, roughly chopped
1 tablespoon roughly chopped flat-leaf (Italian) parsley

Put 750 ml (26 fl oz/3 cups) water in a saucepan and bring to the boil. Add the rice, reduce the heat and slowly simmer for 45 minutes, or until tender. Drain and set aside.

Put the butter and ½ tablespoon of the sage in a frying pan over medium–high heat. When the butter has melted, add the pumpkin and cook for 10 minutes, or until golden, turning with a slotted spoon. Transfer to a mixing bowl and set aside.

Preheat the oven to 170°C (325°F/Gas 3). Warm the olive oil in the frying pan, then add the onion, celery, fennel, carrot and a pinch of sea salt and freshly ground black pepper. Gently sizzle over low–medium heat for 10 minutes, stirring occasionally.

Stir in the remaining sage leaves, garlic, thyme and apple. Cook for 10 minutes, then add to the pumpkin with the wild rice, tamari and the parsley. Toss together gently using your fingertips, then taste and add more salt and pepper if required.

Spoon the mixture into an ovenproof baking dish — I use a 20 cm (8 inch) square dish. Drizzle in the stock, then cover with foil and bake for 45 minutes.

Meanwhile, make the topping. Melt the butter in a small saucepan, then add the bread and toss until evenly coated. Add the nuts and toss through.

Remove the foil, spread the topping over the vegetables and bake for a further 30 minutes, or until the breadcrumbs are golden. Sprinkle with parsley and serve.

VARIATIONS

You could use this mixture to stuff any poultry. It is also lovely as a stuffing for pumpkin (winter squash), in which case, completely omit the pumpkin and mix the topping into the vegetable mixture.

You could also use it as a base on which to roast a leg or a rolled shoulder of lamb, hogget or mutton. To do this, mix the topping into the vegetables, spread it in a baking dish and place your roast on top.

Use leftover cooked gratin as a stuffing for capsicums (peppers). Slice off their tops, remove the seeds and membranes, pile in the stuffing and bake at 200°C (400°F/Gas 6) for 10–15 minutes, or until the capsicum is soft. Cheese is a delicious addition to the stuffing mixture.

ଓଃ

Time saver

THE GRAIN, PUMPKIN AND MIXED VEGETABLES CAN BE PREPARED IN STAGES. THEY WILL KEEP WELL IN THE FRIDGE UNTIL YOU'RE READY TO PUT IT ALL TOGETHER

Quinoa and vegetable pilaff with Indian flavours

GLUTEN FREE

SERVES 4

If you have a teenage vegetarian, this is the recipe you should give them to master. And if you are a none-too-diligent vegetarian you should master this yourself. Why? It's whole and complete — in every way. While quinoa is protein rich, it is not complete, and the inclusion of mung dal and cashew nuts provides the missing amino acids. Mung dal is also very easy to digest. This pilaff is full of vegetables and quality complex carbohydrates, and the fat ensures all the goodness makes it to your body's cells. And if you want more reasons? It's easy — and quick. Even though the cooking time is about 1 hour, your actual work time is minimal. Put it on when you get home, then go and relax while it's in the oven. You'll be mighty pleased with yourself.

Time saver
YOU DON'T HAVE TO
SOAK THE QUINOA,
BUT IT MAKES
MORE NUTRIENTS
AVAILABLE AND
WILL BE EASIER TO
DIGEST. IF MAKING
THIS RECIPE USING
UNSOAKED QUINOA,
INCREASE THE
STOCK BY 60 ML
(2 FL OZ/¼ CUP)

200 g (7 oz/1 cup) quinoa, soaked overnight in 500 ml
    (17 fl oz/2 cups) water with 1 tablespoon yoghurt,
    or 2 teaspoons whey or lemon juice
2 tablespoons unrefined sesame oil (see Kitchen notes) or
    coconut oil (flavoured coconut oil is fine)
2 tablespoons ghee
1 brown onion, finely diced
½ teaspoon ground coriander
¼ teaspoon ground cumin
½ teaspoon ground turmeric
½ cinnamon stick, or ¼ teaspoon ground cinnamon
3 cardamom pods, gently crushed, or ¼ teaspoon ground
    cardamom
a pinch of nutmeg
2 whole cloves
1 tablespoon finely grated fresh ginger
1 teaspoon crushed garlic, or a pinch of asafoetida
125 g (4½ oz/½ cup) mung dal, checked for stones
    (see Kitchen notes)
1 carrot, cut into 1 cm (½ inch) dice
½ cauliflower, cut into florets
100 g (3½ oz) green beans, cut into 3 cm (1¼ inch) lengths

625 ml (21½ fl oz/2½ cups) vegetable stock
155 g (5½ oz/1 cup) peas (frozen is fine)
2 tomatoes, peeled, seeded and cut into 1 cm (½ inch) dice
a handful of coriander (cilantro) leaves
155 g (5½ oz/1 cup) roasted cashew nuts

Preheat the oven to 180°C (350°F/Gas 4). Rinse the quinoa, then set aside to drain thoroughly.

Heat the sesame oil and ghee in a large ovenproof frying pan or flameproof casserole dish. When the ghee has melted, add the onion and a good pinch of sea salt, then sauté over a gentle heat, stirring frequently, for 15 minutes, or until the onion is lightly coloured, but not browned.

Stir in all the spices, ginger, garlic and mung dal. Cook gently for a minute or so, then stir in the quinoa, along with the carrot, cauliflower and beans. Add the stock and bring to the boil, then immediately cover with a lid and transfer to the oven.

Bake for 40 minutes, then remove from the oven. Fold the peas and tomato through, then cover and allow to sit for 10 minutes. Stir in the coriander and cashews just before serving.

KITCHEN NOTES: *Be careful not to mistake a dark sesame oil (which is roasted) for the unrefined sesame oil.*

◆

Don't use the whole mung bean, but rather the mung dal, which is broken; the yellow inside is clearly visible.

ೞ

Red-wine braised lentils with beetroot and root vegetables

GLUTEN FREE

SERVES 4 – 6

Time saver

ROAST EXTRA
BEETROOT FOR
WEEKDAY SALADS
AND SANDWICHES

Brown and green lentils are not as easy to work with as you might think — their extreme astringency needs tempering to provide a full-flavoured and satisfying result. Enter the root vegetables carrot, parsnip and especially beetroot, whose sweetness does the job beautifully. The inherent sweetness in shallots is also brought out by browning them in butter, adding further depth of flavour. You could use only olive oil for this dish, but it wouldn't be anywhere near as good — butter really softens the astringent lentil. While you can also use the larger brown lentils, this dish is best with the small blue-green or black lentils.

IF USING OLIVE
OIL RATHER THAN
BUTTER OR GHEE
TO MAKE THIS DISH
(IN WHICH CASE IT
WILL BE VEGAN),
YOU MAY NEED
TO INCREASE THE
QUINCE PASTE A
LITTLE TO BALANCE
THE FLAVOURS

Red-wine braised lentils
1 tablespoon olive oil
1 tablespoon butter or ghee
2 rosemary sprigs
4–5 small bay leaves
3–4 thyme sprigs
10–12 French shallots, peeled and left whole
5 garlic cloves, peeled (the large type of garlic is wonderful here)
250 ml (9 fl oz/1 cup) red wine
1 tablespoon tomato paste (concentrated purée)
150 g (5½ oz/¾ cup) small blue-green lentils, checked for stones
    and rinsed
1 litre (35 fl oz/4 cups) vegetable stock
4 juniper berries (optional)
1 tablespoon quince paste, or mirin, to taste

12 very small beetroot (beets), with leaves still intact
2 tablespoons olive oil
4 large or 8 small parsnips
8 small carrots (about 300 g/10½ oz), skin on, scrubbed and left whole
1 tablespoon butter or ghee
2 tablespoons roughly chopped flat-leaf (Italian) parsley

Preheat the oven to 200°C (400°F/Gas 6). To prepare the braised lentils, heat the olive oil and butter in a large heavy-based saucepan. Add the rosemary sprigs, bay leaves, thyme sprigs, shallots and whole garlic cloves and cook over medium–high heat for 10 minutes — stir every now and then, but resist stirring too often as the shallots need continued contact with the base of the pan to caramelize.

While the shallots are caramelizing, cut up the root vegetables. Trim the leaves from the beetroot, keeping the smaller and healthier ones. Wash the beetroot well, but don't peel. Peel the parsnips and trim off the skinny tips. If they are very young, fresh and small, simply cut them in half lengthways. If they are large, cut the thickest section into quarters and remove the woody core, then cut the middle section in half and keep the root end whole.

Stir the wine into the shallot mixture with the tomato paste, lentils, stock, juniper berries if using, some sea salt and a good pinch of freshly ground black pepper. Simmer for about 1 hour, stirring every now and then until the liquid becomes a sauce and the lentils are tender. Taste and balance with quince paste or mirin if required.

While the lentils are braising, roast the root vegetables. Place the whole beetroot in a small baking dish, drizzle with 1 tablespoon of the olive oil and add 125 ml (4 fl oz/½ cup) water. Cover with a lid or foil. Place the parsnips on a baking tray with the carrots, drizzle with the remaining olive oil, some sea salt and freshly ground black pepper and mix well. Bake the beetroot for 45 minutes to 1 hour, or until soft when pierced with the tip of knife; bake the parsnip and carrot for 30–45 minutes, or until cooked and golden.

Allow the beetroot to cool a little before peeling off the skin, wearing a pair of gloves so your hands don't get stained. If the beetroot are larger, cut them into chunks.

Just before serving, heat the butter in a frying pan and quickly wilt the reserved beetroot leaves over high heat.

Arrange the roast vegetables on a large platter, top with half the wilted beetroot leaves, and spoon the lentils over. Top with the remaining leaves, sprinkle with parsley and serve.

ಛ

IF YOU'VE FOUND YOUNG HEIRLOOM CARROTS OF ALL COLOURS AT A FARMERS MARKET, THIS IS A GREAT WAY TO USE THEM. SIMPLY WASH THEM AND USE WHOLE — IF THEY ARE VERY YOUNG AND FRESH, THEY WON'T NEED PEELING

Spanish capsicum, chickpea and fennel pie

WHEAT FREE

SERVES 6 - 8

IF YOU'RE NOT
VERY CONFIDENT
ABOUT MAKING
PASTRY, THIS IS A
GREAT ONE FOR
YOU — IT'S A
CROSS BETWEEN A
PASTRY AND A
DOUGH. THE FAT
GIVES MOISTNESS
AND MOUTHFEEL,
WHILE KNEADING
MAKES IT STURDY,
WHICH IS SO HANDY
FOR GRABBING A
SLICE AND EATING
IT FROM YOUR
HAND — THE
ORIGINAL IDEA
OF A PASTIE

My original influence for this pie was a wonderful Spanish tuna and capsicum (pepper) pie. Tuna, unfortunately, is becoming more problematic due to extensive overfishing and the presence of methyl mercury and PCBs (polychlorinated biphenyls) — hence this alternative version. Nevertheless, this pie remains the perfect place to use fish. Use one of your local, sustainable options: the more robustly flavoured ones such as herring, mackerel or mullet would be perfect. This is a lovely pie for lunch, easy to put together, and is great hot, warm or cold the day you make it, and equally good the next. The filling also makes a great sauce for pasta or polenta (see Basics, page 245). Beautiful served with the Salad of Orange, Fennel and Olives on page 109.

Pastry

185 g (6½ oz/1¼ cups) plain (all-purpose) wholemeal spelt flour
155 g (5½ oz/1¼ cups) plain (all-purpose) white spelt flour
60 g (2¼ oz) butter, melted
80 ml (2½ fl oz/⅓ cup) olive oil
1 egg, beaten
40 g (1½ oz/¼ cup) sesame seeds

Filling

2 tablespoons olive oil, plus extra, for brushing
1 red onion, sliced
½ teaspoon dried basil
1 large red capsicum (pepper), cut lengthways into 5 mm (¼ inch) strips
1 large green capsicum (pepper), cut lengthways into 5 mm (¼ inch) strips
1 fennel bulb, woody tips removed, cut lengthways into 5 mm (¼ inch) slices
3 garlic cloves, crushed or finely diced
½ teaspoon ground cumin
½ teaspoon ground paprika
1 tablespoon balsamic vinegar
400 g (14 oz) tin chopped tomatoes
150 g (5½ oz/1 cup) cooked chickpeas, or a 400 g (14 oz) tin of chickpeas,
   drained and rinsed

To make the pastry, put all the flour in a bowl with the butter, olive oil and 120 ml (3¾ fl oz) water. Mix together well — the dough will most likely be quite wet. Turn onto a work surface and knead, adding a tablespoon more water. The dough should be firm, but not resistant, and depending on the spelt, may need another 2–3 teaspoons water. Knead well for a further 5 minutes, or until the dough is soft and elastic — you should feel it begin to give and soften underneath your hands as you are kneading. Form into a ball, return to the bowl and cover. Set aside.

To make the filling, heat the olive oil in a frying pan and sauté the onion and basil over medium heat with some sea salt and freshly ground black pepper for 10 minutes, stirring from time to time. Stir in the capsicum, fennel, garlic, cumin and paprika and gently sizzle over low–medium heat for 20 minutes, stirring often.

Stir in the vinegar, tomatoes and chickpeas and gently simmer, stirring frequently, for 20–30 minutes, or until no liquid remains. Taste and add a little more black pepper if needed.

Meanwhile, preheat the oven to 200°C (400°F/Gas 6). Brush a 2.5 cm (1 inch) deep, 24 cm (9½ inch) loose-based tart tin with olive oil.

Divide the pastry in half and roll one portion into a 33 cm (13 inch) circle. (This is an oily pastry, so you may not need any extra flour for dusting.) Fold the pastry into quarters, pick it up and align the corner over the centre of the tin. Unfold the pastry and line the tin. Roll out the remaining pastry to the same diameter.

Spoon the filling into the pie and top with the remaining pastry. Using scissors, trim the pastry to give a 1 cm (½ inch) overhang, then fold the edges of the pastry from underneath towards the top. Brush with the beaten egg and sprinkle with the sesame seeds. Bake for 10 minutes, then reduce the oven temperature to 190°C (375°F/Gas 5) and bake for a further 20–30 minutes, or until golden.

VARIATIONS

If using fish, make sure it is filleted and skinned, with any remaining bones removed. I leave out the chickpeas, cook and reduce the filling as above, then fold lovely big chunks of fish through the filling before it goes into the pie shell. You'll need about 300 g (10½ oz) of fish.

ଔ

SMOKED PAPRIKA IS A GROWN-UP FLAVOUR BOOSTER TO THIS PIE. YOU COULD ADD SOME TO THE FILLING WITH THE GROUND SPICES

Meat or vegetarian Sunday night pasties

MAKES 4 LARGE PASTIES

A simple and tasty Sunday night dinner for the cooler weather. The vegetarian option does take longer to put together unless you have some filling in the freezer — it really pays to plan ahead. Pasties are fabulously cheap to make using chuck steak and turnips or swedes (rutabaga). Meat pasties need to be served with a tomato sauce (see recipe on page 227; a commercial one is also fine), tomato relish or chutney. Salsa is a perfect match for the vegetarian pasties.

Steak filling
300 g (10½ oz) chuck steak
1 onion, finely diced
1 small–medium swede (rutabaga), peeled and cut into 5 mm (¼ inch) dice
2 potatoes, scrubbed and cut into 1 cm (½ inch) dice
2 thyme sprigs, leaves picked

Vegetarian filling
1 quantity of Quick Beanie Mix (see page 113; reduce it down a bit to
    make it thicker)

4 sheets of home-made puff pastry (see Basics, page 247), or ready-made
    puff pastry (see Kitchen notes)
1 egg, beaten

If making the steak filling, trim the gristle and fat from the steak and cut the meat into 1.5 cm (⅝ inch) chunks. Toss in a mixing bowl with the onion, swede, potato and thyme. Generously sprinkle with sea salt and freshly ground black pepper and toss well.

Remove the pastry from the freezer. Take one sheet, invert a 20 cm (8 inch) plate onto it and cut around the plate using a small sharp knife. Place the pastry round on a plate lined with baking paper. Repeat with the remaining pastry sheets, stacking the rounds one on top of the other with a sheet of baking paper between each to stop them sticking together. Chill for a couple of minutes in the freezer.

Line a baking tray with baking paper. Remove the pastry from the freezer, keeping each pastry round on its sheet of baking paper. Spoon your preferred filling down the centre of each pastry round.

Using the baking paper, fold the pasties over into a semi-circle. Press the edges together with your fingers to seal — the meat pastie will be full, but it will reduce as it cooks. Lift the pastie and turn it slightly so it is standing upright with the seam on the top. Twist the ends, folding the pastry from right to left over itself and towards you, creating a rope-like design. If the pastry is too soft to manage, place it in the freezer for a few minutes to firm up, and use a bit of flour on your hands.

Set the pasties on the baking tray and refrigerate for 30 minutes to firm. Meanwhile, preheat the oven to 180°C (350°F/Gas 4).

Brush the pasties with the beaten egg and bake until the pastry is fully cooked and crisp — this will take about 50–60 minutes for the meat pasties, and 35–40 minutes for the vegetarian ones.

KITCHEN NOTES: *Using the home-made or a commercial butter puff pastry will give you four 24–26 cm (9¹/₂–10¹/₂ inch) sheets of pastry. As you cut out your 20 cm (8 inch) circle, you will be left with scraps. Layer these, then wrap and freeze to use for a quiche pastry. These pasties are also the perfect place to use any scraps of puff pastry you already have, rolled out again to a 20 cm (8 inch) square, 2–3 mm (¹/₁₆–¹/₈ inch) thick.*

ೞ

Time saver

A QUICK WAY TO SEAL THE PASTIES IS TO SIMPLY CRIMP THE EDGES TOGETHER WITH A FORK

Gumbo ya-ya

GLUTEN FREE / DAIRY FREE

SERVES 4 – 6

This is my version of the Cajun classic — nowhere near as spicy or rich, and with a bit of West Australian ease thrown into it. Gumbo is a beautiful dish and such a fabulous example of peasant cooking, where ingenuity makes something quite amazing out of so little. If my daughter hasn't made pasta, we generally have gumbo for Christmas Eve dinner — it's a brilliant dish to make ahead, tastes better the next day, and extends to feed many. My version is with chicken (it's perfect for an older chicken) and prawns (shrimp), but spicy sausage is a traditional and tasty addition.

Time saver

INSTEAD OF USING A WHOLE CHICKEN, YOU COULD USE 1 KG (2 LB 4 OZ) CHICKEN PIECES AND A FROZEN HOME-MADE CHICKEN STOCK INSTEAD OF MAKING A NEW BATCH OF STOCK. YOU WILL NEED ABOUT 750 ML (26 FL OZ/3 CUPS)

THIS DISH IS BEST MADE IN A HEAVY, CAST IRON POT — I USE A 26 CM (10½ INCH) FRENCH OVEN. IF YOU ARE USING STAINLESS STEEL, TAKE CARE WHEN MAKING THE ROUX — YOU WILL NEED TO TURN DOWN THE HEAT A LITTLE

1.5 kg (3 lb 5 oz) whole chicken
400 g (14 oz) raw prawns (shrimp)
4 tablespoons olive oil
40 g (1½ oz/⅓ cup) plain (all-purpose) white spelt flour
2 green capsicums (peppers), finely chopped
3 celery stalks, finely sliced
2 spring onions (scallions), including the greens, finely sliced
6 garlic cloves, squashed
3 bay leaves
4 thyme sprigs
a pinch of cayenne pepper, or to taste
¼ teaspoon freshly ground black pepper, or to taste
400 g (14 oz) tin chopped tomatoes
a handful of flat-leaf (Italian) parsley, finely chopped
steamed brown or white rice, to serve

For the stock

1 onion, roughly chopped
1 carrot, roughly chopped
2 celery stalks, roughly chopped
3 thyme sprigs
2 bay leaves
2 tablespoons white wine, or 1 teaspoon wine or apple vinegar

If using a whole chicken, put it on a chopping board. First cut around the leg joint and then, with your hands, move the leg from the body until the ball joint pops out. Cut the whole leg from the body, then repeat with the other leg joint. Cut through the middle of each leg at the thigh joint — you now have two legs, and two thighs. Cut the wings from the body, leaving the base of the wing attached to the breast. Finally, cut down through the breast and remove the meat from the rib cage. The knife should run parallel to and about 2 cm (³/₄ inch) from the middle bone. Place all the chicken pieces in a bowl, sprinkle with sea salt and freshly ground black pepper, then cover and refrigerate.

To make the stock, put the chicken carcass in a stockpot with all the other stock ingredients and enough water to just cover the chicken. Season with sea salt and freshly ground black pepper, bring to a gentle boil and simmer for 1 hour.

Meanwhile, peel the prawns, discarding the heads, but reserving the shells and tails. Place the prawns in a bowl, then cover and refrigerate. (If you are using ready-made chicken stock, freeze the prawn trimmings for use in another stock.)

Add the prawn shells and tails to the stock and simmer for a further 30 minutes. Sit a colander over a large saucepan and pour in the stock. Discard the solids.

Heat the olive oil in a 26 cm (10½ inch) heavy-based saucepan or flameproof casserole dish. Brown the chicken pieces in batches over a good heat until lightly golden. Remove to a plate, allow to cool and return to the fridge.

Add the flour to the oil — it will sizzle — and stir well to scrape up any chicken bits. Stirring frequently, cook over low–medium heat for 10–15 minutes, or until the flour is a lovely golden brown, edging to a dark brown. The mixture will be gently bubbling, but take care it doesn't burn. The time this takes will greatly depend on the type of pan you are using.

Reduce the heat to low and add the capsicum, celery, spring onion and garlic. Cover and cook over a very low heat for 20 minutes, stirring frequently. Stir in the bay leaves, thyme sprigs, cayenne and black pepper. Stirring well, pour in 750 ml (26 fl oz/3 cups) of the chicken stock — the mixture will immediately smooth out and thicken. Add the tomatoes and chicken. (If using sausage, add it now — 100–200 g/3½–7 oz will be enough, sliced about 1 cm/½ inch thick. There is no need to cook it first.) Gently simmer for 15–20 minutes, or until the chicken is cooked.

IF YOU ARE MAKING THE GUMBO AHEAD, LET IT COOL A LITTLE AFTER YOU HAVE THICKENED THE SAUCE AND PUT THE CHICKEN PIECES BACK IN, THEN COVER AND REFRIGERATE

TO REHEAT THE GUMBO, PLACE OVER VERY GENTLE HEAT UNTIL THE GELATINE HAS 'RELAXED' AND THE GUMBO LOOKS MORE LIQUID. ADD THE RAW PRAWNS, THEN INCREASE THE HEAT AND GENTLY SIMMER, STIRRING, FOR 8–10 MINUTES, OR UNTIL THE DISH IS WARMED THROUGH AND THE PRAWNS ARE JUST COOKED

Remove the chicken and set aside. Spoon off and discard any oil sitting on top of the gumbo. If the sauce is too thin, cook at a sturdy (but not rapid) boil to reduce, stirring frequently — generally about 10 minutes. The consistency should be that of a stew, with lovely sauce to run over the rice. Return the chicken to the pot.

Add the prawns and simmer for 8 minutes, or until the prawns are just opaque. Taste and adjust for salt and pepper. Stir in the parsley and serve with steamed rice.

VARIATIONS

Gumbo is traditionally spicy, so feel free to increase the heat by upping the cayenne pepper. You can use either fish or chicken stock — this recipe suggests chicken, as this takes into account the carcass you are left with after cutting away the meat. If using fish stock, you may need to add a little rapadura sugar or apple juice concentrate to the gumbo to balance the acidity in the tomatoes. You'll need about 750 ml (26 fl oz/3 cups) fish stock.

℅

Cupboard love shoulder chop stew

GLUTEN FREE / CAN BE DAIRY FREE

SERVES 4 – 6

SHOULDER CHOPS ARE THE BEST HERE — THEY ARE CHEAP, BUT MORE IMPORTANTLY, WILL BE MELTINGLY TENDER WHEN COOKED

Cupboard love is the name I give to a meal put together with what is left in the pantry or fridge. This old recipe is incredibly easy, very forgiving and always tastes fabulous, but it's a perfect example of how the transfer of heat affects the end result. It is best made in an enamel-coated, cast-iron casserole dish or French oven. This holds great heat, which is reflected from the lid, as well as the bottom and sides. I like this stew served with steamed peas tossed in butter, but any green vegetable is fine — Garlic Runner Beans (page 103) would also be delicious.

1 kg (2 lb 4 oz) lamb, hogget or mutton shoulder chops, trimmed of fat
1 large brown onion, roughly sliced
5–6 garlic cloves, roughly chopped
4 rosemary sprigs

310 ml (10¾ fl oz/1¼ cups) red wine

400 g (14 oz) tin chopped tomatoes

300 g (10½ oz) pumpkin, peeled and cut into 3–4 cm (1½ inch) dice

300 g (10½ oz) potatoes, scrubbed and left whole if small, cut in half
   if a bit bigger, or into 3 cm (1¼ inch) pieces if very large

4 carrots, skin on, scrubbed and cut into 1 cm (½ inch) slices, or in half
   if very thick

1 teaspoon rapadura sugar, apple juice concentrate or brown sugar

80 (2¾ oz/½ cup) fresh or frozen peas per person, to serve

2 teaspoons butter or ghee

Preheat the oven to 170°C (325°F/Gas 3). Put the chops in a wide, shallow flameproof casserole dish, sprinkle with sea salt and freshly ground black pepper and place over low–medium heat. After a few minutes, add the onion and garlic.

Turn the chops — they should be lightly golden in spots — and add the rosemary sprigs. After 2 minutes, increase the heat and add the wine, letting it bubble. Stir in the tomatoes, turn off the heat and add the pumpkin, potatoes, carrots and sugar.

Cover and bake for 1 hour, then reduce the oven temperature to 160°C (315°F/Gas 2–3) and cook for a further 1 hour. Remove from the oven and remove the lid. There will probably be a layer of golden fat sitting on the top — remove as much as you like with a tablespoon.

Put the casserole dish back on the stovetop over medium–high heat and allow the liquid to reduce until lovely and thick. (If you prefer, remove the chops from the stew before reducing the liquid, cut the meat from the bones, then return the meat before serving the stew.)

Meanwhile, steam the peas for 5 minutes, or until tender. Toss the steamed peas with the butter. Spoon the stew into serving bowls, adding the peas as you go.

VARIATIONS

This stew is very versatile. Try using baby onion, turnip, swede (rutabaga), broccoli and/or cauliflower in the stew.

ঙ৩

Mango and cashew nut chicken

GLUTEN FREE

SERVES 4 – 6

My take on mum's Cashew Chicken, which is a firm favourite with all the grandchildren. It's a lightly curried and fragrant stew — a great, quick family meal. Serve with any cooked grain, though I really like a basmati rice here.

2 tablespoons ghee, unrefined sesame oil, or olive oil
1 onion, roughly chopped
1½ tablespoons finely chopped or grated fresh ginger
2 garlic cloves, crushed
60 g (2¼ oz/heaped ⅓ cup) roasted cashew nuts
3 tomatoes, roughly chopped
1 tablespoon yoghurt
500 g (1 lb 2 oz) chicken (thigh meat is best), cut into 2.5 cm
    (1 inch) chunks
1 teaspoon garam masala
1 teaspoon sweet curry powder
¼ teaspoon ground turmeric
250 ml (9 fl oz/1 cup) vegetable or chicken stock
1 mango, flesh roughly diced
4 tablespoons roughly chopped coriander (cilantro)

A SWEET, FRAGRANT CURRY POWDER IS BETTER THAN A HOT CHILLI VARIETY HERE AS IT WILL GIVE THE DISH A MORE ROUNDED FLAVOUR

Put the ghee in a frying pan, and when melted and very warm, add the onion, ginger, garlic and some sea salt. Sauté over low–medium heat for 10 minutes, taking care that the onion lightly sizzles but does not fry, stirring from time to time.

Meanwhile, put the cashews, tomatoes and yoghurt in a food processor or blender and pulse until the sauce is smooth, but the nuts are still a little chunky. Set aside.

Add the chicken, garam masala, curry powder and turmeric to the frying pan and stir through. Cook for 5–6 minutes over low–medium heat, then stir in the cashew nut mixture, stock, mango and half the coriander. Slowly simmer for 25–30 minutes, or until the chicken is cooked and the sauce is thick. Check for taste and add more sea salt if desired. Fold the remaining coriander through and serve.

ભ

Quick roasted lemon, thyme and garlic chicken

GLUTEN FREE / DAIRY FREE

SERVES 4

Everybody loves a roast chicken, but sometimes there's not time to roast a whole bird. Cutting the chicken into smaller pieces allows more browning of the skin, greater opportunity to flavour the flesh and a much shorter cooking time. This version is simply paired with the classic ingredients lemon, thyme and garlic, but you could also flavour the chicken with Nessie's Herby Chicken Paste, which follows this recipe and is my daughter's delicious take on the same thing.

Both options are equally good pulled out of the oven and packed into the car for a picnic dinner. Serve with Garlic Runner Beans (page 103).

4 tablespoons lemon thyme
2–3 garlic cloves
grated zest of ½ lemon
400 g (14 oz) potatoes, skins on, scrubbed (see Kitchen notes)
1–1 ½ tablespoons olive oil
1.6 kg (3 lb 8 oz) whole chicken, or 4 chicken leg quarters — or 4 thighs
    (bone in and skin on), 2 wings and 4 drumsticks
juice of ½ lemon

Preheat the oven to 200°C (400°F/Gas 6). Finely chop the lemon thyme and garlic and place in a bowl with the lemon zest.

If using kipfler (fingerling) potatoes, simply cut them in half, leaving any small ones whole. If using larger potatoes, slice them about 1 cm (½ inch) thick. Spread the potatoes on a baking tray and sprinkle with sea salt and freshly ground black pepper. Drizzle with about 2 teaspoons of the olive oil and massage in well.

If using a whole chicken, put it on a separate chopping board. First cut around the leg joint and then, with your hands, move the leg from the body until the ball joint pops out. Cut the whole leg from the body, then repeat with the other leg joint. Cut through the middle of each leg at the thigh joint — you now have two legs, and two thighs. Cut the wings from the body, leaving the base of the wing attached to the breast. Finally, cut down through the breast and remove the meat from the rib cage.

The knife should run parallel to and about 2 cm (³⁄₄ inch) from the middle bone. The remaining carcass (with a little bit of breast meat) can be used for stock.

Stuff part of the lemon and herb mix under the skin of the chicken pieces and into any crevices. Place the chicken on the baking tray with the potatoes, and sprinkle well with sea salt and freshly ground black pepper. Drizzle with the remaining olive oil — enough to lightly cover the skin. Press the remaining herb mix onto the chicken, and drizzle with the lemon juice. Roast for 50–60 minutes, or until the chicken and potatoes are golden and cooked.

KITCHEN NOTES: *Any potato will work, but kipfler (fingerling) are especially delicious. There's absolutely no reason you couldn't add other vegetables to the baking tray — pumpkin (winter squash), sweet potato, parsnip or carrot.*

VARIATIONS

NESSIE'S HERBY CHICKEN PASTE
GLUTEN FREE

4 tablespoons fresh mixed herbs such as thyme and oregano, including
    4 small or 2 large sage leaves
3 garlic cloves, peeled
30 g (1 oz) butter or ghee

Using a mortar and pestle, pound the herbs and garlic with a good pinch of sea salt and freshly ground black pepper until well broken down. Add the butter and mix until smoothish and well combined.

(Alternatively, finely blend the herbs and garlic in a food processor, then add the butter, some sea salt and black pepper, and pulse until combined. Or very finely chop the herbs and garlic together using a knife and mix them into the butter.)

Sprinkle the chicken pieces with sea salt and freshly ground black pepper, rub well with the herb mix and stuff some under the skin. Roast as directed in the recipe, but without drizzling any oil or lemon juice over the chicken.

ɔ঵

Fish: local, seasonal, sustainable, unfarmed

These recipes cover two categories: white-fleshed and sweeter-tasting, and dark-fleshed and strongly flavoured. You can easily swap your fish options within these two categories. You'll also note that many of the recipes for stronger-flavoured, oily fish use butter or ghee — this tempers and softens the flavours, and ensures optimum usage of the valuable omega-3 essential fatty acids. ❧

Pirates pie

GLUTEN FREE

SERVES 4 - 6

This is the kind of pie I would make for my pirate husband when he returned from sea with his crew and a handful of freshly caught fish. In this fantasy, I imagine myself living on a Greek island, with a wood oven and a bounty of tomatoes, olive oil and olives. This pie does need a hot oven to reduce the tomato, giving it a deep and rounded taste, and is another example of how important heat transfer can be in producing a good end result. I would be serving this with much red wine, and lashings of greens — the Braised Garlic Kale on page 105 is perfect.

700 g (1 lb 9 oz) potatoes (larger are better), skin on, scrubbed well
4 good-sized garlic cloves
a large handful of basil
12 oregano leaves
1 tablespoon balsamic vinegar
3 tablespoons olive oil
2 x 400 g (14 oz) tins chopped tomatoes
30 g (1 oz) unsalted butter, melted
500 g (1 lb 2 oz) strongly flavoured fish fillets, checked over for bones
115 g (4 oz/¾ cup) pitted kalamata olives, roughly chopped

Preheat the oven to 220°C (425°F/Gas 7). Add a generous pinch of sea salt to a large pot of water and bring to the boil.

Add the potatoes to the boiling water and boil until nearly cooked — take care not to overcook; they should offer some resistance to a skewer. Drain well and set aside.

Put the garlic and a good pinch of sea salt in a mortar and pound a little. Add the basil and oregano and pound to a lovely paste. Add the vinegar and 1 tablespoon of the olive oil and mix it through the paste. (Alternatively, chop the garlic, basil and oregano. Put them in a small bowl, add the vinegar, tomatoes and 1 tablespoon of the olive oil and mix together well.) Turn out the mixture into a bowl, add the tomatoes and mix well.

Pour the melted butter into a 30 x 20 cm (12 x 8 inch) metal baking dish (see Kitchen notes), add the tomato mixture and spread to cover the base. Lay the fish fillets on top; they will sink into the sauce. Sprinkle with the olives and a little freshly ground black pepper.

Slice the boiled potatoes 5 mm (¼ inch) thick and place in a bowl. Drizzle with the remaining olive oil and toss until well coated. Arrange the potato slices in rows on top of the fish, then drizzle with any oil remaining in the bowl.

Bake for 30 minutes — the tomato sauce should be bubbling as it cooks and will be well reduced. If the sauce is not thick and well reduced, return to the oven for a further 10 minutes. If the potatoes are not golden, place under a hot grill (broiler) for 10 minutes to finish the job.

KITCHEN NOTES: *I use an enamel-coated, cast-iron baking dish here as it holds the heat brilliantly and enables a quicker reduction of the liquid. You could instead use an enamel-coated tin (the old camping ones) or stainless steel roasting tin, but you will need to increase the oven temperature to about 235–240°C (475°F/Gas 8), and the pie may take 10 minutes or so longer to cook.*

☙

Lemon and herb polenta-crumbed fish with chips

GLUTEN FREE

SERVES 4

This is a fabulous way to serve strongly flavoured fish to children — the colour is bright and funky, and chips are always a winner.

Crumb mixture
150 g (5½ oz/1 cup) polenta, or 4 large, thick pieces of stale sourdough
    bread, crusts removed
zest of 1 lemon
12 chives, chopped
2 parsley stalks, leaves picked
a good handful of lemon thyme, woody stems discarded

12–15 kipfler (fingerling) potatoes, skins on, washed well
3–4 tablespoons olive oil
1 egg
4 fish fillets (400 g/14 oz in total), such as mullet or herring, skin removed
2 tablespoons ghee
lemon wedges, to serve (optional)

Preheat the oven to 220°C (425°F/Gas 7). Put all the ingredients for the crumb mixture in a food processor with a good pinch of sea salt and freshly ground black pepper. Pulse until the herbs (and breadcrumbs, if using) are quite fine. Tip the mixture out onto a flat plate.

Cut the potatoes in half lengthways and place on a baking tray. Drizzle with 1 tablespoon of the olive oil and rub the oil all over all the potatoes. Sprinkle with a generous pinch of sea salt, then bake for 20 minutes, or until the potatoes are soft, golden and a little puffed.

Meanwhile, break the egg into a flat bowl or dish and beat. Dip each fish fillet in the beaten egg, then into the crumb mixture, pressing gently on the crumbs to help them stick to the fish.

About 10 minutes before the chips are ready, add the ghee and remaining olive oil to a frying pan. If your frying pan is very large, you may need more oil — the fat

CHOOSE STRONGLY FLAVOURED, OILY FISH SUCH AS SEA MULLET, RED MULLET OR HERRING. A MIXED SELECTION IS FINE

THIS IS A
GREAT DISH FOR
CHILDREN, SO IT
IS ESPECIALLY
IMPORTANT TO
REMOVE ANY
BONES. LAY THE
FISH ON A PLATE,
RUN YOUR CLEAN
HANDS OVER
TO FEEL ANY
BONES, THEN
REMOVE WITH
FISH TWEEZERS

should be about 5 mm (¼ inch) deep. When the oil is sizzling, but not smoking, add half the fish fillets (see Kitchen notes). Cook over medium heat for 3–5 minutes, then turn and cook the other side for a further 2–3 minutes — the actual cooking time will depend on the type and thickness of the fillet. Remove and drain on paper towels while cooking the remaining fish. Serve the fish with the hot chips and lemon wedges, if desired.

KITCHEN NOTES: *The best heat for frying the fish depends a lot on the thickness of the fish. If the fillets are very thin, the heat will need to be higher, to ensure the polenta or crumbs brown by the time the fish is cooked. If they are thicker, the heat can be a little lower, as the coating will have more time in which to brown. If the heat is too low, the coating will be soggy, rather than lovely and browned.*

⅋

Fish stew with Moroccan flavours

GLUTEN FREE / DAIRY FREE

SERVES 4 - 6

Many of the more sustainable fish are very strongly flavoured, which you can temper by pairing with other robustly flavoured ingredients. I prefer to make my own fish stock (see Basics, page 253) — it is absurdly cheap, provides an exceptionally nourishing meal, and you can freeze any leftover stock for another day. Leftover stew should jell, indicating a powerful stock.

Spice paste
2 tablespoons extra virgin olive oil
5–6 coriander (cilantro) stalks
2 flat-leaf (Italian) parsley stalks, leaves picked
3 garlic cloves
1½ teaspoons ground cumin
½ small red chilli, or to taste
½ teaspoon saffron threads
1 tablespoon lemon juice
1 teaspoon paprika

1 tablespoon extra virgin olive oil

1 small fennel bulb, thinly sliced lengthways

1 large brown onion, roughly chopped

2 carrots, cut in half lengthways, then sliced 1 cm (½ inch) thick
    on the diagonal

¼ preserved lemon, flesh discarded, the rind roughly chopped

4 ripe tomatoes, roughly chopped

10 baby potatoes

600 ml (21 fl oz) fish stock (see Basics, page 253)

10 pitted kalamata olives

600–700 g (1 lb 5 oz–1 lb 9 oz) fish fillets (such as red mullet, sea mullet,
    mackerel or leather jacket), skin removed, checked over for bones,
    then cut into chunks

1 tablespoon finely chopped mint

1–2 coriander (cilantro) stalks, finely chopped

1 flat-leaf (Italian) parsley stalk, leaves picked and finely chopped

Put the spice paste ingredients in a blender with a pinch of sea salt. Blend until combined but still chunky. Set aside.

Warm the olive oil in a large heavy-based saucepan. Add the fennel, onion, carrot and a good pinch of sea salt and fry gently for 5 minutes. Add half the preserved lemon and two-thirds of the spice paste, the tomatoes, potatoes and stock. Simmer for 30 minutes, or until the vegetables are tender.

Stir in the olives, fish, mint, coriander and parsley and simmer for a further 5 minutes. Check for taste, adding the remaining spice mix, preserved lemon and some freshly ground black pepper as desired. Ladle into bowls and serve.

ಌ

Japanese ginger fish balls with a sweet and sour sauce and bok choy

GLUTEN FREE / DAIRY FREE

WILL ONLY BE GLUTEN FREE IF THE TAMARI IS WHEAT FREE

SERVES 4 – 6

This is a lovely way to use a strongly flavoured white fish to create a meal that is nourishing and delicious.

300 g (10½ oz/1½ cups) long-grain brown rice, soaked overnight if desired
    with 2 teaspoons whey or yoghurt, or 1 teaspoon lemon juice
2 tablespoons unrefined sesame oil or flavourless coconut oil
1 tablespoon flavourless coconut oil (or olive oil)
550 g (1 lb 4 oz) bok choy (pak choy), larger leaves cut in half lengthways
1 tablespoon lightly roasted sesame seeds
chopped red chilli, to serve (optional)

Fish balls
3 tablespoons chopped chives, or 2 roughly chopped spring onions
    (scallions)
finely grated zest of 1 lime
1 tablespoon lime juice
1 tablespoon grated fresh ginger
1 tablespoon coconut milk
¼ teaspoon umeboshi paste, or a good pinch of sea salt
500 g (1 lb 2 oz) mixed white fish fillets, checked over for bones,
    then roughly chopped

UNFARMED MULLOWAY IS A SUSTAINABLE AND LOCAL WHITE FISH FOR ME. AS IT ISN'T OVERLY SWEET, I TRY TO FIND A SWEETER FISH TO PAIR WITH IT — A TREVALLY OR SOMETHING FROM THE BREAM FAMILY

Sweet and sour sauce
5 small dried shiitake mushrooms
a 3 cm (1¼ inch) strip of kombu
3 'coins' or slices of ginger (you can keep the skin on)
2 teaspoons cornflour (cornstarch) or kudzu (kuzu)
1 tablespoon tamari
1 tablespoon dark brown sugar
1 teaspoon brown rice vinegar
1 teaspoon fish sauce
2 tablespoons mirin

If soaking the rice, turn it into a strainer, rinse, then drain well. Place in a saucepan with 375 ml (13 fl oz/1½ cups) water if soaked, and 435 ml (15¼ fl oz/1¾ cups) if unsoaked. Cover and bring to the boil, then immediately turn the heat down low and simmer for 45–50 minutes. About 5 minutes before the end of cooking time, check if there is any water left by tipping the pot at an angle — if so, continue to cook until there is no water left. When the rice is ready, small steam holes should appear on the surface. Remove from the heat, place a clean tea towel (dish towel) or paper towel over the rice, then cover and set aside.

Meanwhile, make the fish balls. Put the chives, lime zest, lime juice, ginger, coconut milk and umeboshi paste in a food processor and pulse a few times to break down. Add the fish and process until fully combined, but take care not to overmix. Form the mixture into 20 balls, place on a plate, then cover and refrigerate.

To make the sweet and sour sauce, put the mushrooms, kombu and ginger in a small saucepan with 375 ml (13 fl oz/1½ cups) water. Cover and bring to the boil, then immediately turn off the heat and set aside. Put the cornflour in a small bowl with the tamari and sugar and stir until smooth. Stir in the vinegar, fish sauce and mirin.

Remove the mushrooms from the soaking liquid and cut off any tough stems. Very thinly slice the mushrooms and set aside. Pour the soaking liquid through a fine sieve to measure 250 ml (9 fl oz/1 cup), then stir it into the cornflour mixture (discard the ginger and kombu). Pour the sauce back into the saucepan, place over medium heat and bring to the boil, stirring constantly, then remove from the heat and set aside.

Warm the sesame oil in a frying pan over medium heat. Add the fish balls — they should sizzle when they touch the oil. Cook the fish balls, in batches if necessary, for 5–7 minutes on each side, or until cooked through, taking care not to overcook them. Drain on paper towels.

Heat the coconut oil in a large wok. When the oil is very hot, add all the bok choy and cook for 3–5 minutes, or until just barely cooked, tossing frequently. Add the fish balls and sweet and sour sauce, gently mix through, then bring the sauce to the boil. Immediately remove from the heat.

Stir the sesame seeds through the steamed rice. Spoon the rice into bowls, then spoon the fish balls, bok choy and sauce over the top. If desired, top with chilli.

 beta

Time saver
SERVE WITH WHITE STEAMED BASMATI FOR A QUICKER RICE OPTION

Fragrant coconut fish and vegetable curry

GLUTEN FREE / DAIRY FREE

SERVES 4 – 6

This is my fail-safe recipe that I know I can throw together into a delicious meal. It's lovely with the cabbage and snow pea (mangetout) shoots, but other vegies such as English spinach, broccoli, capsicum (pepper), zucchini (courgette) or green beans work just as well. The protein element is infinitely flexible also — that's why this is such a great recipe. It's divine with fish, giving otherwise bland varieties a wonderful flavour. It's also great with leftover or tinned black (turtle) beans, gorgeous with tofu, and when you're absolutely desperate and depending on your pantry, a small tin of wild salmon does the job brilliantly. If you have any leftover Crunchy Green Salsa (see page 120), this is the perfect place to use it up. Pick out the avocado (if it's still okay, keep it for another use), and use the salsa instead of the cabbage, snow peas, snow pea shoots and lime below. The shoots will be more cooked, but that's fine.

THE QUALITY OF CURRY POWDER USED HERE MAKES A BIG DIFFERENCE. I USE AN ORGANIC SWEET, FRAGRANT CURRY POWDER, BUT YOU COULD ALSO USE A GREEN CURRY PASTE — JUST CHECK IT ISN'T TOO HOT!

1 tablespoon coconut or unrefined sesame oil

1 small red onion, finely chopped

a good knob of fresh ginger, peeled and cut into thin julienne strips

1 garlic clove, finely diced

1–2 teaspoons curry powder, or 2 tablespoons green curry paste (depending on the heat of your curry paste), to taste

250–310 ml (9–10¾ fl oz/1–1¼ cups) coconut milk

3 makrut (kaffir lime) leaves

1–2 red chillies, or to taste, seeded and cut on the diagonal (optional)

2 carrots, peeled, cut in half lengthways, then sliced on the diagonal 5 mm (¼ inch) thick

300 g (10½ oz) butternut, jap or kent pumpkin (winter squash), peeled and cut into batons 3 cm (1¼ inches) long and 1 cm (½ inch) wide

100 g (3½ oz) orange sweet potato, peeled and cut into 1.5 cm (⅝ inch) chunks

¼ savoy or Chinese cabbage, very finely sliced

½ small lime, cut in half, plus extra lime as needed

10 snow peas (mangetout), cut lengthways into julienne strips

300 g (10½ oz) sweet-tasting fish fillets, such as wild mulloway,
    red mullet or nannygai (redfish), checked over for bones,
    then cut into small pieces
a large handful of coriander (cilantro) leaves
a handful of snow pea (mangetout) shoots, the woody stems cut off
1 teaspoon pear juice concentrate, to taste
steamed basmati rice, to serve

Put the oil, onion, ginger and garlic in a heavy-based saucepan. Cook over gentle heat for 5 minutes, or until the onion starts to soften. Stir in the curry powder and cook for a further 3 minutes.

Add 250 ml (9 fl oz/1 cup) of the coconut milk, 125 ml (4 fl oz/½ cup) water, lime leaves, chilli (if using), carrot, pumpkin and sweet potato. Don't be too alarmed if it seems there is not enough liquid — the vegetables release liquid as they cook. Cover and gently simmer for 15–20 minutes, or until the vegetables are just soft and still a little firm. Taste and add more curry powder if desired.

Add the cabbage, squeeze in the juice from the lime, then drop the lime rind into the curry. Again, it may look as if there is not enough liquid, but this will be released from the cabbage. (If you're using leftover Crunchy Green Salsa, also add that now, but you may need a little more lime; taste when the cabbage is cooked and adjust if necessary.) Cover and cook for 5 minutes. Taste and add more curry if desired.

Add the snow peas and fish, gently stir through, and if you feel there is absolutely not enough liquid, add the remaining coconut milk. Cover and cook for a further 10 minutes. Stir in the coriander and snow pea shoots and check for taste. Adjust the flavour if needed with a squeeze more lime, or a dash of pear juice concentrate. Serve with steamed basmati rice.

VARIATIONS

Instead of the fish, you could add 170 g (6 oz/1 cup) cooked black (turtle) beans or 150–200 g (5½–7 oz) firm tofu, cut into 1.5 cm (5/8 inch) cubes.

 C3

Pizza

Pizza is a great dinner for a relaxed Friday or Saturday night — one we don't have a lot of, but certainly enjoy when we do. It's a guaranteed hit with children and teenagers, and my philosophy is to enjoy it, but make it as 'real' and wholesome as possible. Pizza definitely does not need cheese — you have to put a bit more work into it, but it's equally delicious. I prepare and knead the dough in my stand mixer — it makes the whole thing painless and very easy; you could even do it in a breadmaker. Any leftover dough freezes well for another time.

I've included two pizza base options here — a basic spelt-based dough, and a gluten-free polenta alternative. You'll also find a base tomato sauce, and several favourite toppings, including a dairy-free version. ☙

KITCHEN NOTE: *For very little money, a pizza stone can give you an even better pizza and the dough will take a little less time to cook. Preheat the oven to 250°C (500°F/Gas 9), or 230°C (450°F/Gas 8) if fan-forced. Place the pizza stone on the floor of the oven and heat for 15 minutes. Meanwhile, put the pizza dough (rolled to the full 33 cm/13 inches) on a polenta-dusted pizza peel or open-sided baking tray. Top with your favourite ingredients and slide the pizza from the peel or tray onto the preheated stone — this sometimes takes a bit of wrist flicking. Bake for 10–15 minutes.*

The pizza dough

WHEAT FREE / DAIRY FREE / VEGAN

MAKES ONE 33 CM (13 INCH) PIZZA BASE OR 4 SMALL BASES

I have always liked to use spelt flour for pizza, with equal quantities of wholemeal and white. The quality of both white and wholemeal spelt varies enormously. Whites can be lovely and light, or almost of a light wholemeal consistency. Wholemeals can be coarse and hefty, or sometimes fine and smooth. When the wholemeal is soft and fine, I use 100%; when hefty and coarse, I use half wholemeal and half white. Every time you change the ratio and batch of flour, the grain will absorb differing amounts of water. It's enough to drive you crazy, but that's the nature of the beast.

7 g (⅛ oz) dried yeast
1 teaspoon rapadura sugar or honey
250 g (9 oz/2 cups) plain (all-purpose) spelt flour — I generally use
    half white and half wholemeal, but you could also use wheat flour
½ teaspoon sea salt
olive oil, for brushing

Put the yeast, sugar and 160 ml (5¼ oz) lukewarm water in a large bowl. Leave to sit for 10 minutes, or until froth appears. Add the flour, sea salt and olive oil and begin to mix the dough together — the dough should be moist, but not wet. (For half white and half wholemeal flour, you may need an extra tablespoon of water. If using white spelt only, you may need a little less; if using all wholemeal, you will need a little more.) If the dough is really wet, add a little more flour.

Knead the dough on a lightly floured surface for 10 minutes, or until smooth and elastic. Do not add too much flour as you knead — the dough will eventually come together and become less sticky as you knead. You should begin to feel it relax and 'give' as you roll — small air bubbles as you knead is a good sign that the dough is nearly ready. (If you are using a stand mixer to knead, do so at a very slow speed for about 5 minutes.)

Rub a little olive oil around the bowl. Return the dough to the bowl and rub some oil over the top. Cover the dough and place in a warm place to rise for 40 minutes to 1 hour, or until doubled in size.

Lightly oil a baking tray. Turn the dough onto a lightly floured surface. Gather the dough back, then knead a little, forming a ball. Dust a rolling pin with flour and roll the dough out to a 33 cm (13 inch) circle about 5 mm (¼ inch) thick, using extra flour for dusting as needed. (If you prefer a thinner pizza, freeze half the dough and roll out a thinner base, though you may need to use your hands to press it out over the tray.)

The pizza base is now ready for topping — it is best to do this straight away as the dough will begin to rise. If it needs to sit, cover it with plastic wrap.

ۼ

Polenta pizza base

GLUTEN FREE / DAIRY FREE / VEGAN

MAKES ONE 25 CM (10 INCH) PIZZA

Most gluten-free pizza is made from highly refined starches — potato, tapioca, rice — with a few gums thrown in to help it all stick together. It will do the same thing in your digestive system: stick together! Corn (maize) is naturally gluten free, and makes a fabulous pizza base. At a pinch, you could use instant polenta for a quicker base, but your results will be more flavoursome and nutritious without. Look for a polenta that has the germ intact — many are sold without the germ to improve the shelf life.

75 g (2½ oz / ½ cup) polenta
Basil and Garlic Paste (see page 161), for brushing

Preheat the oven to 220°C (425°F/Gas 7). Line a baking tray with baking paper.

YOU CAN SIMMER THE POLENTA IN STOCK RATHER THAN WATER FOR A STRONGER FLAVOUR

Bring 500 ml (17 fl oz/2 cups) water to the boil, with a pinch of sea salt. Slowly sprinkle the polenta into the water, whisking so it doesn't clump. Reduce the heat to a gentle simmer and begin to stir with a spoon. Make sure the heat is very gentle — you only want a gentle blip and bubble in the polenta. Cook for 20 minutes, stirring frequently.

Spoon the hot polenta (don't let it cool) onto the baking tray and spread into a free-form 25 cm (10 inch) circle about 5 mm (¼ inch) thick.

INSTEAD OF THE BASIL AND GARLIC PASTE YOU COULD BRUSH THE POLENTA BASE WITH OLIVE OIL

When the base has cooled a little, brush with the Basil and Garlic Paste and bake for 10–15 minutes. Remove from the oven and top as desired, taking care to extend your sauce and toppings to the edge of the base. Bake for a further 15 minutes, or until the edges are lovely and golden and crisp.

૭ઠ

The tomato sauce

MAKES ENOUGH FOR 1 LARGE PIZZA

If you have a mortar and pestle, try this method for making the sauce. Pound and grind the basil and garlic together, add 1½ tablespoons olive oil, mix and crush to infuse the flavour, then tip into the saucepan. Add the onion and gently cook for about 5 minutes, before adding the tomatoes and sugar. Some chopped sun-dried tomatoes are a great addition to the tomato sauce.

    1 tablespoon olive oil
    ½ small red onion, finely diced
    8–10 fresh basil leaves, or ¼–½ teaspoon dried basil
    2–3 garlic cloves, crushed or finely chopped
    400 g (14 oz) tin chopped tomatoes
    ½ teaspoon rapadura sugar, or 1 teaspoon apple juice concentrate,
        or other sweetener, to taste

Put the olive oil, onion and basil in a saucepan and sauté over gentle heat for 5 minutes. Add the garlic and cook for 1 minute, then stir in the tomatoes and sugar. Gently simmer for 20 minutes, or until the sauce is thick and no watery liquid remains, stirring now and then. Leave to cool a little before spreading.

ങ

Time saver
THIS TOMATO SAUCE FREEZES WELL, SO WHY NOT MAKE EXTRA FOR FUTURE USE?

My classic family pizza

WHEAT FREE

MAKES ONE 33 CM (13 INCH) PIZZA OR 4 SMALL PIZZAS

Time saver

I SOMETIMES USE
A TINNED, ORGANIC
PIZZA SAUCE FOR A
QUICKER OPTION

I've been making this version for years, and still love it. It includes pineapple (it's my sweet/savoury personal thing) but feel free to omit it. Sometimes I also give the whole thing a fine grating of parmesan or pecorino on top of the other cheese … yum!

1 quantity of Tomato Sauce (see page 159)
1 ready-rolled 33 cm (13 inch) pizza base (see page 156)
6 small mushrooms, finely sliced
1 small red capsicum (pepper), finely diced
12 pitted kalamata olives, roughly chopped or torn
3 slices of tinned pineapple in natural juice, cut into small bits
(or use some fresh ripe pineapple, cut into small chunks)
50 g (1¾ oz) tin or jar of anchovies
80 g (2¾ oz) mozzarella cheese, or to taste
7–10 small basil leaves

Preheat the oven to 220°C (425°F/Gas 7). Spread as much tomato sauce over the pizza base as desired. Scatter with the mushroom, capsicum, olives, pineapple and anchovies. Pinch small bits off the cheese and scatter over the top (it's much easier than grating it!).

Bake for 15–18 minutes, or until the dough is lightly golden and cooked. If the edges are cooking more quickly than the centre, reduce the oven temperature after 5 minutes. Scatter the basil leaves over the top of the pizza and serve.

☙

Dairy-free pizza

WHEAT FREE / DAIRY FREE / VEGAN

MAKES ONE 33 CM (13 INCH) PIZZA OR 4 SMALL PIZZAS

My complaint with dairy-free cheeses is that they are made from highly refined vegetable oils, gums, flavours and colours — there's nothing 'real' or good about them. Try this pizza, and you'll never miss the cheese.

Balsamic onion
1 tablespoon olive oil
1 red onion, finely sliced
2 teaspoons balsamic vinegar

Basil & garlic paste
a generous handful of basil leaves
3 garlic cloves
2 tablespoons olive oil

½ red capsicum (pepper), cut in half, seeds removed
5 slices of eggplant, each about 1.5 cm (⅝ inch) thick
½ tablespoon olive oil
½ teaspoon dried basil
1 ready-rolled 33 cm (13 inch) pizza base (see page 156)
1 quantity of Tomato Sauce (see page 159)
10–12 pitted kalamata olives, roughly torn or chopped

Preheat the oven to 200°C (400°F/Gas 6). To prepare the balsamic onion, put the olive oil and onion in a frying pan and cook over a very gentle heat for 15 minutes, or until the onion is very soft. Stir in the vinegar and cook over a gentle heat, stirring often, for a further 10 minutes. Take care not to brown the onion. Set aside.

Meanwhile, to make the basil and garlic paste, put the basil and garlic in a mortar and pound and grind gently to blend. Add the olive oil and mix and crush to infuse all the flavours.

Place the capsicum on a baking tray, skin side up, with the eggplant. Drizzle the olive oil over the capsicum, taking care to rub it over the skin. Brush the eggplant with some of the basil and garlic paste, then sprinkle with the dried basil. Roast for

20 minutes, or until the vegetables are just lightly coloured — they will finish cooking on the pizza. Allow to cool a little, peel the skin from the capsicum, then slice the capsicum and eggplant.

Increase the oven temperature to 220°C (425°F/Gas 7). Brush the outer border of the pizza base (about 1.5 cm/⅝ inch) with more basil and garlic paste. Spread the tomato sauce around the inside of the border. Scatter the balsamic onion, eggplant, capsicum and olives over the top, then drizzle with the remaining basil and garlic paste.

Bake for 15–18 minutes, or until the dough is lightly golden and cooked. If the crust is cooking more quickly than the centre, reduce the oven temperature after 5 minutes.

VARIATIONS

The options for pizza toppings are huge. My favourites include cooked English spinach; sliced artichoke hearts; grilled vegetables (fennel is particularly good); cooked and thinly sliced potato; seafoods; meats such as salami, ham, bacon, pancetta and prosciutto; pesto (see Basics, pages 255–256); herbs of all types; and cheeses of all descriptions, including goat's cheese and cream cheese (cheeses such as feta can be dotted on after cooking). I also like to serve a cooked pizza with lightly dressed rocket (arugula) scattered on top.

૩

Pasta and noodles

I have nothing against pasta — I love it! — but it's not something to be had every night for dinner. Unfortunately that's what I see a lot of people doing. At the end of a busy day, pasta is a quick and appealing option. It's also a big trap for vegetarian teenagers — especially when the only pasta they have is made from white flour. Pasta should be a delicious part of a broad diet that is rich in all the other food groups. My feeling with pasta is to have it well done and less often.

My daughter Nessie is the pasta queen in the family. I gave her a recipe book with photos for her 14th birthday — a proper one by an Italian pasta guru. At that time, she was responsible for one meal a week. I wanted her to learn about real pasta, and how to make good, proper sauces. She now makes her own pasta and fabulous sauces!

I have included two simple pasta recipes here — the first is Nessie's and reflects the more traditional teachings that were instilled by Giuliano Hazan in *The Classic Pasta Cookbook*. The second is dairy free and reflects my own twist on Nessie's style. Both recipes are relatively quick to make, but when you have more time there's also a wonderful Cannelloni recipe on page 128. ☙

Creamy mushroom and snow pea pasta

SERVES 4

CAN BE WHEAT OR GLUTEN FREE DEPENDING ON THE PASTA USED

The best pasta to use here is one that has a few nooks and crannies to catch all the lovely, creamy sauce: penne, shells of all descriptions, and even bow ties. If you would like to reduce the amount of cream in this recipe, replace half with chicken or vegetable stock.

30 g (1 oz) butter
1 red onion, finely diced
2 slices of nitrate-free bacon, roughly chopped (including the fat)
5 garlic cloves, finely diced or crushed
100 g (3½ oz) mushrooms, sliced 1 cm (½ inch) thick
2 thyme sprigs, leaves picked
1 zucchini (courgette), cut into quarters lengthways, then into 5 mm (¼ inch) slices

300-375 g (10½-13 oz) pasta
20 snow peas (mangetout), cut in half on a slight diagonal
300 ml (10½ fl oz) cream
3 tablespoons grated parmesan cheese, or to taste

Bring a large pot of water to the boil.

Meanwhile, melt the butter in a frying pan. Add the onion, bacon and a pinch of sea salt and cook over medium heat for 5–10 minutes, stirring often. Add the garlic, mushrooms, thyme and zucchini and cook for a further 15 minutes, keeping the heat at medium — the vegetables, especially the mushrooms, must not stew, but gently sizzle the whole time. Keep stirring often.

Add the pasta to the boiling water and cook according to the packet directions. Place a colander in the sink and carefully pour in the pasta to drain.

Meanwhile, add the snow peas, cream and some freshly ground black pepper to the mushroom mixture. Increase the heat to a boil and cook, stirring often, for 5 minutes, or until the sauce is thick. Taste and add sea salt if needed.

Tip the pasta into a large bowl or serving dish. Add the mushroom mixture and parmesan and mix through.

ᴄꙅ

Dairy-free pasta with mushrooms, zucchini, tomato and pesto

DAIRY FREE

SERVES 4 GENEROUSLY

CAN BE WHEAT
OR GLUTEN FREE
DEPENDING ON THE
PASTA USED

Dairy-free pesto provides the moistness and flavour that cream and cheese usually would here, without any loss of deliciousness. It's equally good the next day as a salad for lunch. I like to use a kamut spiral for this, and sometimes a spelt wholemeal. Kamut is a wonderful grain — an ancient non-hybrid relative of wheat, with a nuttier flavour.

2 tablespoons olive oil
1 red onion, finely diced
100 g (3½ oz) well-flavoured mushrooms, sliced 1 cm (½ inch) thick
1 zucchini (courgette), cut into quarters lengthways, then into 5 mm
    (¼ inch) slices
5 garlic cloves, finely diced
250 g (9 oz) pasta — any shape is fine
450 g (1 lb) tomatoes, skinned, seeded and diced
115 g (4 oz/¾ cup) pitted kalamata olives, roughly chopped
3 tablespoons roughly chopped flat-leaf (Italian) parsley
5 tablespoons Dairy-Free Pesto (see Basics, page 256)

Bring a large pot of water to the boil.

THIS RECIPE IS
BEST ENJOYED IN
SUMMER WHEN
TOMATOES ARE AT
THEIR PEAK

Meanwhile, heat the olive oil in a frying pan. Add the onion and cook over medium heat for 8 minutes, stirring often; there should be a light sizzle. Add the mushroom, zucchini, garlic, some sea salt and a good grind of black pepper. Stirring often, cook for 15 minutes, or until the vegetables have cooked down and no mushroom juices remain.

Add the pasta to the boiling water and cook according to the packet directions. Place a colander in the sink and carefully pour in the pasta to drain.

Tip the pasta into a large bowl or serving dish. Add the mushroom mixture, tomato, olives, parsley and pesto and gently stir everything together. Check for taste and add more black pepper if necessary.

ଓଃ

165   *dinner*

Sesame chicken with buckwheat noodles and bok choy

GLUTEN FREE / DAIRY FREE

SERVES 4 – 6

WILL ONLY BE
GLUTEN FREE IF
THE TAMARI IS
WHEAT FREE

My approach with expensive meat is to use only enough to make the dish work. This is a very quick and easy meal to put together (especially when the chicken has been poached the day before), and is rich in goodness — especially calcium from both the sesame seeds and bok choy. This dish is best eaten as soon as it is made, as the sauce tends to set a bit, and the noodles dry out when cold.

400 g (14 oz/2 bunches) bok choy (pak choy), washed well and dried
3 spring onions (scallions), greens only
a large handful of coriander (cilantro)
1 tablespoon sesame seeds
250 g (9 oz) poached chicken breast (see Basics, page 252)
250 g (9 oz) soba (buckwheat) noodles
2 tablespoons unrefined sesame oil

CHECK YOUR
SOBA NOODLES
ARE MADE FROM
100% BUCKWHEAT
— MANY ARE
CUT WITH
WHEAT FLOUR

Tahini dressing
1 tablespoon roasted sesame oil
2 teaspoons finely grated fresh ginger
1½ tablespoons tamari
1 tablespoon mirin
60 ml (2 fl oz/¼ cup) hulled tahini
1 teaspoon umeboshi vinegar or rice vinegar
2 teaspoons sweet chilli sauce

WHEN BUYING
HULLED TAHINI,
ORGANIC IS THE
BETTER OPTION —
THE SEEDS HAVE
BEEN HULLED
MECHANICALLY,
RATHER THAN
WITH CHEMICALS

Place a large pot of water on the stove to boil.

Meanwhile, cut the larger bok choy leaves in half lengthways and leave the others whole. Set aside. Slice the spring onion greens on the diagonal and pick the leaves from the coriander. Set aside.

Lightly toast the sesame seeds in a dry frying pan and set aside.

Shred the chicken breast, being sure to keep any jelled stock clinging to the meat.

Put all the tahini dressing ingredients in a small bowl with 60 ml (2 fl oz/¼ cup) water. Whisk together and set aside.

Add the noodles to the boiling water and stir through. When the water returns to the boil, add 250 ml (9 fl oz/1 cup) cold water. When it returns to the boil again, add another 250 ml (9 fl oz/1 cup) cold water. After 3 minutes from the time the noodles were first added to the water, check for doneness: it is very important that they be *just* cooked, otherwise they will break up.

Immediately pour the noodles into a colander in the sink and rinse with cold water to stop them cooking. Add 1 teaspoon or so of the sesame oil to the noodles and gently toss through. Set aside.

Warm the remaining sesame oil in a wok or large frying pan over moderate heat. Add the bok choy — it should sizzle, not burn — and toss for 3 minutes, or until beginning to wilt.

Stir in the chicken and any jelled stock, then add the noodles. Gently keep tossing the mixture and cook for a further 5 minutes, or until all the ingredients are heated through. Turn off the heat and gently stir the spring onion, coriander and tahini dressing through. Serve sprinkled with the sesame seeds.

VARIATIONS

For even more goodness, add some blanched broccoli florets to the dish when adding the shredded chicken.

ଔ

THE TAHINI DRESSING IS ALSO A GREAT STIR-FRY SAUCE. ADD IT AT THE LAST MOMENT WHEN ALL THE VEGIES ARE COOKED

cakes, cookies and desserts

I recently ran a course titled 'Don't Skip the Dessert', aimed at people who believe sweets have no place in a wholesome, healthy diet. We all love a little something sweet and delicious — and that yearning does not go away, no matter how strong your willpower. But enjoying a delicious sweet treat is very different from *craving* chocolate and sweets. Craving is an indication that your diet is out of balance, that you are not eating a nutrient-dense breakfast, lunch and dinner. I've used a variety of wholesome ingredients in the following recipes, and even though some of them might seem expensive, the result will still be far cheaper than those you buy.

You'll find both high- and low-fat cakes, cookies and desserts in the following recipes. I prefer higher-fat options in winter when the body requires more fuel — this is especially important for children.

Unsalted organic butter is the most stable and delicious fat for baking. If you are dairy intolerant, you may be able to use ghee instead, but note that ghee is 100% fat while butter contains roughly 20% milk solids and water. When using any pure fat (oil, ghee) instead of butter, you will need to reduce the amount by 20%, and adjust the liquid accordingly.

Unrefined coconut oil is an excellent dairy-free option, but is not always easy to use. In a cake, it will toughen the crumb when cooled — thus the cake is lovely warm but not so good cold or reheated. This oil is wonderful for some pastries and cookies. It comes in both a full coconut-flavoured version, and another where that flavour is removed, generally by filtering the oil through clay. (Different brands call this flavourless coconut oil by different names, so you'll need to check.) Almond oil, with its good oleic fatty acid level, is my next preference. I don't use canola, sunflower or safflower oils as these are generally too refined, highly coloured, highly flavoured or unstable. And I never use hydrogenated oil products (spreads and margarines), no matter how healthy they are claimed to be.

The following recipes use spelt flour and are wheat (but not gluten) free; however, you can use wheat flour if you prefer. For best results, please read the section 'Flours and baking powder' on pages 24–26 *before* you start baking.

Biscuits, bars and cakes

When you bake a cake, bar or biscuit (cookie) to tuck into a lunchbox or for afternoon teas, you'll end up with more Domestic Goddess/God brownie points than you'll know what to do with. You'll smile and be entirely delighted with yourself — and so you should be! ○

Apricot and oat bars

WHEAT FREE

MAKES 12 BARS

The inclusion of oatmeal gives a delicious chewiness to these bars. They keep extremely well; in warmer weather, store them in an airtight container in the fridge. (If your school has banned nuts, leave these out.)

280 g (10 oz/1½ cups) roughly chopped dried apricots
1–2 teaspoons lemon juice
125 g (4½ oz/1 cup) plain (all-purpose) white spelt flour
100 g (3½ oz/1 cup) rolled (porridge) oats
½ teaspoon ground cinnamon
¼ teaspoon baking powder
75 g (2½ oz/heaped ⅓ cup) rapadura or raw sugar
80 g (2¾ oz) unsalted butter, melted and cooled a little
1 teaspoon natural vanilla extract
50 g (1¾ oz/½ cup) pecans or walnuts, finely chopped

SULPHUR DIOXIDE-FREE APRICOTS VARY ENORMOUSLY IN FLAVOUR — SOME ARE FAR SWEETER THAN OTHERS. IF USING VERY TART DRIED APRICOTS, OMIT THE LEMON JUICE FROM THE RECIPE. YOU COULD ALSO USE DRIED PEACHES INSTEAD — YOU'LL NEED ABOUT 200 G (7 OZ), ROUGHLY CHOPPED

Put the apricots in a saucepan with 250 ml (9 fl oz/1 cup) water. Bring to the boil, then turn off the heat. Add 1 teaspoon lemon juice and taste, adding more if required — the brew should be a little tart, as the base is sweet. Set aside to cool.

Preheat the oven to 180°C (350°F/Gas 4). Line a 20 cm (8 inch) square biscuit tin with baking paper, cutting the corners to allow the paper to fold.

Put the flour, oats, cinnamon, baking powder and sugar in a bowl and whisk through to combine. Add the butter and vanilla and mix well — the mixture will probably be a little crumbly.

Spoon a little over half the mixture into the biscuit tin, pressing it in well with your hands or the back of a spoon — this will help bring the mixture together and make it look more like a dough, rather than a crumble.

Mash the soaked apricots well to form a thick mixture and spread this gently over the dough. Stir the nuts into the remaining oat mixture and sprinkle over the fruit. Using your hands, very gently pat the topping down so it's a little flattened.

Bake for 20–25 minutes, or until the top is golden. Allow to cool well to firm up, then cut into 12 bars.

VARIATIONS

For a cheaper option, use stewed apples. Peel and roughly chop 4 apples (about 500 g/1 lb 2 oz in total). Add them to a saucepan with 1½ tablespoons water and 2 teaspoons sugar. Cover and cook over a very gentle heat for about 5 minutes (the apples will sweat out their juices). Gently simmer for a further 5 minutes, or until the apples are just tender. Remove the lid and increase the heat to reduce all the juice. Roughly mash and use, adding a little grated lemon zest if desired.

℃

Peach Anzacs

WHEAT FREE

MAKES 10

I've been making these since my daughter (now 25) was very little. The original idea was to make 'healthier' Anzacs, and I needed the moistness of fruit to soften the biscuit (cookie) mix. My approach to what constitutes healthy food has changed, but I still make this version of the traditional Australian biscuit using my trusty crumble mix. Whenever I include them in a class, they are the most popular of the recipes. Peach Anzacs are equally delicious warm or cold and are excellent packed in a lunchbox. They are delicious for dessert served with Honey and Cinnamon Yoghurt Cream (page 196).

5 peaches
50 g (1¾ oz / ½ cup) rolled (porridge) oats or oatmeal
60 g (2¼ oz / ½ cup) plain (all-purpose) white spelt flour
90 g (3¼ oz / ½ cup) light brown or rapadura sugar
25 g (1 oz / ¼ cup) desiccated coconut
½ - 1 teaspoon ground cinnamon
100 g (3½ oz) unsalted butter or ghee
50 g (1¾ oz / ½ cup) walnuts, roughly chopped (optional)
1 teaspoon natural vanilla extract

Preheat the oven to 180°C (350°F/Gas 4). Wash the peaches and shake off any excess water. Cut in half and remove the stones. Lay the peaches in a large ovenproof dish, cut side up.

Combine the oats, flour, sugar, coconut, cinnamon and butter in a bowl, or place in a food processor. Rub the butter into the dry ingredients until combined, or pulse until the mixture is just coming together, taking care not to overmix. Add the walnuts and fold through, or give a quick pulse.

Divide the mixture into 10 portions, or lightly mould into 10 balls, using about 1 heaped tablespoon for each. Place one on each peach half and gently pat to spread over the peach, but don't cover the entire peach. Pour 250 ml (9 fl oz/1 cup) water into the dish with the vanilla. Bake for 20–30 minutes, or until the peaches are just soft and the crumble is golden. The crumble topping will firm up a little as the peaches cool.

VARIATIONS

Nectarines work beautifully in this recipe, following the instructions above. Pears are also great — you'll need 4 small–medium ripe (but not over-ripe) ones. Cut them in half, scoop out the core, continue as above and cook for 30–40 minutes, or until the pears just 'give' when gently squeezed. When making Pear Anzacs, I like to add 1 tablespoon or so finely chopped glacé ginger.

ଔ

Luscious lemon bars

GLUTEN FREE / DAIRY FREE / VEGAN

MAKES 16

As the name says, these bars are absolutely luscious, and easy to make. They are best eaten on the day they are made, but will keep for a couple of days in an airtight container — the base will soften a little, but they will still be delicious. Rather than making bars, you could also pour the filling into a pre-cooked 24 cm (9½ inch) tart shell.

145 g (5 oz/¾ cup) brown rice flour
25 g (1 oz/¼ cup) desiccated coconut
70 g (2½ oz/⅔ cup) ground almonds
2 tablespoons maple syrup
80 ml (2½ fl oz/⅓ cup) coconut oil (melted for measuring, if solid)
1 teaspoon natural vanilla extract

Topping
185 ml (6 fl oz/¾ cup) lemon juice
3 teaspoons agar powder
1 tablespoon cornflour (cornstarch)
500 ml (17 fl oz/2 cups) coconut milk
125 ml (4 fl oz/½ cup) brown rice syrup
125 ml (4 fl oz/½ cup) maple syrup
1 tablespoon grated lemon zest
a pinch of ground turmeric

THE ACID IN LEMONS CAN INTERFERE WITH AGAR'S ABILITY TO SET. DEPENDING ON HOW ACIDIC YOUR LEMONS ARE, THE TOPPING WILL SET EITHER FAIRLY FIRM, OR SLIGHTLY SOFTER

Preheat the oven to 180°C (350°F/Gas 4). Line a 20 cm (8 inch) square biscuit tin with baking paper, cutting the corners to allow the paper to fold.

Put the rice flour, coconut and ground almonds in a bowl and whisk through to combine. In a small bowl, mix together the maple syrup, coconut oil and vanilla, then add to the dry ingredients and mix to combine. The mixture will be quite wet and oily, but will soften the rice flour and result in a lovely shortbread.

Spoon the mixture into the prepared tin and press it in with your hands. Bake for 15–20 minutes, or until lightly golden. Set aside to cool.

To make the topping, put the lemon juice and agar powder in a saucepan and mix together well, making sure the agar is evenly distributed, and has not clumped together. Place over a very gentle heat for 5 minutes, stirring often, then increase the heat to a gentle boil. Continue to very gently simmer for 8 minutes, stirring often.

Meanwhile, put the cornflour in a bowl with 125 ml (4 fl oz/½ cup) of the coconut milk and mix to a smooth slurry. Mix in the remaining coconut milk, brown rice syrup and maple syrup. Set aside.

Remove the lemon agar from the heat and slowly add the coconut milk mixture, whisking constantly. Return to the heat and bring to the boil, using a whisk to stir gently but constantly until just boiled. Do not over-boil.

Remove from the heat and stir in the lemon zest and turmeric (don't add too much turmeric or the colour will be too bright). Allow to cool a little, then very gently pour the mixture over the biscuit base.

Leave to cool for about 30 minutes, before gently placing in the fridge to set for 2–3 hours. Cut into 16 squares and serve.

VARIATIONS

If you would prefer not to use a gluten-free base, try this spelt one.

90 g (3¼ oz/1 cup) desiccated coconut
125 g (4½ oz/1 cup) plain (all-purpose) white spelt flour
½ teaspoon baking powder
80 ml (2½ fl oz/⅓ cup) flavourless coconut oil (melted for measuring, if solid)
60 ml (2 fl oz/¼ cup) maple syrup
1 teaspoon natural vanilla extract

Put the coconut, flour and baking powder in a bowl and whisk through to combine. In a small bowl, mix together the coconut oil, maple syrup and vanilla, then add to the wet ingredients and mix through — the mixture will be a bit crumbly. Spoon into the biscuit tin and press it in with your hands, then cook as per recipe.

ↄ𝅺

Chocolate chip cookies

WHEAT FREE / DAIRY FREE / VEGAN

MAKES 20 COOKIES

A deliciously sustaining choc chip cookie, and a great way to enjoy a wholesome treat. These cookies will last for a couple of weeks in an airtight container.

150 g (5½ oz/1½ cups) rolled (porridge) oats
155 g (5½ oz/1 cup) raw almonds (skin on)
125 g (4½ oz/1 cup) plain (all-purpose) white spelt flour
¼ teaspoon baking powder
170 g (5¾ oz/1 cup) chocolate chips
125 ml (4 fl oz/½ cup) almond oil or flavourless coconut oil (melted for measuring, if solid)
125 ml (4 fl oz/½ cup) maple syrup
2 teaspoons natural vanilla extract

Preheat the oven to 180°C (350°F/Gas 4). Line a baking tray with baking paper.

Spread the oats on a baking tray and bake for 5 minutes. Remove from the oven and immediately tip into a bowl to stop the cooking process. Spread the almonds on the same baking tray and bake for 7–10 minutes, taking care they don't burn.

Put the oats in a food processor or blender and grind to a coarse meal. Tip into a mixing bowl. Roughly grind the almonds and add to the oats. Add the flour, baking powder and chocolate chips and whisk through to combine.

Mix together the almond oil, maple syrup and vanilla, then pour into the dry ingredients and mix to form a dough.

Spoon tablespoons of the dough onto the prepared baking tray, then flatten and shape into neat circles 8 mm–1 cm (⅜–½ inch) thick.

Bake for 10–15 minutes, or until ever so slightly golden. Remove from the oven and allow to sit on the tray for 10 minutes before removing to a wire rack.

☙

Brownies

WHEAT FREE / DAIRY FREE / VEGAN

MAKES 16

Rich and delicious, these brownies are made using good-quality real chocolate — full of wonderful goodness. The mix of sweeteners is important. Rice syrup provides a lovely chew to the brownies, and is a very body-compatible sweetener, but too much can make the mixture unworkable. Maple syrup is also a nutrient-rich, whole sweetener — but too much can be expensive. Raw sugar provides the little bit of sweetening that balances everything perfectly.

NOTE THAT OAT
FLOUR IS NOT
GROUND ROLLED
(PORRIDGE) OATS,
BUT GROUND
OAT GROATS
(KERNELS)

125 g (4½ oz/1 cup) plain (all-purpose) white spelt flour
30 g (1 oz/¼ cup) oat flour
1½ teaspoons baking powder
90 g (3¼ oz/¾ cup) dutched cocoa powder (see Kitchen notes)
185 ml (6 fl oz/¾ cup) almond oil
185 ml (6 fl oz/¾ cup) maple syrup
60 ml (2 fl oz/¼ cup) rice syrup
55 g (2 oz/¼ cup) raw sugar
1 teaspoon natural vanilla extract
60 ml (2 fl oz/¼ cup) soy, almond or oat milk
50 g (1¾ oz/⅓ cup) roughly chopped good-quality, semi-sweet
    dark chocolate
100 g (3½ oz/1 cup) walnuts, lightly toasted, then roughly chopped

Preheat the oven to 165°C (320°F/Gas 2–3). Grease and line the sides and base of a 20 cm (8 inch) square slice tin.

Put the spelt and oat flour, baking powder and cocoa powder in a bowl and whisk through to combine.

In a separate bowl, mix together the almond oil, maple syrup, rice syrup, sugar, vanilla and milk, then pour into the dry ingredients and mix until combined. Fold the chocolate and walnuts through.

Pour into the prepared tin and bake for 30–35 minutes, or until the edges are puffed and cracked, and the centre is gently puffed and just starting to crack. A skewer should come out a little wet when inserted in the middle, but clean when inserted near the outside edges. If you wobble the tin ever so gently the mixture should wobble a little — it won't be set solid in the middle. Remove from the oven and allow to cool fully before cutting into slices.

KITCHEN NOTES: *Cocoa is really concentrated chocolate, and its natural acidity and tartness is increased when the fat is removed from it. 'Dutching' is a process that uses an alkali to remove some of that acidity, and the result is a 'softer', darker and less bitter and acidic cocoa. Many dutched cocoas use harsh chemicals in the alkalizing process, and some are more dutched than others. I use a moderately dutched cocoa — the organic, fair-trade Green & Black's. It is a beautiful, full-flavoured cocoa, with some of the aggressive acidity and bitterness removed.*

☙

Chocolate, cocoa nib and cherry biscotti

WHEAT FREE / DAIRY FREE / VEGAN

MAKES 32

This is my personal prescription for those who want a little something delicious after dinner with a cup of tea. The biscotti do contain some expensive ingredients, but only in small amounts, and they go a long way.

250 g (9 oz/2 cups) plain (all-purpose) white spelt flour
1 teaspoon baking powder
110 g (3¾ oz/½ cup) rapadura or raw sugar
50 g (1¾ oz/½ cup) walnuts or pecans, or 80 g (2¾ oz/½ cup) almonds, roughly chopped
90 g (3¼ oz/½ cup) dried cherries, roughly chopped
3 tablespoons cocoa nibs (see Kitchen notes)
35 g (1¼ oz/¼ cup) finely chopped good-quality dark (70% cocoa) chocolate
60 ml (2 fl oz/¼ cup) maple syrup
60 ml (2 fl oz/¼ cup) almond oil
165 ml (5¼ fl oz/½ cup plus 2 tablespoons) soy or oat milk
2 teaspoons natural vanilla extract

Preheat the oven to 180°C (350°F/Gas 4). Line a baking tray with baking paper.

Put the flour, baking powder and sugar in a mixing bowl and whisk through to combine. Mix in the nuts, cherries, cocoa nibs and chocolate.

In a small bowl, mix together the maple syrup, almond oil, milk and vanilla, then add to the dry ingredients and mix until just combined — the mixture may be quite moist.

Turn the mixture onto a very lightly floured surface and roll into a log about 35 cm (14 inches) long, 3 cm (1¼ inches) deep and 6–7 cm (2½–2¾ inches) wide. Place on the prepared baking tray and bake for 30–35 minutes, or until firm to the touch. Remove from the oven and allow to cool fully.

When ready to bake the biscotti for the second time, preheat the oven to 170°C (325°F/Gas 3). Have two unlined baking trays at the ready.

Pick up the biscotti log using the baking paper and place on a cutting surface. Using a sturdy, sharp, non-serrated knife, cut the log into slices 1 cm (½ inch) thick. Gently pick up each slice (I use my knife or palette knife to do this) and transfer to the baking trays.

Bake for 12–15 minutes — you don't want the biscotti to colour — then turn the slices over and bake for a further 10–15 minutes. Remove from the oven and allow to cool completely before storing in an airtight container. If you feel the biscotti have not dried out enough, simply bake them a little longer.

KITCHEN NOTES: *Cocoa nibs are becoming more freely available, even organic ones. They are roasted, hulled and broken cocoa beans — this is where chocolate comes from. They are probably the most heavenly food on the planet — rich with cocoa butter, nutty texture and every possible nuance of flavours.*

CB

Nut loaf

WHEAT FREE

MAKES 18 – 20 SLICES

A sturdy, not-too-sweet loaf, perfect for morning tea with a coffee. Not quite a cake and not quite a bread, nut loaf used to be made in round loaf tins and comes from a time when thrift and good sense were abundant. I like it warm with butter. It freezes fabulously (cut it into slices first), and can be warmed in the oven or under the grill (broiler).

45 g (1½ oz) unsalted butter, softened
175 g (6 oz/½ cup) honey, or 90 g (3¼ oz/½ cup) rapadura sugar
1 egg
100 g (3½ oz/1 cup) walnuts or pecans, chopped
180 g (6 oz/1 cup) dried or fresh pitted dates, roughly chopped
125 g (4½ oz/1 cup) sultanas (golden raisins)
110 g (3¾ oz/½ cup) glacé ginger (without the sugar), roughly chopped
250 g (9 oz/2 cups) plain (all-purpose) white spelt flour
3 teaspoons baking powder
1 teaspoon ground cinnamon
250 ml (9 fl oz/1 cup) non-homogenized, full-cream milk

Preheat the oven to 180°C (350°F/Gas 4). Line a 1 litre (35 fl oz/4 cup) loaf (bar) tin with baking paper.

Put the butter, honey and egg in a bowl and mix well. Add the remaining ingredients and mix to combine well — the mixture may look quite moist, but will dry during baking.

Spoon the mixture into the prepared tin and bake for 65–75 minutes, or until a skewer inserted into the centre of the loaf comes out clean. Remove from the oven and allow to cool in the tin for a few minutes before removing.

☙

IF YOU USE LOWER-FAT MILK SUCH AS OAT OR SOY IN THIS RECIPE, YOU WILL NEED TO INCREASE THE BUTTER A LITTLE

Pear harvest cake

WHEAT FREE

This is a cake I've been making for years, and a lovely way to welcome autumn. Beautiful hot or cold.

Crumble mix
50 g (1¾ oz oz/½ cup) rolled (porridge) oats
60 g (2¼ oz/½ cup) plain (all-purpose) white spelt flour
90 g (3¼ oz/½ cup) brown sugar — light muscovado or rapadura
25 g (1 oz/¼ cup) desiccated coconut
1 teaspoon ground cinnamon
80 g (2¾ oz) unsalted butter, diced
100 g (3½ oz/1 cup) walnuts, roughly chopped

125 g (4½ oz) unsalted butter, softened
165 g (5¾ oz/¾ cup) rapadura or raw sugar
2 eggs
1 teaspoon natural vanilla extract
125 g (4½ oz/1 cup) plain (all-purpose) white spelt flour
125 g (4½ oz/1 cup) plain (all-purpose) wholemeal spelt flour
2½ teaspoons baking powder
1 teaspoon ground cinnamon
1 teaspoon ground ginger
250 ml (9 fl oz/1 cup) milk (any type is fine)
2–3 pears (about 450 g/1 lb in total), washed, skin on, cut
    into 1 cm (½ inch) dice (discard the cores)

Preheat the oven to 170°C (325°F/Gas 3). Lightly grease a 24 cm (9½ inch) spring-form cake tin and line the base and side with baking paper.

To make the crumble mix, put the oats, flour, sugar, coconut, cinnamon and butter in a bowl, or place in a food processor. Rub the butter into the dry ingredients until combined, or pulse until the mixture just comes together — take care not to overmix. Add the walnuts and set aside.

Using electric beaters, whisk together the butter and sugar until creamy. Add the eggs one at a time, beating well after each addition. Add the vanilla, all the flour, the baking powder, cinnamon, ginger and milk and mix through until just combined — I prefer to do this by hand, using a spatula. Add the pears and just fold through. Add half the crumble mix, and just fold through.

Turn the batter into the prepared tin and top with the remaining crumble. Bake for 70–80 minutes, or until a skewer inserted into the centre of the cake comes out clean. Check the cake after 50 minutes — if the crumble is browning too much, reduce the heat to 160°C (315°F/Gas 2–3).

Remove from the oven and remove the cake tin. Enjoy warm, or leave to cool.

VARIATIONS

This cake is equally delicious made with rhubarb. Cut 450 g (1 lb) rhubarb into slices 1 cm (½ inch) thick. The cake will need more sugar to counter the rhubarb's tartness, and this will depend a lot on what sugar you use. Rapadura sugar is less sweet than raw sugar, but using more doesn't necessarily mean extra sweetness. I'd suggest using 165 g (5¾ oz/¾ cup) rapadura plus 55 g (2 oz/¼ cup) raw — or if using just raw sugar, 165 g (5¾ oz/¾ cup) in total. Also, omit the ground ginger.

 C3

Apple and berry cake

WHEAT FREE

SERVES 10 – 12

A deliciously moist, beautiful cake. Instead of spelt flour you could use 240 g (8½ oz/2 cups) oat flour — the result will be slightly chewier, but still fabulous. If you prefer the cake to be egg free, use 1 teaspoon egg replacer mixed with 2 tablespoons water — the crumb won't be as textured, but you'll still end up with a great cake.

Fruit mixture
3 large apples, about 550 g/1 lb 4 oz in total
1 tablespoon rapadura or raw sugar
300 g (10½ oz) berries, either one variety or a mixture (frozen berries are fine — there is no need to thaw them first)

Topping
45 g (1½ oz/½ cup) flaked almonds
25 g (1 oz/¼ cup) desiccated coconut
1 tablespoon rapadura or raw sugar
1 teaspoon ground cinnamon

OAT FLOUR IS NOT GROUND ROLLED (PORRIDGE) OATS, BUT FINELY GROUND OAT GROATS (KERNELS)

120 g (4¼ oz/1 cup) oat flour
125 g (4½ oz/1 cup) plain (all-purpose) white spelt flour
2½ teaspoons baking powder
180 g (6 oz/1 cup) rapadura sugar, or 165 g (5¾ oz/¾ cup) raw sugar
1 egg
185 ml (6 fl oz/¾ cup) soy, oat or dairy milk
1 teaspoon apple cider vinegar
60 ml (2 fl oz/¼ cup) almond oil
2 teaspoons natural vanilla extract

IF SERVING THE CAKE WARM, USE MELTED COCONUT OIL INSTEAD OF ALMOND OIL

Preheat the oven to 175°C (335°F/Gas 3–4). Lightly grease a 26 cm (10½ inch) spring-form cake tin and line the base and side with baking paper.

To prepare the fruit mixture, peel and very finely dice one of the apples and place in a small saucepan. Add 1 tablespoon water, cover and cook over a gentle heat for 3–4 minutes, or until entirely softened. Mash until smooth, then continue to cook, stirring until all the liquid has evaporated — you should have 80–125 ml (2^1/$_2$–4 fl oz/^{1}/$_3$–^{1}/$_2$ cup) purée. Set aside to cool.

Peel the remaining apples and slice into eighths, removing the core. Place in a small saucepan with 1^1/$_2$ tablespoons water and the sugar. Cover and cook over a very gentle heat for 10 minutes, or until soft. Drain off any remaining juice, gently stir in the berries and set aside to cool.

Put all the topping ingredients in a small bowl, toss together and set aside.

Put the oat and spelt flour, baking powder and sugar in a bowl and whisk through to break up any lumps.

Crack the egg into a separate bowl. Add the milk, vinegar, almond oil, vanilla and the cooled apple purée. Whisk together, then pour into the dry ingredients and just mix through, taking care not to overmix.

Spoon two-thirds of the batter into the prepared tin. Top with the fruit mixture. Spoon the remaining batter over the top and gently spread over the fruit. Sprinkle with the topping and bake for 60 minutes, or until a skewer inserted into the centre of the cake comes out clean — with so much fruit it can be tricky to tell.

Remove from the oven and allow to cool a little before removing the cake tin. Enjoy the cake warm, or leave to cool.

ꇙ

Lemon tea cake

WHEAT FREE

SERVES 8–10

I love this cake — it's a good example of how the truly wholesome can simply mean using quality, less-refined ingredients. It's quick to put together and because of the syrup, stays moist.

125 g (4½ oz/1 cup) plain (all-purpose) white spelt flour
2½ teaspoons baking powder
45 g (1½ oz/½ cup) desiccated coconut
80 g (2¾ oz) unsalted butter, softened
120 g (4¼ oz/⅔ cup) rapadura sugar
1 egg
1 teaspoon natural vanilla extract
finely grated zest of 1 lemon
60 g (2¼ oz/¼ cup) yoghurt
2–4 tablespoons milk (any type is fine)

Lemon syrup
125 ml (4 fl oz/½ cup) lemon juice
2 tablespoons brown rice syrup
1 tablespoon raw or demerara sugar

Preheat the oven to 175°C (335°F/Gas 3–4). Line a 1 litre (35 fl oz/4 cup) loaf (bar) tin with baking paper. Don't cut the corners of the baking paper to fit — fold them instead. This will allow you to pour the lemon syrup onto the cake when it is cooked without it seeping onto the tin.

Sift the flour and baking powder into a small bowl, add the coconut and whisk through to combine. Set aside.

Using electric beaters, beat the butter and sugar in a bowl until well combined. Add the egg and beat well until fluffy. Add the vanilla, lemon zest, flour mixture, yoghurt and 2 tablespoons of the milk. Gently beat together until just combined. If the batter is still very dry, add the remaining milk.

Spoon the batter into the prepared tin and bake for 40–45 minutes, or until a skewer inserted into the centre of the cake comes out clean.

While the cake is baking, put all the lemon syrup ingredients in a small saucepan. Bring to the boil and check for taste, adding more sweetener if desired. Continue to boil until reduced by about one-third.

As soon as the cake comes out of the oven, spoon half the lemon syrup over it. Leave for about 10 minutes, then spoon the remaining syrup over the cake. Leave for a further 10 minutes to absorb, then remove the cake from the tin.

C8

Iced vanilla and coconut cupcakes

WHEAT FREE / DAIRY FREE / VEGAN

MAKES 10 MUFFIN-SIZE CUPCAKES, 36 MINI MUFFINS, OR A 20 CM (8 INCH) CAKE

These egg- and dairy-free cupcakes can be whipped up quickly and are perfect for birthday treats and school lunchboxes. For a nut-free version, use melted ghee instead of almond oil, although they won't be dairy free. These cupcakes freeze and keep well, and are utterly delicious.

185 g (6½ oz/1½ cups) plain (all-purpose) white spelt flour
1 teaspoon baking powder
¾ teaspoon bicarbonate of soda (baking soda)
45 g (1½ oz/½ cup) desiccated coconut
2 teaspoons apple cider vinegar
1 tablespoon natural vanilla extract
185 ml (6 fl oz/¾ cup) maple syrup
125 ml (4 fl oz/½ cup) coconut milk
60 ml (2 fl oz/¼ cup) rice milk
80 ml (2½ fl oz/⅓ cup) almond oil
1 quantity of Dairy-free Creamy Icing (see page 190)

*cakes, cookies
and desserts*

Preheat the oven to 175°C (335°F/Gas 3–4). Line 10 holes of a 12-hole muffin tin (each 250 ml/9 fl oz/1 cup capacity) with paper cases.

Sift the flour, baking powder and bicarbonate of soda into a mixing bowl. Add the coconut and whisk through to combine.

In a separate bowl, mix together the vinegar, vanilla, maple syrup, coconut milk, rice milk and almond oil. Add to the dry ingredients and mix until just combined. Leave the batter to sit for 5 minutes — it will look wet, but will firm up on sitting.

Spoon the batter into the paper cases and bake for 30 minutes, or until a skewer inserted into the centre of a cake comes out clean. Remove from the oven and allow to cool completely, then spread the icing over the cupcakes before serving.

ය

Orange cake with passionfruit and orange icing

WHEAT FREE

SERVES 10

Sometimes you just want a piece of cake — no healthy fruit or nuts in it, just cake with gorgeous butter icing. This is a simple, very quick throw-together cake based on a recipe my sister used for years. I prefer to use spelt, rapadura sugar and a less-refined icing (confectioners') sugar — it tastes great, and keeps very well.

250 g (9 oz/2 cups) plain (all-purpose) white spelt flour
3 teaspoons baking powder
180 g (6 oz/1 cup) rapadura sugar
1 teaspoon ground cardamom
4 eggs
finely grated zest and juice of 2 large oranges
60 g (2¼ oz/¼ cup) yoghurt
2 tablespoons full-cream, non-homogenized milk, approximately
160 g (5½ oz) unsalted butter, melted

YOU CAN USE ANY TYPE OF MILK IN THIS CAKE WITH GOOD RESULTS

Passionfruit and orange icing
120 g (4¼ oz) unsalted butter, softened
250 g (9 oz/2 cups) unrefined/golden icing (confectioners') sugar, sifted
1 tablespoon orange juice
2 teaspoons finely grated orange zest
1 tablespoon passionfruit pulp (you'll need about 3 passionfruit)

Preheat the oven to 180°C (350°F/Gas 4). Grease and line the base and sides of a deep 20 cm (8 inch) square baking tin with baking paper.

Sift the flour and baking powder into a mixing bowl. Add the sugar and cardamom and whisk through to combine.

Crack the eggs into a 500 ml (17 fl oz/2 cup) measuring jug. Add the orange juice, orange zest and yoghurt, then top up to 500 ml (17 fl oz/2 cup) with milk — if the oranges are very large, you may not need the milk at all. Pour the mixture into the dry ingredients with the melted butter and mix together.

Pour the batter into the cake tin and bake for 40–60 minutes, or until a skewer inserted into the centre of the cake comes out clean. Remove from the oven and allow to cool for 15 minutes before removing from the tin. Turn out onto a wire rack to cool completely before icing.

To make the icing, put the butter and icing sugar in a small bowl and mix together using electric beaters until creamy and fluffy, adding the orange juice 1 teaspoon at a time — the icing will lighten in colour as you beat. Add the orange zest and passionfruit pulp and beat again until the icing is light and fluffy. Spread the icing over the cooled cake before serving.

VARIATIONS

A half-quantity of the cake and icing will make 10 cupcakes using a 12-hole muffin tin. Bake the cupcakes in a 165°C (320°F/Gas 2–3) oven for about 25 minutes.

℃

Better icings

I love iced (frosted) cakes. Typically, a cake is iced to dress it up, and provide a balance of flavour and moistness to a plain cake. Icing makes a cake special and beautiful. Often, though, icings are overly sweet and too rich.

I prefer to use an unrefined (often referred to as 'golden') icing (confectioners') sugar — this gives a wonderful, subtle sweetness, but it does tint the icing more beige than white, and some sugars are whiter than others. This can make it a bit tricky when adding colour — speaking of which, I never use or recommend most of the cheaper commercial food colours. Many are known carcinogens or have adverse effects in the body. Some countries continue to use colours that are banned in others. You can buy good-quality colours made from natural foods, but if these are not available where you live, you can also make your own, using the natural ingredients below. ☙

Red/pink	beetroot juice
Green	parsley or spinach juice
Yellow	turmeric, dissolved in a little water or sugar syrup
Orange	carrot juice
Blue/purple	blueberry juice
Blue/violet	red cabbage juice

Better butter-cream icing

GLUTEN FREE

MAKES ABOUT 265 G (9¼ OZ/1½ CUPS), ENOUGH TO ICE 10 CUPCAKES
DOUBLE THE RECIPE TO ICE 1 LARGE CAKE

Butter-cream icing (frosting) can be very rich, but it remains one of the best. This icing is based on the famous Magnolia Bakery vanilla butter cream, using a thickened milk mixture to reduce the amount of butter. I've played with it a little to suit my needs — a less rich milk, more coconut, lime to cut the sweetness and a less-refined sugar. All in all, it's delicious and nowhere near as rich. This icing holds up well for piping.

1 tablespoon cornflour (cornstarch)
60 ml (2 fl oz/¼ cup) rice milk
60 ml (2 fl oz/¼ cup) coconut milk
125 g (4½ oz) unsalted butter, softened
85 g (3 oz/½ cup) unrefined/golden icing (confectioners') sugar, sifted
2 teaspoons natural vanilla extract or 1 teaspoon vanilla bean paste
2 teaspoons lime juice

Put the cornflour in a small saucepan, add half the rice milk and mix into a completely smooth slurry. Stir in the remaining rice milk and the coconut milk. Place over medium heat and bring to the boil, stirring constantly until thickened. Pour into a small bowl and press some waxed paper directly onto the surface. Place in the refrigerator to cool.

When the milk mixture is cool, beat the butter using an electric mixer until light and fluffy. Add the icing sugar and beat for a few more minutes. Add the cooled milk mixture, vanilla and lime juice and beat well for a couple of minutes, until the icing is beautifully smooth and fluffy. When the weather is warmer, you may need to put the icing in the fridge to set a little before using — don't leave it too long, or the butter will set hard. In winter, the cool air from the beaters will begin to set the butter, and you may need to use a little more coconut milk (about 1 tablespoon) to bring it to a good consistency for spreading and piping.

Place in the fridge to set just a little before using — but don't leave it too long, or the butter will set hard. If the icing has become too firm to use, let it sit at room temperature to soften before using.

VARIATIONS

Try this delicious raspberry version. Put 60 g (2¼ oz/½ cup) of raspberries in a fine sieve (you can use frozen raspberries, but thaw them first) and place over a bowl. Using the back of a spoon, press the berries into the sieve, to release a lovely purée. Discard the seeds and pulp. Omit the lime juice from the recipe and stir 2 tablespoons of the raspberry purée into the icing, adding another 1 tablespoon if necessary to bring it to the desired consistency.

ೞ

YOU CANNOT REPLACE THE CORNFLOUR IN THIS RECIPE WITH ARROWROOT OR KUDZU

FOR A STRONGER COCONUT FLAVOUR, REPLACE THE RICE MILK WITH EXTRA COCONUT MILK

cakes, cookies and desserts

Dairy-free creamy icing

GLUTEN FREE / DAIRY FREE / VEGAN

MAKES ABOUT 350 G (12 OZ/1¼ CUPS), ENOUGH TO ICE 10 CUPCAKES
DOUBLE THE RECIPE TO ICE 1 LARGE CAKE

As some of the individual steps and quantities in this recipe are small, this icing (frosting) can initially be a bit tricky to work with. The first time you make it, double the quantity — this will give you more to work with, and a good understanding of the process. It's worth the effort because this is a fabulous dairy-free icing. Scoop leftovers straight out of the bowl and serve with fruit, or place in a blender and break down a little to a softer, more voluptuous consistency. This icing holds up well for piping, and you can decorate your cake as desired.

Crème

YOU CANNOT
REPLACE THE
CORNFLOUR IN
THIS RECIPE WITH
ARROWROOT OR
KUDZU

1½ tablespoons cornflour (cornstarch)
¾ tablespoon maple syrup
1 teaspoon natural vanilla extract
185 ml (6 fl oz/¾ cup) milk — half rice milk, half coconut milk

175 g (6 oz/1 cup) unrefined/golden icing (confectioners') sugar
1 tablespoon almond oil
¾ tablespoon lime juice
2 teaspoons natural vanilla extract
145 ml (4¾ fl oz) coconut milk
¾ teaspoon agar powder
¾ tablespoon cornflour (cornstarch)
food colour as desired

To make the crème, put the cornflour in a small saucepan with the maple syrup and vanilla. Mix to a smooth slurry and stir in the milk. Stirring constantly, cook over medium heat until thick and boiling — do not overboil. Use a spatula to remove the crème into a bowl and refrigerate until cool.

When the crème is cool, put the icing sugar in a blender or food processor and pulse until fine. (Allow the sugar dust to settle for a few minutes before lifting the lid.)

Break the cooled crème in three and add to the blender with the almond oil, lime juice and vanilla — do not pulse yet.

Put 125 ml (4 fl oz/½ cup) of the coconut milk in a small saucepan. Gently whisk in the agar powder and place over a very gentle heat. Put the cornflour in a small bowl and mix to a smooth paste with the remaining coconut milk. Leave the spoon in the bowl and set aside.

Increase the heat under the agar mixture a little and slowly bring to the boil, stirring frequently to stop the agar sticking to the bottom. Immediately reduce the heat to a very gentle simmer, where just a blip breaks the surface. Stir frequently for 5–6 minutes, or until thickened noticeably. Remove from the heat.

Briefly stir the cornflour mixture again. Stirring constantly, add it to the agar mixture — it will thicken immediately. Return to the heat and bring to the boil, stirring constantly (the 'boil' will just be bubbles lifting from the bottom of the pan without breaking). Allow to boil for 2 seconds, then remove from the heat.

Using a spatula, spoon all the agar mixture into the blender. Process until smooth and creamy — this may take a few minutes — stopping to scrape down the sides as needed. (If using a large processor or blender, process the mixture slowly — this will stop it splattering.) At this stage, you are incorporating air into the icing, so little bubbles are a good sign. Add the desired amount of food colour as you blend.

Immediately pour the icing into a bowl, press a piece of waxed paper directly onto the surface, and place in the refrigerator to set for 2–3 hours.

If piping the mixture, spoon the set icing directly from the bowl into the piping bag. If using a palette knife, also take the icing directly from the bowl — you will find it will 'give' a little as you start to work with it. If it is too firm for icing with a palette knife, simply give it a quick stir before using.

 Cʒ

Luscious dairy-free lemon curd

DAIRY FREE / GLUTEN FREE / VEGAN

MAKES ABOUT 250 G (9 OZ/1½ CUPS), ENOUGH TO ICE 10 CUPCAKES OR 1 LARGE CAKE

Beautiful to fill little cupcakes, or to spread between the layers of a larger cake. The lemon curd keeps well in the fridge — just press a little baking paper directly onto the surface to keep the air out.

90 ml (3 fl oz) lemon juice
1¼ teaspoons agar powder
2 teaspoons cornflour (cornstarch)
250 ml (9 fl oz/1 cup) coconut milk
60 ml (2 fl oz/¼ cup) maple syrup
60 ml (2 fl oz/¼ cup) brown rice syrup
½ teaspoon natural vanilla extract
2 teaspoons finely grated lemon zest
a tiny pinch of turmeric

Put the lemon juice and agar powder in a small saucepan and whisk until the agar is well combined, with no clumps. Place over a very gentle heat for 5 minutes, stirring often, then increase the heat to a gentle boil. Immediately reduce the heat a little and continue to cook at a very gentle simmer for 8–10 minutes, stirring often to stop the agar sinking to the bottom of the pan and sticking.

Meanwhile, put the cornflour in a bowl with 60 ml (2 fl oz/¼ cup) of the coconut milk and mix to a smooth slurry. Add the remaining coconut milk, maple syrup and brown rice syrup and mix together.

Remove the agar mixture from the heat and stir to cool a little. Slowly add the coconut milk mixture, whisking constantly. Return to the heat and bring to the boil, stirring constantly with a spoon until just boiled. Do not overboil.

Remove from the heat and whisk in the vanilla, lemon zest and turmeric (don't add too much turmeric or the colour will be very bright). Allow to cool, then refrigerate for about 1 hour, or until set.

08

Light and simple desserts

It's always good to have a few simple desserts up your sleeve other than fruit — desserts that are deliciously light and simple, and so easy to put together. ☙

Chocolate banana pudding

GLUTEN FREE / DAIRY FREE / VEGAN

SERVES 6

This is my version of the banana custard we enjoyed as children — such an easy dessert to put together, and so delicious. I make this in little glass bowls (130 ml/ 4 fl oz capacity), but in winter when pears are in season, I poach the pears and put them in a slightly larger bowl and spoon the hot pudding around them, leaving them to cool a little before serving. I prefer to use kudzu (kuzu) for thickening this pudding. It is expensive, but extraordinarily health supportive — highly alkalinizing, wonderful for the digestive system and very calming. A great choice for settling young ones before bedtime.

3½ tablespoons kudzu (kuzu) or cornflour (cornstarch)
2 tablespoons dutched cocoa powder (see Kitchen notes on page 177)
2 tablespoons rapadura sugar or maple syrup
375 ml (13 fl oz/1½ cups) rice milk
185 ml (6 fl oz/¾ cup) coconut milk
1 teaspoon natural vanilla extract
2 bananas, peeled and cut into small pieces

Put the kudzu, cocoa powder and sugar in a saucepan with 125 ml (4 fl oz/½ cup) of the rice milk and mix to a smooth slurry. Add the remaining rice milk, coconut milk and vanilla and whisk until well combined. Place over medium heat and bring just to the boil, whisking constantly until thick and smooth. Once you see the bubbles from the boil, give it a couple more stirs and remove from the heat.

Divide the banana among six small pots or bowls. Spoon the warm chocolate pudding over the banana and serve, or allow to cool and serve later.

☙

GOOD KUDZU IS OFTEN QUITE LUMPY. FOR EASIER MEASURING, PLACE IT IN A SMALL BOWL AND GENTLY CRUSH TO A FINE POWDER USING A PESTLE OR THE END OF A ROLLING PIN

THIS PUDDING WILL FIRM UP AS IT COOLS

Yoghurt and almond panna cotta with honey-roasted figs

SERVES 6

A far lighter version of one of my favourite desserts — using yoghurt instead of cream, with some almond milk. Use the best-quality honey, as the flavour comes through. You can serve any fruit with this — I just happen to adore figs, but pears are a fine substitute. In summer, try grilling mangoes and peaches, or serving with a mint-studded fruit salad.

Yoghurt and almond panna cotta
235 g (8½ oz/1½ cups) blanched almonds
1 teaspoon agar powder
2 vanilla beans, split down the centre lengthways
4 teaspoons kudzu (kuzu) or cornflour (cornstarch)
500 g (1 lb 2 oz/2 cups) full-cream, Greek-style organic yoghurt
2–4 tablespoons best-quality honey, or to taste

Honey-roasted figs
1–2 ripe figs per person
2 tablespoons unsalted butter or ghee
2 tablespoons honey
a large pinch of ground cinnamon

A THICK, FIRM-SET YOGHURT IS BEST FOR THIS DISH

FRESH THYME IS A LOVELY MATCH WITH THE FIGS — YOU CAN SPRINKLE A LITTLE ON AS THEY BAKE. IF YOU HAPPEN TO HAVE SOME THYME BLOSSOM, SPRINKLE A LITTLE OVER THE DESSERT BEFORE SERVING

Start by making the panna cotta. Peg four layers of muslin (cheesecloth) onto the rim of a jug or bowl. Put the almonds and 625 ml (21½ fl oz/2½ cups) water in a blender. Blend well, then pour through the muslin to strain. Squeeze out the remaining almond milk from the muslin into the bowl.

Just in case you need some extra milk, squeeze the muslin over a separate bowl to give 80 ml (2½ fl oz/⅓ cup) more almond milk (you may need to add a little more water to the almond mixture). Set aside.

Measure 500 ml (17 fl oz/2 cups) of the almond milk into a saucepan, then immediately whisk in the agar powder and add the vanilla beans. Place over a gentle heat and slowly bring to the boil, stirring regularly to prevent the agar sticking to the bottom of the pan. Once at the boil, reduce the heat to very low (so it just barely simmers) for 8–10 minutes, or until the agar has dissolved, continuing to stir regularly to stop the agar sticking to the bottom. The mixture will be thick. Remove from the heat, then pick out and reserve the vanilla bean.

Put the kudzu in a small bowl, add 80 ml (2½ fl oz/⅓ cup) almond milk and mix to a smooth slurry. Add to the saucepan, whisking all the while, then place back over the heat and bring to the boil, stirring constantly with a wooden spoon rather than a whisk. Because the mixture is thick it may be hard to see the big bubbles that show it has come to the boil, so look carefully and make sure you can see them.

Remove the pan from the heat, then scrape the seeds from the vanilla bean back into the milk.

Put the yoghurt in a bowl and whisk until smooth. Gradually whisk the milk mixture into the yoghurt and add the honey. Test for sweetness and add more if desired, but take into account the sweetness of the fruit you are serving with the panna cotta. Rinse six 200 ml (7 fl oz) moulds with water and shake dry. Divide the mixture among the moulds and refrigerate for 1 hour, or until set.

Meanwhile, preheat the oven to 220°C (425°F/Gas 7). To prepare the figs, cut them into quarters, but without cutting through to the base. Squeeze them gently at the bottom to open them out a little and place in a baking dish. Dot the butter around the figs, drizzle with the honey and sprinkle with cinnamon. Roast for 10–15 minutes.

Run the tip of a small, sharp knife around the edge of each panna cotta. Place a serving plate over the mould and invert. Spoon the figs around and serve.

VARIATIONS

If using pears instead of figs, choose six ripe ones, cut them into quarters and remove the cores. Roast them in a skillet or cast-iron gratin dish, as the direct transfer of heat helps to caramelize the honey.

To grill stonefruit, simply heat a cast-iron grill plate to very hot. Cut the fruit, brush with a little flavourless coconut oil and place on the grill for 1–2 minutes, or until lightly scored.

೦೩

Honey and cinnamon yoghurt cream

GLUTEN FREE

MAKES ABOUT 375 G (13 OZ/1½ CUPS)

Extremely simple to make, this is a sweetened version of the classic yoghurt cheese, Labneh (see page 68). As a bonus, because yoghurt is rich in lactic acid, it will help you digest your meal. Use yoghurt that is not already sweetened, and does not have a large amount of milk solids in it (a home-made yoghurt is perfect — see Basics, page 240). The whey that drips from the yoghurt into the bowl will keep for weeks in a sealed container in the fridge, and is perfect for soaking grains.

> 500 g (1 lb 2 oz/2 cups) full-cream plain, non-homogenized yoghurt
> 1 tablespoon maple syrup or honey, or to taste
> ½ teaspoon natural vanilla extract, or to taste
> a pinch of ground cinnamon (optional)

Place a sieve lined with four layers of muslin (cheesecloth) over a bowl. Pour or spoon in the yoghurt and allow it to drain in the fridge for 2–3 hours. The longer it sits, the firmer it will become.

Sweeten to taste with honey and vanilla, stirring through to combine. Flavour with cinnamon if desired.

ೞ

Cooked fruit desserts

A bowl of seasonal fresh, stewed, poached or baked fruit in all its glory can be one of the most perfect of desserts. These are the easiest desserts on the planet, and some of the most underrated. Custard, cream and ice cream complement cooked fruit desserts beautifully.

Generally, I prefer to poach summer fruits and bake winter fruits. When poaching, I use a couple of tricks. I prefer raw sugar to sweeten as it doesn't interfere with the flavour of the fruit, and I start with just a little — you can always add more, but you can't take it away. Secondly, add only the tiniest bit of liquid to protect the fruit from burning before it sweats out its juices — this gives you a truer-flavoured result. I'm not big on flavouring agents apart from vanilla (the bean or extract), though in winter spices such as cinnamon and clove are delicious.

I don't use exotic or expensive fruits. Sometimes, when a fruit is in season, I gratefully accept nature's offerings from a friend's tree. Seconds and windfalls cook up beautifully and leftovers are ready the next day to put on pancakes, porridge or in a bowl with yoghurt. For more stewed and baked fruit recipes, see Cinnamon Stewed Apples (page 43), Honey-Roasted Figs (page 194) and Peach or Pear Anzacs (page 171). ↝

Poached summer fruits

GLUTEN FREE / DAIRY FREE / VEGAN

SERVES 4 – 8

Near closing time at produce markets, you can often pick up fruit at discounted prices; some may be discounted because it is overripe. Buy it, go home and poach it and the fruit will last for several days.

- 4 peaches
- 4 apricots
- ½ – 2 tablespoons raw sugar
- 1 vanilla bean, split down the centre lengthways, or 1 teaspoon natural vanilla extract

Cut the peaches into quarters and remove the stones. Cut the apricots in half and remove the stones. Place the fruit in a saucepan with ½ tablespoon sugar, the vanilla bean or extract and 125 ml (4 fl oz/½ cup) water. Cover and place over a gentle heat for 10–15 minutes, or until the fruit starts to release its juices. Taste for sweetness and add more sugar as required.

Increase the heat a little and simmer for a further 5 minutes, or until the fruit is just soft. If using a vanilla bean, remove it from the saucepan, then scrape the seeds back into the fruit using the tip of a small knife. Serve the fruit warm or chilled.

ↂ

Poached winter fruits

GLUTEN FREE / DAIRY FREE / VEGAN

SERVES 4 – 6

Organic, sulphur-free dried fruits are expensive, but it's easy to mix them with traditional winter fruits to extend their delicious flavour. The following recipe is wonderful for dessert served with Yoghurt and Almond Panna Cotta (page 194) or Honey and Cinnamon Yoghurt Cream (page 196), and perfect spooned onto porridge for breakfast. It keeps very well in the fridge for about 1 week.

10 dried apricot halves
7 dried peach segments
6 prunes, stones removed
4 dried figs
1 cinnamon stick
1 orange
125 ml (4 fl oz/½ cup) grape, apple or pear juice
1 vanilla bean, 1 teaspoon natural vanilla extract, or 1 teaspoon vanilla bean
    paste
2 small pears, peeled and cut into quarters, cores removed
2 small apples, peeled and cut into quarters, cores removed
1 tablespoon rapadura sugar or honey, or to taste

GOLDEN DELICIOUS
APPLES ARE A
GOOD CHOICE FOR
POACHING AS THEY
HOLD THEIR SHAPE

Put the apricots, peaches, prunes, figs and cinnamon stick in a saucepan. Using a vegetable peeler, remove the peel from half the orange (avoiding the white pith) and add it to the pot. Juice the orange, pour into a measuring jug, and add enough water to give 250 ml (9 fl oz/1 cup) liquid. Pour into the pot and add the grape juice. If using a vanilla bean, split it down the middle using a sharp knife and add it to the pot (reserve the vanilla extract or paste for a little later). Cover, bring to a gentle boil and simmer for 5 minutes.

Remove the lid, add the pear and apple pieces and add only just enough water to barely cover — this will probably be about 185 ml (6 fl oz/³⁄₄ cup). Cover and cook over a gentle heat for 5–6 minutes, or until the pear and apple are just soft — take care not to overcook. Remove the lid and discard the orange peel. Test for sweetness and add sugar as desired. If using vanilla extract or paste, stir it in now. If using the vanilla bean, remove it and set it on a plate.

Increase the heat and cook at a rapid boil for 2 minutes to reduce the liquid, taking care not to stir the fruit too much or break it up. When the liquid has reduced, discard the cinnamon stick. If using a vanilla bean, run the tip of a small sharp knife down the bean and scrape the seeds back into the fruit, then gently stir through. Taste again and adjust the sweetness as desired.

ᚼ

Honey and cinnamon poached quinces

GLUTEN FREE / DAIRY FREE

SERVES 4 – 6

Quinces are probably the cheapest fruits around, and with just a little bit of work will repay you with the most beautifully ruby-coloured, fragrant poached fruit. You do need to be quite careful peeling and coring quinces as they are very tough.

4 quinces (not too large)
1 tablespoon honey, or more to taste
2 cinnamon sticks
1 vanilla bean, split down the centre lengthways, or 1 teaspoon natural
   vanilla extract

199   *cakes, cookies*
       and desserts

Peel and slice each quince into eight wedges, removing any cores. Place in a saucepan (an enamel-coated cast-iron one is best) with 250 ml (9 fl oz/1 cup) water and the remaining ingredients. Cover and simmer over the gentlest of heat for 50–90 minutes, adding a little more water as needed. The longer the quinces cook, the more deeply coloured they will become — they will turn a beautiful ruby.

Check for taste, adding a little extra honey if needed. If using a vanilla bean, remove it from the saucepan, then scrape the seeds back into the fruit using the tip of a small knife. Serve warm.

ೞ

Honey-baked pears

GLUTEN FREE

SERVES 4 – 6

BAKING THE PEARS IN A HEAVY-BASED METAL DISH ENABLES THE HEAT TO TRANSFER THROUGH AND CARAMELIZE THEM

So easy to prepare, and so very delicious. As an alternative to serving with custard, try serving the cooled pears with roasted new-season walnuts and goat's cheese. They are also divine with the Honey and Cinnamon Yoghurt Cream (page 196), but are sweet enough without adding the maple syrup to the yoghurt.

    1 tablespoon butter
    1 tablespoon best-quality honey
    1 teaspoon natural vanilla extract
    4 small or 3 large ripe pears, cut into quarters, cores removed

THE BUTTER AND HONEY WILL SET AS THE PEARS COOL. TO EXTEND THE BAKING JUICES, STIR IN A SMALL AMOUNT OF WATER AND SERVE WITH THE PEARS

Preheat the oven to 200°C (400°F/Gas 6). Melt the butter in a cast-iron gratin dish or skillet, or an ovenproof stainless steel frying pan. Turn off the heat, then stir in the honey and vanilla. Add the pears and toss through, then turn the pears so the flesh, rather than the skin, is touching the base of the pan.

Bake for 15 minutes, then remove from the oven and turn the pears over so the skin is touching the base. Bake for a further 10 minutes, or until the pears are just soft — this will depend on their size and variety. Remove from the oven and serve.

ೞ

Sweet and spicy baked apples

GLUTEN FREE

SERVES 6

Such a simple and quick dessert to put together, for such a great result. Leftovers are easily warmed and make a lovely breakfast, morning or afternoon tea.

Stuffing

30 g (1 oz/¼ cup) sultanas (golden raisins) or raisins, chopped if large
2 tablespoons desiccated coconut
¾ tablespoon dark brown sugar
3–4 pieces of glacé ginger, finely chopped
a pinch of ground cinnamon
1 teaspoon grated lemon zest
2 teaspoons butter, slightly softened
25 g (1 oz/¼ cup) walnuts or pecans, roughly chopped

6 apples (granny smiths are excellent)
375 ml (13 fl oz/1½ cups) apple or pear juice
maple syrup, rice syrup, or rapadura or raw sugar, to sweeten (optional)

Preheat the oven to 180°C (350°F/Gas 4). Put all the stuffing ingredients in a bowl and toss together.

Core the apples and trim the base so they sit flat. Using a vegetable peeler, peel around the very top of the apples, into the slight depression around the open core — this will enable more stuffing to sit on top. Generously pile the stuffing into the apples and place them in a baking dish so they fit fairly snugly. Pack as much of the remaining stuffing as possible onto the top of the apples.

Pour the fruit juice over and bake for 40 minutes to 1 hour, or until the apples are soft — it's a good sign to see some of the cooked apple oozing from the top. Remove the apples and pour the baking juices into a small saucepan. Boil over high heat until reduced to a syrupy consistency. Taste the sauce and add extra sweetener if desired, taking into account what you are serving the apples with (such as a sweet custard, or sweetened yoghurt cream).

ೞ

ANY FINELY CHOPPED DRIED FRUIT CAN BE USED IN THE STUFFING

BUTTER OR WHITE MISO (SHIRO) CAN BE ADDED TO THE STUFFING TO HELP BIND IT, SO YOU CAN USE MORE STUFFING ON TOP OF THE APPLES

Baked rhubarb

GLUTEN FREE / DAIRY FREE / VEGAN

SERVES 4 - 6

I far prefer to bake rather than poach rhubarb — it holds its shape so much better. If you happen to have some organic berry cordial or liqueur on hand, use it to replace some of the sugar. It's a lovely match, as is a handful of raspberries or strawberries added to the rhubarb. If you have time, it's good to let the rhubarb macerate in the sugar and liquid before cooking.

350 g (12 oz) rhubarb, washed and cut into 7.5 cm (3 inch) lengths
1½ tablespoons raw sugar
1 vanilla bean, or 1 teaspoon natural vanilla extract

Preheat the oven to 180°C (350°F/Gas 4). Choose an ovenproof baking dish that can fit all the rhubarb snugly — it doesn't matter if five or six pieces have to sit on top of the others.

Arrange the rhubarb in the dish and sprinkle with the sugar (if using a berry cordial, reduce the sugar to 1 tablespoon, and add 1 tablespoon of cordial). Drizzle 2 tablespoons water over the rhubarb, and the vanilla extract. If using a vanilla bean, cut it down the centre lengthways using a small knife and add to the rhubarb.

Cover and bake for 20–30 minutes, or until the rhubarb is tender. Remove from the oven. If using a vanilla bean, remove it and place on a flat surface. Run the tip of a small sharp knife down the bean and scrape the seeds back into the fruit, then gently stir through. The rhubarb is equally delicious served warm or cold.

℅

Custards

In summer, a superb vanilla ice cream is always hard to beat, but if you're after a dairy-free dessert, the Dairy and Egg Free Custard below is just as delicious cold as it is warm. In winter, custard of any sort is the number one star to drizzle or scoop over beautiful fruit and winter puddings, especially the richer, more traditional custard on the following page. ∽

Dairy and egg free custard

GLUTEN FREE / DAIRY FREE / VEGAN

MAKES 375 ML (13 FL OZ/1½ CUPS)

I'm not a big fan of soy-based custards; I prefer using a mixture of rice and coconut milk, or even almond and coconut milk. I wouldn't recommend using arrowroot in this custard as it makes it a bit viscous.

    2 tablespoons kudzu (kuzu) or cornflour (cornstarch)
    250 ml (9 fl oz/1 cup) rice milk
    125 ml (4 fl oz/½ cup) coconut milk
    1 tablespoon maple syrup, or to taste
    1 teaspoon natural vanilla extract, or 1 vanilla bean

Measure the kudzu into a saucepan. Add 60 ml (2 fl oz/¼ cup) of the rice milk and mix to a smooth slurry with a wooden spoon. Stir in all the remaining milk, maple syrup and vanilla extract. If using a vanilla bean, cut it down the centre lengthways and, using the tip of a small knife, scrape the seeds into the saucepan.

Place over medium heat and stir constantly until just boiled. Taste and add extra maple syrup if desired.

VARIATIONS

For a chocolate custard, add 1 tablespoon cocoa powder to the kudzu and continue as above. You may need to increase the sweetener to accommodate the cocoa.

∽

Stove-top custard

GLUTEN FREE

MAKES 500 ML (17 FL OZ/2 CUPS)

It's hardly worth making a traditional custard with anything less than full-cream, organic milk. Thick clumps of cream from the milk melt into the custard, making it creamy and silky smooth. Leftover custard keeps well for gentle reheating.

2 large organic eggs
1 egg yolk, extra
2 tablespoons maple syrup or raw sugar, or to taste
500 ml (17 fl oz/2 cups) organic, full-cream milk
1 teaspoon natural vanilla extract, or 1 vanilla bean

Put the eggs, extra egg yolk and maple syrup in a saucepan. Whisk until well combined and slightly creamy, then whisk in the milk and vanilla extract. If using a vanilla bean, cut it down the centre lengthways and, using the tip of a small knife, scrape the seeds into the saucepan. Whisk well.

Place over low–medium heat and stir constantly with a wooden spoon. The custard must not boil — or you will have scrambled eggs! — but should become thick and coat the back of the spoon. This will take 12–15 minutes, and at the most 20 minutes, so do be patient. The custard is thick enough when you are able to draw a line down the back of the spoon with your finger and it stays there. Immediately take the custard off the heat and whisk for a couple of minutes to cool it down a little. The custard will thicken more on cooling.

VARIATIONS

To make chocolate custard, mix 1 tablespoon cocoa powder to a smooth slurry with a little of the milk, then add to the saucepan with the milk. You may need to increase the sweetener to accommodate the cocoa.

෪

A handful of puddings

Mostly traditional, these are the desserts used by women like my mum to feed and fill hungry growing tummies, and bring joy to the day. They use simple ingredients and epitomize thrifty yet wholesome cooking. I've also included a few desserts that aren't really traditional, but are firm favourites and big on deliciousness. ❧

Apple, rhubarb and raspberry cobbler

GLUTEN FREE

SERVES 4 – 6

A cobbler is essentially stewed fruit topped with a traditional sponge consisting of butter, sugar, egg and flour. This is a perfect dessert for a gluten-free cake mix, where the moist fruit softens the harder gluten-free grains. You can use any berries in place of raspberries.

4 apples, peeled, cored and cut into 1.5 cm ($\frac{5}{8}$ inch) slices
5 rhubarb stalks, washed and cut into 5–6 cm (2–2$\frac{1}{2}$ inch) lengths
1 teaspoon natural vanilla extract
$\frac{3}{4}$ tablespoon maple syrup
200 g (7 oz/1$\frac{2}{3}$ cups) raspberries (frozen berries are fine)

Batter
185 g (6$\frac{1}{2}$ oz/1 cup) brown rice flour
50 g (1$\frac{3}{4}$ oz/$\frac{1}{2}$ cup) ground almonds
2 teaspoons baking powder
2 teaspoons egg replacer, or 1 egg
60 ml (2 fl oz/$\frac{1}{4}$ cup) almond oil
80 ml (2$\frac{1}{2}$ fl oz/$\frac{1}{3}$ cup) maple syrup
1 teaspoon natural vanilla extract
125 ml (4 fl oz/$\frac{1}{2}$ cup) milk, malt-free soy or rice milk

Preheat the oven to 180°C (350°F/Gas 4). Put the apple, rhubarb, vanilla and maple syrup in a saucepan with 60 ml (2 fl oz/$\frac{1}{4}$ cup) water. Cover and cook over a gentle heat for 5 minutes, or until just soft.

Transfer the mixture to a 1–1.5 litre (35–52 fl oz/4–6 cup) capacity baking dish. (A large, shallow dish is better than a smaller, deeper one — mine is 5 cm/2 inches deep, with a 22 cm/8½ inch diameter.)

To make the batter, put the flour, ground almonds and baking powder in a bowl and whisk through to break up any lumps.

In a separate bowl, mix the egg replacer and 2 tablespoons water to a smooth paste (or beat the egg). Whisk in the almond oil, maple syrup, vanilla and milk. Pour into the flour mixture and stir through until smooth — the mixture will be wet.

Scatter the raspberries over the apples, then pour the batter over the top. Place the baking dish on a baking tray (the pudding will drizzle fruit juice as it cooks) and bake for 1 hour, or until the sponge topping is lightly golden and springs back when gently pushed, or when a skewer inserted only a short way into it comes out clean (push too deep and you'll get the fruit). The juices should be bubbling and often running over the side of the dish.

慲

Apple brown betty

SERVES 4

This is a very old-fashioned pudding which rates as one of my favourites. It's a great autumn or winter dessert that consists mainly of fruit, with a bit of bread, butter and sugar thrown in. Use fruit seconds or windfalls, with the bruises cut out. If any leftovers survive, they make a fabulous breakfast.

½ teaspoon freshly grated nutmeg
110 g (3¾ oz/½ cup) demerara or raw sugar
4-5 pieces of good sourdough bread, crusts removed, then cut into 1 cm
    (½ inch) dice to give about 150 g (5½ oz/3 loosely packed cups)
grated zest of 1 lemon
40 g (1½ oz) butter, melted
5 apples, about 800 g (1 lb 12 oz) in total

Preheat the oven to 200°C (400°F/Gas 6). Combine the nutmeg and sugar in a bowl. Scoop 2 tablespoons of the mixture into a smaller bowl and set aside.

Add the bread cubes and lemon zest to the larger bowl and toss through. Add the melted butter and toss through to coat.

Peel the apples and cut into quarters. Remove the cores and cut each quarter into wedges about 1 cm (½ inch) thick. Place one-third of the bread cubes over the base of a 1.25 litre (44 fl oz/5 cup) baking dish. Choose a dish with a good surface area, rather than a deeper one with less surface area — ideally, one that is about 4.5 cm (1¾ inches) deep and 22 cm (8½ inches) long. The dish will be very, very full but the pudding will bake down.

Layer half the apples over the bread, then top with 20 g (¾ oz/½ cup) bread cubes. Layer the remaining apples over the top and drizzle with 60 ml (2 fl oz/¼ cup) water. Top with the remaining bread cubes, then sprinkle with the reserved sugar mixture. Pat down and cover with a sheet of baking paper, then a sheet of foil.

Bake for 40–45 minutes, or until the apples are bubbling and noticeably cooked. Remove the foil and paper and bake for a further 15 minutes, or until lightly golden.

ঙ

Little tapioca puddings

GLUTEN FREE / DAIRY FREE / VEGAN

MAKES 6

Old-fashioned tapioca makes the most delicious, incredibly cheap little puddings, and they are a great balance for a bowl of fruit salad. I prefer to buy my tapioca pearls in an Asian grocery store — not only are they far cheaper than those in the supermarket, but they are also free of preservative 220 (sulphur dioxide). Set into little plastic containers (about 150 ml/5 fl oz capacity), these puddings are an excellent addition to a lunchbox.

I have used passionfruit juice here, simply because I needed some way to use the prolific bounty from my sister's vine and because I love passionfruit — but any fruit juice is fine. If you go with lemon or lime juice, use 60–125 ml (2–4 fl oz/ ¼–½ cup) of the juice, and make up the required 500 ml (17 fl oz/2 cups) of liquid with water, to end up with a strength of citrus juice that suits you. I also add 1 teaspoon of finely grated citrus zest.

The amount of sweetener used will depend heavily on the juice used, as some require more than others. I do prefer palm sugar (jaggery) as a sweetener here, but rapadura sugar, maple syrup and agave nectar are all good options.

90 g (3¼ oz/½ cup) tapioca or sago pearls
30-40 passionfruit, cut in half
palm sugar (jaggery), for sweetening as needed
4½ teaspoons kudzu (kuzu) or cornflour (cornstarch)
310 ml (10¾ fl oz/1¼ cups) coconut milk

Put the tapioca and 250 ml (9 fl oz/1 cup) water in a saucepan and allow to soak for 1 hour.

Scoop the passionfruit pulp into a sieve set over a bowl. Press and work the pulp through the sieve with a large spoon, allowing the juice to drip through to the bowl. This should yield 500 ml (17 fl oz/2 cups) juice. If you get tired of this, stop at 375 ml (13 fl oz/1½ cups) juice, then add 125 ml (4 fl oz/½ cup) water to the sieve, then mix it through to bring the liquid up to the required 500 ml (17 fl oz/2 cups). Discard the seeds left in the sieve.

Stir the passionfruit juice through the soaked tapioca and place over a gentle heat. Cook for 10–15 minutes, or until the tapioca is clear, stirring frequently to avoid sticking. After 5 minutes of cooking, check for taste and add palm sugar as desired. Allow to cool for 10 minutes, then divide among six serving bowls or little plastic containers of about 150 ml (5 fl oz) capacity.

While the puddings are cooling, measure the kudzu into a saucepan. Add 60 ml (2 fl oz/¼ cup) water and mix to a smooth slurry. Stir in the coconut milk, then place over medium heat, stirring until just boiled. Remove from the heat, allow to cool slightly, then spoon onto the tapioca puddings. Refrigerate for 30 minutes to set.

cs

Chocolate self-saucing pudding

WHEAT FREE

SERVES 4

You must have this at least once during winter. I have adapted this recipe over the years from an original by Margaret Fulton. Using less-refined sugars and organic cocoa powder gives it the most gorgeous flavour — unlike the intense sweetness of many chocolate puddings and cakes. It is delicious served with cream.

125 g (4½ oz) unsalted butter, softened
115 g (4 oz/½ cup) dark brown sugar or muscovado sugar
2 eggs
1 teaspoon natural vanilla extract
90 g (3¼ oz/¾ cup) plain (all-purpose) white spelt flour, sifted
¾ teaspoon baking powder
1 tablespoon dutched cocoa powder (see Kitchen notes on page 177)
2–3 tablespoons milk — dairy, soy or a mix of coconut and rice

Sauce
160 g (5½ oz/⅓ cup) light brown sugar or muscovado sugar
1 tablespoon cocoa powder

Preheat the oven to 180°C (350°F/Gas 4). Using electric beaters, cream the butter and sugar until creamy. Add the eggs one at a time, beating well after each addition, then add the vanilla and mix well.

Sift in the flour, baking powder and cocoa powder, then add 2 tablespoons of the milk and mix together. The batter should be soft and moist; stir in the remaining tablespoon of milk if needed. Spoon the batter into a wide, shallow baking dish — the batter should come halfway up the side of the dish.

Put the sauce ingredients in a small saucepan with 250 ml (9 fl oz/1 cup) water and place over a gentle heat. Stir until the sugar has dissolved — do not allow to boil. Pour the sauce over the pudding and bake for 30–40 minutes, or until a skewer inserted into the centre of the pudding comes out clean. (The sauce will have sunk to the bottom, so just insert the skewer into the top cakey bit.) Serve warm.

ೞ

INSTEAD OF SPELT FLOUR YOU COULD USE OAT FLOUR IN THIS PUDDING

Buckwheat, pistachio and coconut pudding

GLUTEN FREE / DAIRY FREE / VEGAN

SERVES 4 – 6

A wonderful twist on a baked rice custard, this pudding is delicious served after a vegetable-based main, to complete the meal. It's equally good and wholesome for breakfast.

flavourless coconut oil, for brushing
200 g (7 oz/1 cup) buckwheat groats
375 ml (13 fl oz/1½ cups) soy, almond or dairy milk
3 teaspoons maple syrup
1 teaspoon natural vanilla extract
½ teaspoon ground cinnamon
⅛ teaspoon freshly ground nutmeg
60 g (2¼ oz/½ cup) raisins or sultanas (golden raisins)
160 g (5 oz/1 cup) grated apple (with or without skin)
35 g (1¼ oz/¼ cup) roughly chopped pistachio nuts
125 ml (4 fl oz/½ cup) coconut cream
3 teaspoons dark brown sugar or dark muscovado sugar
3 teaspoons molasses sugar

MOLASSES SUGAR IS SIMILAR TO DARK BROWN SUGAR, BUT IS STICKIER, WITH A RICH FLAVOUR

Preheat the oven to 180°C (350°F/Gas 4). Grease a 5 cm (2 inch) deep, 22 cm (8½ inch) baking dish with coconut oil.

Put the buckwheat groats in a frying pan and place over a gentle heat. Toast for 6–10 minutes, or until lightly coloured, shaking the pan now and then. At no time should the pan smoke — you may need to take it off the heat from time to time to stop this happening. You now have 'kasha' (roasted buckwheat groats).

Put the kasha, milk and 375 ml (13 fl oz/1½ cups) water in a saucepan over a gentle heat. Bring to the boil, stirring occasionally, then simmer gently for 5 minutes. Stir in the maple syrup, vanilla, cinnamon, nutmeg, raisins and apple, then pour the mixture into the baking dish and bake for 10 minutes.

Remove from the oven and sprinkle the pistachios over the top. Bake for a further 15–20 minutes, or until the pudding is almost set.

Mix together the remaining ingredients. Remove the pudding from the oven and drizzle with the coconut cream mixture. Bake for a further 10 minutes, or until the pudding has set — it should feel lightly firm, while still a little soft.

ℭჳ

Pumpkin pie

WHEAT FREE

SERVES 6 – 8

I grew up on pumpkin pie and love it hot or cold. It's especially wonderful in autumn. I like it fairly spicy, but you can reduce the nutmeg and cloves.

Pastry
100 g (3½ oz/¾ cup) plain (all-purpose) wholemeal spelt flour
100 g (3½ oz/¾ cup) plain (all-purpose) white spelt flour
100 g (3½ oz) chilled butter
1 tablespoon golden caster (superfine) sugar
50-60 ml (1½ – 2 fl oz/¼ cup) iced water

360 g (12¾ oz/1½ cups) cooked and cooled butternut pumpkin (squash) or jap pumpkin (winter squash) — start with about (425 g/15 oz) uncooked, unpeeled pumpkin
115 – 165 g (4 - 5¾ oz/½ – ¾ cup) dark brown sugar
1¼ teaspoons ground cinnamon
¼ teaspoon ground nutmeg
¼ teaspoon ground cloves
1 tablespoon plain (all-purpose) white spelt flour
125 ml (4 fl oz/½ cup) milk (any type is fine)
3 eggs

First, make the pastry. Put all the flour in a bowl. Using your fingertips, rub the butter into the flour until it is incorporated, then add the sugar and quickly rub through until only small chunks of the mixture remain. Alternatively, place the flour, butter and sugar in a food processor, pulse once or twice until combined, then turn out into a bowl.

PUMPKINS VARY ENORMOUSLY IN SWEETNESS, HENCE THE LARGE VARIATION IN THE AMOUNT OF SUGAR GIVEN IN THIS RECIPE

cakes, cookies and desserts

Using a butter knife, begin to 'cut' the iced water gradually into the flour. Use only as much water as you need — some flours will absorb more water than others. Once the mixture looks evenly moist, gather it together into a ball, but don't knead or work it too much. Flatten the pastry slightly, then cover and refrigerate for 20 minutes, or until cold to the touch.

While the pastry is resting in the fridge, preheat the oven to 190°C (375°F/Gas 5). Place a baking tray in the oven to heat up.

Lightly butter a 20 cm (8 inch) tart tin, preferably one about 5 cm (2 inches) deep. To roll out the pastry, use as little flour as possible, but enough to make sure the rolling surface is covered. Lightly flour a heavy rolling pin. Roll it once or twice over the pastry, then run a palette knife underneath, move the pastry firmly and quickly, lightly redust the rolling area with flour and turn the pastry over. Continue to repeat this process, folding the pastry if necessary to move it, until the pastry is about 3 mm (⅛ inch) thick. Line the tart tin with the pastry and trim the edges. Chill in the freezer for a few minutes.

Meanwhile, make the filling. Put the pumpkin, 115 g (4 oz/½ cup) of the sugar, the ground spices, flour and milk in a food processor or mixing bowl and mix until smooth. Check for taste, adding the extra sugar if needed. Add the eggs and mix until smooth.

Line the chilled pastry shell with baking paper and fill with baking beans or uncooked rice. Place on the hot baking tray and blind-bake for 15 minutes. Remove from the oven, lift away the baking paper and tip the beans out into a bowl to cool.

Reduce the oven temperature to 170°C (325°F/Gas 3). Pour the filling into the pastry shell and bake for about 45 minutes, checking after 30 minutes. If the pie filling is rising and cracking, turn the oven down to 160°C (315°F/Gas 2–3) for the final 15 minutes. The pie is cooked when the filling around the outside is lightly puffed, and the middle is firm but not puffed. Serve warm or cold.

ഗ്രദ

Coconut cream tart

WHEAT FREE / DAIRY FREE / VEGAN

SERVES 6 - 8

An amazingly quick and delicious dessert. If you can't be bothered making the crust, simply pour the coconut cream into little ramekins or small glass containers and top with fruit of your choice. In summer I prefer to make a luscious fruit salad full of mango, cherry, peach, apricot and passionfruit and spoon this over the tart just before serving, so the juices don't weep into the white coconut. In winter I serve it with Baked Rhubarb (page 202).

Oatmeal pastry

2½ tablespoons almond oil, or 3 tablespoons flavourless coconut oil
185 g (6½ oz/1½ cups) oatmeal
45 g (1½ oz/½ cup) desiccated coconut
80 g (2¾ oz/½ cup) macadamia nuts or almonds
1½ – 2½ tablespoons maple syrup

800 ml (28 fl oz) coconut milk
125 ml (4 fl oz/½ cup) maple syrup, or 110 g (3¾ oz/½ cup) raw sugar
½ teaspoon agar powder
1 vanilla bean, split down the centre lengthways, or 1 teaspoon
  natural vanilla extract
3 tablespoons cornflour (cornstarch) or kudzu (kuzu)

Preheat the oven to 180°C (350°F/Gas 4). Brush a 24 x 4 cm (9½ x 1½ inch) loose-based round tart tin with some of the almond or coconut oil.

To make the pastry, lightly chop the oatmeal, coconut and nuts in a food processor until the nuts are just broken. Add the remaining oil and 1½ tablespoons of the maple syrup and pulse until just combined. The mixture should stick together well when pressed together; add the remaining maple syrup if needed to bind the pastry.

Press the pastry into the prepared tart tin and bake for 20–30 minutes, or until lightly golden. Remove from the oven.

OATMEAL IS NOT GROUND ROLLED (PORRIDGE) OATS, BUT RATHER A COARSE OAT FLOUR GROUND FROM OAT GROATS (KERNELS)

THIS TART HAS A LOVELY SOFT SET. IF YOU PREFER IT A LITTLE FIRMER, ADD ANOTHER ¼ TEASPOON AGAR POWDER TO THE FILLING

While the pastry is baking, put the coconut milk, maple syrup and agar powder in a saucepan and whisk together. Add the vanilla bean now, if using. Bring to a gentle simmer, stirring frequently to stop the agar from sinking to the bottom of the pan and sticking. Simmer for 6–8 minutes, then remove from the heat. Remove the vanilla bean from the saucepan, if using, then scrape the seeds back into the saucepan using the tip of a small knife. If using vanilla extract, stir it in now.

Put the cornflour in a small bowl and mix to a smooth slurry with 60 ml (2 fl oz/ ¼ cup) water. Whisk into the coconut milk mixture, then return the saucepan to the heat and bring to the boil, stirring constantly. Allow to boil for a few seconds, then remove from the heat and set aside to cool a little.

Pour the cooled filling into the tart shell (or into little ramekins). Allow the filling to cool in the tart shell until it starts to firm up a little, then refrigerate for 1 hour, or until set.

ભ

Lime delicious

DAIRY FREE / WHEAT FREE

SERVES 4

Every year, we holiday down in the southwest of Western Australia, and there is a huge Tahitian lime on the property, laden with fruit. It has the best limes I've ever tasted, with a heavy coconut scent. As it's dead winter, this is the dessert I turn to — it's a classic, with the resulting pudding having a lovely spongy top and sauce below. There are never leftovers.

80 g (3 oz) unsalted butter, softened
110 g (3¾ oz/½ cup) raw sugar
2 eggs, separated
1 teaspoon natural vanilla extract
4 tablespoons white spelt flour
½ teaspoon baking powder
zest from 2 limes, approximately 2 teaspoons

juice from 2 limes, approximately 60 ml (2 fl oz/¼ cup)

300 ml (10 fl oz/1¼ cups) full cream, non homogenized or organic milk or
125 ml (4 fl oz/½ cup) rice milk and 180 ml (6 fl oz/¾ cup) coconut milk

Preheat the oven to 180°C (350°F/Gas 4).

Prepare a 1.25 litre (44 fl oz/5 cup) capacity baking dish. Place it in a larger baking dish and add enough water to come approximately 1 cm (½ inch) up the sides of the baking dish.

Put the butter and sugar in a medium mixing bowl, and using an electric beater, mix until creamy. Add the egg yolks and mix until soft and creamy. Add the vanilla, flour, baking powder and lime zest, and beat gently until combined and no lumps remain. Add the lime juice and mix through, then the milks. Stir through to combine.

Using clean and dry beaters, beat the egg whites until soft and fluffy. Pour the lime mix into the egg whites and gently whisk through. Pour into baking dish and carefully carry to the oven — it will move in the water a little. Bake for 30–35 minutes or until lightly golden and just softly firm in the centre.

☙

preserving the harvest

Preserving is one of the things I love to do most — for some reason a pantry filled with jams, chutneys and bottled fruit makes me feel I can cope with anything that life might throw my way. Preserving is one of the ways mankind has survived through the years, holding over nature's unlimited bounty from the growing seasons for the leaner and dormant times. Nowadays, food is available year round and we are disconnected from this cycle.

Technically, the object of preserving is to slow down the process of decay. Food spoils from the continued activity of natural enzymes in all fruits and vegetables, and the continued work of micro-organisms in the form of moulds, yeasts and bacteria present in the food and air. There are many ways to delay this deterioration. Bottling, salting, pickling, sweetening, alcohol, freezing and drying are the most commonly used.

It's true that preserving does take time, but it remains one of the best ways to reduce your costs and provide nutritious, 'real' and delicious food that doesn't cost a fortune. Quality jams, chutneys and sauces — especially those made from organic ingredients — are ridiculously expensive, and most of them still can't match the taste of those you make at home. Once it's all done and dusted, you and those you love will give thanks every day for nature's generosity.

The following recipes are all easy, safe and make use of the less expensive fruit and vegetables — do give them a try. I think you will be pleasantly surprised at how easy and how deeply rewarding it is. ❧

Low-sugar jams

Jam relies on sugar to saturate the natural moisture of the fruit and thus preserve it. Many people ask me if they can use something other than cane sugar to make jam — the answer is complex. Many of the 'sugar free' jams you find in shops are sweetened with white grape juice concentrate. Making jams with grape juice concentrate is a technique that was developed in France and other parts of Europe centuries ago, when no sugar was available but grapes were in plentiful supply. Even today, some of the best jams made with grape juice concentrates are the French ones.

Making jam with fruit juice concentrates is possible, but the process is very different. Using apple and pear concentrates, which have a far lower sweetening power than grape juice, does not work well. Large quantities are required to gain any level of molecule saturation and even then, fruit-sweetened jams will always spoil when the vacuum top is broken — if not before.

Cane sugar helps a jam to 'set', and any jam made with fruit juice concentrates will have added pectin in it to assist setting. So, my answer is yes, you can make low-sugar jam, but you may not be entirely thrilled with the flavour of the finished result, and it will have a limited life. Preservation is best achieved with a boiling water bath (see page 221). Once opened, low-sugar jams will need to be stored in the fridge. At times a little mould forms on top and this I just spoon off.

My preference when making jam is to use organic raw sugar in the smallest possible amounts. Most jam recipes call for equal quantities of sugar to fruit by weight. You need about 60–70% sugar for good jelling to take place. I find this way too much sugar and prefer a ratio of 30% sugar to fruit. Because the holy trinity of acid, sugar and pectin is disrupted, this will result in a softer 'set'. I happen to prefer this, disliking the overly firm texture of many commercial jams, which are mostly made with added pectin.

Even though it is harder to achieve a natural 'set' with low-sugar jams, you still need to consider the pectin and acid content of the fruit being used. Low-pectin fruits benefit from the addition of lemon to boost the acidity — and thus the setting. Using unripe (sour) fruit will also increase the acidity of the mixture. ଔ

LOW PECTIN AND ACID FRUITS

Raspberries, blueberries, strawberries, rhubarb, pears, peaches and apricots.

HIGH PECTIN AND ACID FRUITS

Apples, citrus, cranberries, crab apples, gooseberries, currants, plums and quinces.

Jam is best made with just-ripe fruit. Pectin breaks down as fruit ages, so fruit that is fully ripe or overblown won't contribute to a good set. A percentage of fruit (about 30%) that is slightly under-ripe and even a little green helps.

If needed, add a lemon (skin and all, chopped into about eight pieces) to the cooking jam — about 1 medium-sized lemon to 3–4 kg (6 lb 12 oz–9 lb) fruit. Lemons are high in pectin and acid and will help set the jam.

PICK THE RIGHT POT

A good pot is critical to making low-sugar jam. Mine is a traditional French copper preserving pan — shallow and wide. It's about 12 cm (4½ inches) high, 36 cm (14¼ inches) across the base, and 39 cm (15½ inches) across the top (measured internally), with a 10 litre (350 fl oz/40 cup) capacity. The wide surface area encourages evaporation and reduction, thus cooking the jam quickly.

It is very difficult to make jam in a deep pot with a small surface area. Tall pots are a major cause of runny jam.

However, you can make smaller amounts in your average large home saucepan. You can use a simple stainless steel pot — just make sure it is not too deep. A wider and more shallow pot with less capacity — for example, a sauté pan with a 5 litre (175 fl oz) capacity and a depth of 8 cm (3¼ inches) — is better than a pot with a 10 litre (350 fl oz) capacity, but a depth of 16–18 cm (6¼–7 inches). It will mean you can only make small amounts at a time — approximately 2 kg (4 lb 8 oz); check each individual recipe — but your jam will be more successful.

You can also use a 20–24 cm (8–9½ inch) typical home saucepan, but keep the amount of fruit to 1 kg (2 lb 4 oz).

Never make jam in large quantities — another cause of runny jam — and never crowd your pot. The weight of the fruit will depend on the size of your jam pan. The maximum amount for my pot is 4 kg (9 lb). A good guide is to fill your pot two-thirds full.

preserving the harvest

JARS AND LIDS

Always use 'tempered' jars that can withstand the temperatures involved in sterilizing, jam making and storage. Some jars manufactured for products such as coffee, peanut butter and mayonnaise are not tempered and do not have strong seals on the lids. Jars must not be cracked, chipped or damaged in any way, and lids must not be scratched or dented. Jars can be re-used, but lids are good for one usage only.

STERILIZING YOUR EQUIPMENT

WHEN LIFTING JARS OUT OF BOILING WATER IT IS VERY IMPORTANT TO USE THE RIGHT EQUIPMENT FOR MAXIMUM SAFETY

GOOD KITCHEN SHOPS OR THOSE SPECIALIZING IN PRESERVING SELL THE TONGS YOU NEED FOR LIFTING JARS OUT OF HOT WATER SAFELY

DESIGNS VARY, BUT JAR TONGS ARE MADE TO GRIP THE JAR UNDER THE LIP OF THE OPENING

GOOD JAR TONGS ARE ENCASED IN A BIT OF PLASTIC TO ENSURE THEY DON'T SCRATCH THE GLASS

If you are not using a boiling water bath (see opposite), your jars, lids, ladles and funnels must all be sterilized. This is best done by boiling them for 10 minutes (this means 10 minutes of actual boiling time, after the water has come to the boil). Using sterile tongs (you can buy special jar tongs for this job), lift the sterilized jars carefully from the boiling water, tip very gently to drain off the boiling water and place them base down on a metal tray lined with a clean tea towel (dish towel).

The lids are a little trickier. Lift them carefully from the boiling water with sterile tongs and shake a little to remove as much water as possible. Place the lid on a metal tray lined with a clean tea towel so that the inside of the lid is facing up.

Place both the jars and lids in a low oven to keep warm until the jam is ready. This sounds like a lot of trouble, but it will ensure a safe and sterile end result.

If using a boiling water bath, your jars, lids, ladles and funnels do not need to be sterilized — simply clean, dry and warm.

PUTTING THE JAM INTO JARS

Bottling technique is the other very important part of making low-sugar jams — the jam must be spooned with a sterile ladle through a sterile funnel into warm sterilized jars *as soon as it is ready*. Make sure the jars are warm (either from sterilizing or being kept warm in the oven) and sitting on a wooden surface or on towels. This will ensure your jars seal properly and the jam does not spoil.

After ladling the jam into the jars, put the lids on, taking care to touch only the outside of the lids. Holding the jars with a damp cloth (for a good grip), turn the lids until firm. Hot jam into cool or cold jars will cause the jars to break.

Let the jars sit until fully cool — do not move them for 12 hours, or you could disrupt the vacuum process. A concave dip in the middle of the lid indicates a good seal. If there is no concave dip, store the jam in the fridge and use it straight away.

ONCE YOU HAVE SEALED YOUR JARS AND LEFT THEM TO COOL, DON'T BE ALARMED IF YOU HEAR THE LIDS 'POP' — THIS SIMPLY INDICATES THAT A VACUUM HAS FORMED IN THE JAR, MEANING THE LID HAS SEALED WELL

THE BOILING WATER BATH

Another way to kill bacteria and halt decay is to place the warm jar of warm jam or chutney in a pot of boiling water. This process destroys any remaining bacteria and harmful micro-organisms inside the jar. This is particularly important if you have used fruit juice as a sweetener.

The technique described here is not suitable for preserving vegetables, fish or animal products as their acid levels are too low.

You will need a very large pot, deep enough for the water to cover the tops of the jars and to boil freely — allow about 12 cm (4½ inches) above the jar tops for brisk boiling. Place a wire rack on the bottom of the pot — a circular cake cooling rack works well, or you can make your own. Sitting the jars on a wire rack stops them hitting the bottom of the pan and cracking, and also ensures the water boils freely around the bottom of the jars. Fill the pot with water and bring it to the boil.

Fill the warm jars with warm jam or chutney and place the lids on. Screw them on tight, with just that little bit more to go before they are really tight. Some people then wrap the jars in paper or cloth to stop the jars rattling in the boiling water bath, but I have never done this.

Using jar tongs, gently lower the jars into the boiling water, then allow to boil for at least 12 minutes from the time the water returns to the boil. Using the jar tongs, remove the jars and place them on a towel or wooden surface. Tighten the lids that last tiny bit — you will need to hold the jar, and maybe even the lid, with a tea towel (dish towel).

THE BOILING WATER BATH UTILIZES THE SAME PRESERVING PRINCIPLE USED FOR TINNED FOODS — BUT COMMERCIAL UNITS USE A PRESSURE CANNER, WHICH OPERATES AT VERY HIGH TEMPERATURES

Let the jars sit until totally cool — overnight is ideal. When cool, there should be a concave dent in the middle of the lid. If this has not occurred, store the jam in the fridge and use it straight away.

Universal jam recipe

4 KG (9 LB) FRUIT WILL YIELD ABOUT 3.5 KG (7 LB 14 OZ/12 CUPS) JAM

Jam made from 4 kg (9 lb) fruit with 30% sugar in a 10 litre (350 fl oz/40 cup) jam pot (with the dimensions described on page 219) will take about 1 hour from beginning to end. Using 1 kg (2 lb 4 oz) fruit in a smaller 20–24 cm (8–9½ inch) saucepan will take about 45 minutes. Make sure you have enough sterile jars ready to put the warm jam straight into.

> 4 kg (9 lb) fruit (if using stonefruit, weigh it with the stones still in)
> 1.2 kg (2 lb 11 oz) raw sugar
> 1 medium-sized lemon, skin on, cut into 8 bits

Sterilize all your jars and lids (see 'Sterilizing your equipment', page 220), place them on a baking tray lined with a clean tea towel (dish towel) and keep warm in a low oven.

Wash the fruit (there is no need to dry it) and cut it into smaller portions. As a general guide, leave blueberries whole; leave small strawberries whole, but chop any larger ones; cut apricots and plums into halves or quarters; and cut figs into quarters or even smaller segments.

Put the fruit in your jam pot, together with the sugar and lemon. Gently stir the sugar through.

Stage 1: Place the pot over a very low heat, allowing the sugar to dissolve — this takes about 15 minutes, or a bit longer, depending on the size of your pot.

Stage 2: Once the sugar is visibly starting to dissolve, increase the heat slightly until you see a gentle bubbling. Stir frequently. Continue to cook for 15 minutes (or longer if using a deeper pot) — the juices will have weeped out from the fruit, thus increasing the amount of liquid in the pot. As the jam cooks, your home will be filled with the most amazing smells of cooking fruit!

Stage 3: Increase the heat to a high boil until a 'set' is achieved. As you are now cooking at a high boil, you will need to stir frequently to check the feel of the jam, and to make sure it isn't sticking to the bottom of the pot. As the jam reduces, it will thicken. You may need to reduce the heat to a slower boil as the jam thickens, but keep stirring frequently. This stage should take about 30 minutes, but the deeper your pot, the longer it will take (having less surface area, the jam will take longer to reduce and thicken in a deeper pot). It should only take about 10 minutes if you are cooking a small 1 kg (2 lb 4 oz) amount.

'Set' is generally considered to occur when the jam reaches 105°C (220°F), but this general guide can be unreliable for low-sugar jams, where the relationship between sugar, acid and pectin has been disrupted. You will need to rely on other techniques to judge when your jam is ready. I go by appearance and 'feel', and cook the jam until it is fairly thick. Placing a small amount of jam on a saucer or dish and chilling it is another good method for checking the consistency: when cool, run your finger through the middle — you want to see a clear line of plate underneath. Any juices that flow into the line should look like lovely liquid jam, and not at all watery, and they should have some 'body'.

Meanwhile, about 30 minutes before your jam is ready, put a pot of water on to boil. Sterilize your funnel and ladle by boiling for 12 minutes. While they are boiling, remove the jars and lids from the oven, keeping them on their trays. Remove the funnel and ladle from the boiling water and shake a little to remove the water, allowing the air to dry them off. As soon as the jam is ready, ladle the warm jam through the funnel, into the warm jars. Seal the lids tightly, then leave to sit until totally cool. There should be a concave dent in the middle of the lid — if there isn't, store the jam in the fridge and use it straight away.

CB

Chutneys, pickles and sauces

These are exceptionally easy to make, and any large kitchen pot can be used —
with the exception of copper pots, as the acid in the chutney will break down the
copper. Chutneys and sauces are the perfect place to use ripe, bruised fruits and
vegetables or seconds. When made with sugar, the jars will not need a boiling
water bath to ensure preservation, but they will need to be clean, sterile and warm.
Chutneys and sauces made with fruit juice concentrate will need a boiling water
bath to ensure safe preservation, but it's not essential for the jars to be sterile —
only clean, dry and warm. Pickles, which rely on salting and packing in vinegar
for preservation, also simply need sterile, clean, warm jars. ∽

Mango chutney

GLUTEN FREE / DAIRY FREE / VEGAN

MAKES ABOUT 1.4 KG (3 LB 2 OZ/5 CUPS)

Mango chutney is one of my favourite things — cheese and mango chutney
toasties are simply delicious! I prefer chutney to have vivid flavour, with a subtle
sweet and sourness. This is one of the few places I use fruit juice concentrate — it
makes beautiful chutney.

> 2 kg (4 lb 8 oz) mangoes (weighed whole)
> ½ - 1 teaspoon ground allspice
> 180 g (6 oz/1½ cups) sultanas (golden raisins)
> 60 g (2¼ oz/⅓ cup) finely diced fresh ginger
> 1-2 small red chillies, seeded and finely chopped, or to taste
> 185 - 250 ml (6-9 fl oz/¾-1 cup) apple cider vinegar
> 250 - 375 ml (9-13 fl oz/1-1½ cups) apple juice concentrate

Wash your jars and lids, place them on a baking tray lined with a clean tea towel
(dish towel) and keep warm in a low oven. Wash and dry your ladle and funnel.

Peel the mangoes and cut the flesh into 1 cm (½ inch) dice. Add to a 26 cm
(10½ inch) pot with the allspice, sultanas, ginger, a small amount of chilli to start,
185 ml (6 fl oz/¾ cup) of the vinegar and 250 ml (9 fl oz/1 cup) of the apple juice
concentrate. Stir through.

Very gently bring to the boil, then slowly simmer for 1–1½ hours, or until thick, stirring frequently. After about 40 minutes, check for taste, adding more vinegar, apple juice concentrate and chilli if required. The chutney is cooked when the fruit has lost its bright colour and takes on a much darker tone; the liquid should have reduced considerably, and appear syrupy rather than watery. Towards the end of cooking time, stir the chutney frequently so it doesn't burn.

Meanwhile, bring a very large pot of water (see 'The boiling water bath' on page 221) to the boil. Remove the jars and lids from the oven, keeping them on their trays, and ladle the warm chutney into the jars, through the funnel. Put the lids on the jars, then screw them tight, with just that little bit more to go before they are really tight. Using jar tongs, lower the jars into the boiling water. When the water comes back to the boil, set the timer for 12 minutes.

Using the jar tongs, remove and place the jars on a towel or wooden surface. Tighten the lids that last tiny bit — you will need to hold the jar and maybe the lid with a tea towel (dish towel). Let them sit until totally cool — there should be a concave dent in the middle of the lid. If there isn't, store the chutney in the fridge and use it straight away.

❧

Orange and date chutney

GLUTEN FREE / DAIRY FREE / VEGAN

MAKES 750 G (1 LB 10 OZ/3 CUPS)

A fabulous chutney to serve with cold meats — especially duck — and wonderful with the Shiitake Mushroom, Walnut and Lentil Terrine on page 79. Because this chutney is sweetened with sugar, the jars, lids, ladle and funnel must be sterile. There is no need to process it in a boiling water bath.

1 kg (2 lb 4 oz) oranges, peeled, all pith removed, then cut
      into 1 cm (½ inch) dice
250 g (9 oz/1½ cups) fresh dates, pitted and roughly chopped
2 tablespoons very finely diced fresh ginger
1 teaspoon ground coriander

1 cinnamon stick
250 ml (9 fl oz/1 cup) apple cider vinegar
180 g (6 oz/1 cup) rapadura or light brown sugar

Sterilize your jars and lids (see 'Sterilizing your equipment', page 220), place them on a baking tray lined with a clean tea towel (dish towel) and keep warm in a low oven.

Put all the chutney ingredients in a medium-sized pot (I use a 24 cm/9½ inch French oven). Bring to the boil, immediately reduce to a slow simmer, then simmer for 60–70 minutes, or until the chutney is lovely and thick. Stir frequently, especially as the chutney reduces towards the end of the cooking time.

Meanwhile, about 30 minutes before your chutney is ready, put a pot of water on to boil. Sterilize your funnel and ladle by boiling for 12 minutes. While they are boiling, remove the jars and lids from the oven, keeping them on their trays. Remove the funnel and ladle from the boiling water and shake a little to remove the water, allowing the air to dry them off. As soon as the chutney is ready, ladle the warm chutney through the funnel, into the warm jars. Seal the lids tightly, then leave to sit until totally cool. There should be a concave dent in the middle of the lid — if there isn't, store the chutney in the fridge and use it straight away.

og

Bengal chutney

GLUTEN FREE / DAIRY FREE / VEGAN

MAKES ABOUT 1.125 KG (2 LB 8 OZ/4 CUPS)

Because this chutney is sweetened with sugar, the jars, lids, ladle and funnel must be sterile. There is no need to process it in a boiling water bath.

2 carrots, peeled and finely diced
1 onion, finely diced
3 apples, peeled, any bruised spots discarded, then finely diced
100 g (3½ oz/heaped ¾ cup) raisins
chopped fresh chilli, to taste
400 g (14 oz/2 cups) brown sugar, approximately

3 teaspoons finely chopped fresh ginger, approximately
3 teaspoons curry powder
1 teaspoon mustard seeds
600 ml (21 fl oz) apple cider vinegar, approximately

Sterilize your jars and lids (see 'Sterilizing your equipment', page 220), place them on a baking tray lined with a clean tea towel (dish towel) and keep warm in a low oven.

Put all the ingredients in a good-sized saucepan. Very gently bring to the boil, then simmer, stirring often, for 50 minutes, or until reduced and thickened. Halfway through, check for taste, adjusting the chilli, sugar and vinegar if needed.

Meanwhile, about 30 minutes before your chutney is ready, put a pot of water on to boil. Sterilize your funnel and ladle by boiling for 12 minutes. While they are boiling, remove the jars and lids from the oven, keeping them on their trays. Remove the funnel and ladle from the boiling water and shake a little to remove the water, allowing the air to dry them off. As soon as the chutney is ready, ladle the warm chutney through the funnel, into the warm jars. Seal the lids tightly, then leave to sit until totally cool. There should be a concave dent in the middle of the lid — if there isn't, store the chutney in the fridge and use it straight away.

☙

Tomato sauce (ketchup)

GLUTEN FREE / DAIRY FREE / VEGAN

MAKES ABOUT 1.5 LITRES (52 FL OZ/6 CUPS)

Almost a kitchen essential, and so cheap and easy to make. Because it is processed in a boiling water bath, it's not essential to sterilize the jars, lids, ladle and funnel.

1 tablespoon olive oil
3 kg (6 lb 12 oz) ripe tomatoes (any variety is fine), roughly chopped
2 brown onions, roughly chopped
4 – 5 garlic cloves, crushed
½ –1 teaspoon ground cinnamon
¼ – ½ teaspoon ground cloves

Time saver
INSTEAD OF FRESH TOMATOES, YOU COULD INSTEAD USE 3 LITRES (105 FL OZ/12 CUPS) PASSATA (PURÉED TOMATOES)

1/8 – 1/4 teaspoon cayenne pepper

1/4 – 1 teaspoon celery salt

1/4 – 1 teaspoon ground ginger

1/2 – 1 teaspoon freshly ground black pepper

1 – 2 teaspoons ground cumin

1 – 2 teaspoons yellow mustard powder

375 – 500 ml (13 – 17 fl oz/1½ – 2 cups) apple cider vinegar

270 – 360 g (9½ – 12¾ oz/1½ – 2 cups) rapadura sugar, or 375 – 500 ml
(13 – 17 fl oz/1½ – 2 cups) apple juice concentrate

FEEL FREE TO
ADJUST THE
GROUND SPICES
ACCORDING TO
HOW SPICY YOU
LIKE YOUR SAUCE

Wash your jars and lids, place them on a baking tray lined with a clean tea towel (dish towel) and keep warm in a low oven. Wash and dry your ladle and funnel.

Put the olive oil, tomatoes, onion and garlic in a large pot and cook over low–medium heat for 30–40 minutes, or until they are well broken down. Purée directly in the pot using a stick blender, or allow to cool a little before spooning into a blender to purée in batches. (If using tomato passata, omit this step.)

Return the purée to the pot and add the remaining ingredients. Stirring from time to time, gently simmer for 45 minutes to 1 hour, or until the sauce is thick and of the desired consistency. As it gets thicker it will need to be stirred frequently. Taste the sauce from time to time — depending on the quality of the tomatoes, you may need to adjust the spices, vinegar and sweetener. Add sea salt to taste.

IF YOU PREFER
A VERY SMOOTH
KETCHUP, PEEL
THE TOMATOES
BEFORE CHOPPING
AND COOKING. TO
DO THIS, BRING A
LARGE POT OF
WATER TO THE
BOIL. USING A
SHARP KNIFE,
CUT A SMALL CROSS
INTO THE SKIN
ON THE BASE OF
EACH TOMATO.
SUBMERGE IN
BOILING WATER
FOR 30 SECONDS,
THEN REMOVE
FROM THE WATER
— THE SKIN WILL
PEEL OFF EASILY

Meanwhile, bring a very large pot of water to the boil (see 'The boiling water bath' on page 221). Remove the jars and lids from the oven, keeping them on their trays, and ladle the warm tomato sauce into the jars, through the funnel. Put the lids on the jars, then screw them tight, with just that little bit more to go before they are really tight. Using jar tongs, lower the jars into the boiling water. When the water comes back to the boil, put the timer on for 12 minutes. Using the jar tongs, remove and place the jars on a towel or wooden surface.

Tighten the lids that last tiny bit — you will need to hold the jar and maybe the lid with a tea towel (dish towel). Let them sit until totally cool — there should be a concave dent in the middle of the lid. If there isn't, store the ketchup in the fridge and use it straight away.

ख

Basil tomatoes

GLUTEN FREE/ DAIRY FREE / VEGAN

MAKES ABOUT 1 KG (2 LB 4 OZ/4$^{1}/_{2}$ CUPS)

Because of their high acid content, tomatoes are the only vegetable you can safely preserve at home using a boiling water bath. Because these tomatoes are processed in a boiling water bath, it is not essential to sterilize the jars, lids, ladle and funnel. To be on the safe side, however, you will need to add extra acid — it's worth it for peace of mind.

> 125 ml (4 fl oz/$^{1}/_{2}$ cup) olive oil
> 2 kg (4 lb 8 oz) ripe, delicious tomatoes, peeled (see the side column note
>   on the opposite page), quartered and seeded
> 3 garlic cloves, crushed
> 1 teaspoon sugar
> a good handful of basil leaves, finely sliced
> lemon juice or citric acid

Wash your jars and lids, place them on a baking tray lined with a clean tea towel (dish towel) and keep warm in a low oven. Wash and dry your ladle and funnel.

Warm the olive oil in a good-sized saucepan, then add the tomatoes, garlic, sugar and basil. Season to taste with sea salt and freshly ground black pepper, then cover and cook over a gentle heat for 30 minutes.

Purée the mixture using a stick blender, or in batches in a blender. It can be bottled as is, or returned to the pot and simmered until reduced to the desired consistency.

Meanwhile, bring a very large pot of water to the boil (see 'The boiling water bath' on page 221). Remove the jars and lids from the oven, keeping them on their trays, and ladle the warm sauce into the jars, through the funnel.

Add lemon juice or citric acid to each jar, using the following guide. For jars up to 500 ml (17 fl oz/2 cups) in size — 2 teaspoons lemon juice or $^{1}/_{4}$ teaspoon citric acid. For jars up to 1 litre (35 fl oz/4 cups) — 1 tablespoon lemon juice or $^{1}/_{2}$ teaspoon citric acid.

HERE YOU HAVE A READY-MADE TOMATO BASE TO ENRICH AND FLAVOUR STEWS AND SOUPS, OR TO TURN INTO BOLOGNESE SAUCE OR PIZZA OR PASTA TOPPING. MANY DELICIOUS MEALS ARE JUST A MOMENT AWAY WITH SOME OF THIS SAUCE IN THE PANTRY

Put the lids on the jars and screw them tight, with just that little bit more to go before they are really tight. Using jar tongs, lower the jars into the boiling water, making sure they are completely covered. When the water comes back to the boil, continue boiling for 30 minutes for jars up to 500 ml (17 fl oz/2 cups) in size, or 45 minutes for jars up to 1 litre (35 fl oz/4 cups) in size.

Using the jar tongs, remove and place the jars on a towel or wooden surface. Tighten the lids that last tiny bit — you will need to hold the jar and maybe the lid with a tea towel (dish towel). Leave to sit until totally cool. There should be a concave dent in the middle of the lid — if there isn't, store the sauce in the fridge and use straight away.

അ

Fruit mince

DAIRY FREE / GLUTEN FREE / VEGAN

MAKES ABOUT 1.5 KG (3 LB 5 OZ/6 CUPS)

This is the loveliest fruit mince I know. Make it in early autumn when apples are cropping and in season. It's perfect for using up seconds or windfalls. You can safely keep this in a clean, sterile, sealed jar in the fridge, but if you want to keep it in the pantry, you'll need to give it a boiling water bath.

300 ml (10½ fl oz) apple juice
250 ml (9 fl oz/1 cup) apple juice concentrate
1 kg (2 lb 4 oz) granny smith apples, peeled, cored and finely diced
1 teaspoon mixed spice
¼ teaspoon freshly grated nutmeg
½ teaspoon cinnamon
225 g (8 oz/1¾ cups) seeded raisins, roughly chopped
110 g (3¾ oz/¾ cup) currants
125 g (4½ oz/1 cup) sultanas (golden raisins)
60 g (2¼ oz/⅓ cup) almonds, finely chopped
finely grated zest of 1 lemon
150 ml (5 fl oz) brandy

YOU CAN USE ANY TYPE OF APPLE FOR THE FRUIT MINCE, ALTHOUGH SOME VARIETIES WON'T BREAK DOWN AS MUCH AS OTHERS

Wash your jars and lids, place them on a baking tray lined with a clean tea towel (dish towel) and keep warm in a low oven. Wash and dry your ladle and funnel.

Put all the ingredients except the brandy in a saucepan. Cover and bring to a gentle simmer, then cook for 20 minutes, allowing the apples to sweat out their juices. Remove the lid and continue to simmer for a further 30 minutes, or until the mixture is thick and the apples have cooked down. Stir frequently, especially towards the end of cooking.

Meanwhile, bring a very large pot of water to the boil (see 'The boiling water bath' on page 221).

When the fruit mince is ready, remove from the heat and allow to cool a little. Stir in the brandy.

Remove the jars and lids from the oven, keeping them on their trays, and ladle the warm fruit mince into the jars, through the funnel. Put the lids on the jars, then screw them tight, with just that little bit more to go before they are really tight. Using jar tongs, lower the jars into the boiling water. When the water comes back to the boil, put the timer on for 15 minutes.

Using the jar tongs, remove and place the jars on a towel or wooden surface. Tighten the lids that last tiny bit — you will need to hold the jar and maybe the lid with a tea towel (dish towel). Leave to sit until totally cool. There should be a concave dent in the middle of the lid — if there isn't, store the fruit mince in the fridge and use straight away.

CB

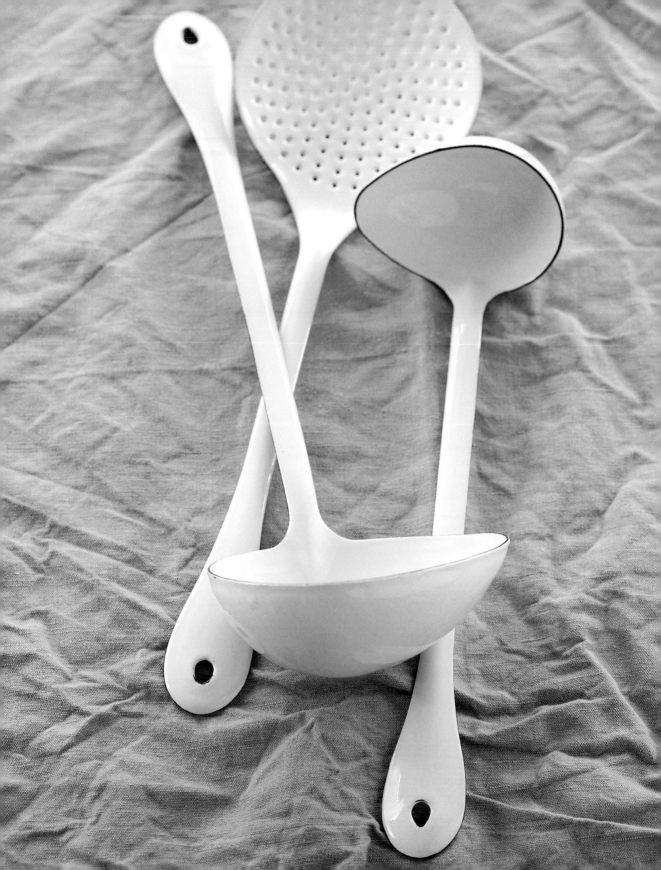

basics

Included in this chapter are recipes for a range of basic essentials such as beans, grains, stocks, yoghurt and puff pastry. These basic items are simply invaluable to have at hand and lend themselves to a huge range of uses. Making these basic pantry or fridge staples from scratch is the single easiest way to reduce your food costs, and provide quality, nutrient-dense dishes for you and your family.

Some of the recipes may take a little time, but only in the sense that you will need to be around to keep an eye on them — your actual work time will be minimal. The finished goods will store happily in the freezer, fridge or pantry until you're ready for them. ✦

Beans

Tinned beans are very handy to have in the pantry, but they are relatively expensive, are not always the most digestible (many are not pre-soaked), and don't taste anywhere near as good as the ones you make yourself. Once soaked, dried beans are easy to cook — you just need to keep an eye on them while they simmer.

A slow cooker is perfect for beans. Make more than you need, and freeze the rest in portions for another time. If you are adding frozen beans to a soup or stew, you won't need to thaw them first as they will simply thaw in the hot pot.

Here you'll find all the information you need for cooking a large variety of beans, with extra recipes for cooking a white bean and a black bean, just to help you on your way. Before you know it, you'll be finding it the simplest of things to put them on to cook yourself, rather than relying on tinned beans. og

HOW TO PREPARE BEANS

It's true that beans take a long time to cook, but once they are ready, you have either a great meal or the beginnings of one. Beans take planning, that's all. If you are cooking them from scratch, you'll need to organize soaking and cooking time. A good habit is to cook beans in bulk and then freeze them for future use. There are many ways to use beans; as a rule, deeply flavoured stews and soups benefit from the addition of uncooked beans, while pre-cooked beans are great for spreads, dips, stir-fries and lighter, quicker-cooking stews.

SOAKING BEANS

Pre-soaking beans for 6–8 hours makes them more digestible. A useful routine is to soak them overnight in a large pot, covered with water and 2 teaspoons of whey, buttermilk or yoghurt stirred gently through. Soaking is recommended at room temperature, allowing a little fermentation to occur.

IF YOU NEED TO HURRY THE SOAKING PROCESS, BRING THE BEANS TO THE BOIL FIRST AND LEAVE THEM TO SOAK FOR A FEW HOURS

COOKING BEANS

Beans must be well cooked to ensure optimum digestion, and can take 1–4 hours to cook on the stove. They need to be well covered with liquid as they swell considerably. The yields given here for cooked beans are approximate as they will vary depending on the age of the beans, length of soaking time and other factors.

TIPS

KOMBU *Adding a small portion of this sea vegetable at the beginning of cooking will soften the beans and improve their digestibility. A 3–5 cm (1¼–2 inch) piece will be adequate for the quantities of beans cooked in the following recipes.*

◆

DO NOT ADD SALT *Salt only helps to toughen beans. If you must add salt, do it when they have finished cooking. Usually, though, the addition of kombu will add a saltiness for you.*

◆

THINK SMALL *Beans are concentrated and powerful foods — a little goes a long way. A good-sized serving is about ½ cup of cooked beans per person.*

◆

TINNED BEANS *These are a great standby and handy to have in the cupboard, but they shouldn't be the only beans you use. Tinned beans are often harder to digest due to the reliance on pressure to create a soft bean rather than long soaking and cooking times. When using, it's best to rinse them well to take away some of the 'tinned' taste.*

GENERAL METHOD FOR COOKING BEANS

SERVES 4 - 6

After the beans have been soaked, discard the water, drain well and place in a large, heavy-based saucepan. Add enough water to cover the beans by 10 cm (4 inches) and bring to the boil over medium heat.

As soon as the water reaches boiling point, turn the heat down very low (a heat diffuser is useful here). Begin timing, based on the cooking times below.

220 g (7¾ oz/1 cup) dried adzuki beans, 1–1½ hours
  makes 520 g (1 lb 2 oz/3 cups)

200 g (7 oz/1 cup) dried black (turtle) beans, 1½–2 hours
  makes 450 g (1 lb/2¼ cups)

200 g (7 oz/1 cup) dried borlotti (cranberry) beans, 1½–2 hours
  makes 450 g (1 lb/2¼ cups)

BAKING BEANS IN THE OVEN GIVES A BETTER-TEXTURED BEAN, BUT WILL TAKE LONGER (4–6 HOURS). DRAIN THE SOAKED BEANS, PLACE IN A FLAMEPROOF BAKING DISH AND COVER WITH 4 CM (1½ INCHES) WATER. PLACE OVER MEDIUM HEAT AND BRING TO THE BOIL, SKIMMING OFF ANY FOAM. COVER WITH A LID AND BAKE IN A PREHEATED 140–180°C (275–350°F/ GAS 1–4) OVEN UNTIL TENDER

200 g (7 oz/1 cup) dried cannellini beans, $1^1/_2$ – 2 hours
    makes 500 g (1 lb 2 oz/$2^1/_2$ cups)

200 g (7 oz/1 cup) dried chickpeas, $2^1/_2$ – 4 hours
    makes 450 g (1 lb/3 cups)

175 g (6 oz/1 cup) dried broad (fava) beans, $1^1/_2$ – 2 hours
    makes 480 g (1 lb 1 oz/3 cups)

200 g (7 oz/1 cup) dried great northern beans, $1^1/_2$ hours
    makes 480 g (1 lb 1 oz/$2^3/_4$ cups)

200 g (7 oz/1 cup) dried red kidney beans, 2 – 3 hours
    makes 450 g (1 lb/$2^1/_2$ cups)

190 g ($6^3/_4$ oz/1 cup) dried butterbeans (lima beans), 1 – $1^1/_2$ hours
    makes 400 g (14 oz/2 cups)

200 g (7 oz/1 cup) dried navy beans, 1 – $1^1/_2$ hours
    makes 480 g (1 lb 1 oz/$2^1/_2$ cups)

190 g ($6^3/_4$ oz/1 cup) dried pinto beans, 1 – $1^1/_2$ hours
    makes 420 g (15 oz/$2^1/_3$ cups)

60 g ($2^1/_4$ oz/1 cup) dried soya beans, 3 – 4 hours
    makes 550 g (1 lb 4 oz/3 cups)

Check the beans regularly to ensure that they are always well covered with liquid.

Some beans, particularly chickpeas, produce a large amount of froth, foam and scum — this needs to be removed as they cook. You can tell when they are cooked — they begin to yield their soft, starchy centres to light pressure.

ভ

White beans with sage

GLUTEN FREE / DAIRY FREE / VEGAN

MAKES ABOUT 400 G (14 OZ/2 GENEROUS CUPS) COOKED BEANS

Cannellini, great northern or butterbeans (lima beans) are all gorgeous white beans. Cooking them with herbs such as sage, rosemary and thyme adds a little more flavour, as well as a delicious broth. Ham and bacon bones are also a wonderful addition to the cooking liquid.

200 g (7 oz/1 cup) dried white beans, soaked overnight in
    2.5 litres (87 fl oz/10 cups) water, then drained and rinsed well
a 5 cm (2 inch) piece of kombu
3 bay leaves
3 large sage leaves
3 thyme sprigs

Put all the ingredients in a large pot with enough water to cover them by 10 cm (4 inches). Simmer over medium heat for 1½ hours, or until the beans 'give' easily and show a creamy texture when pressed on a board, and no hard, pebbly bits of starch remain. The broth will be beautifully flavoured and can be reduced over high heat to intensify the flavour if desired. The beans are now ready to use. If freezing them, include some of the cooking liquid.

VARIATIONS

For a quick and delicious stew, add roughly chopped kale to the pot, with lots of garlic, and braise the kale in the cooking liquid. Add sea salt and freshly ground black pepper to taste before serving.

Alternatively, pour some olive oil into a frying pan, add 1 roughly chopped onion and 2 tablespoons roughly chopped herbs such as basil, oregano and/or marjoram. Cook over medium heat for a few minutes. Add 2–3 sliced zucchini (courgettes) and 4 finely diced garlic cloves. Sauté for 10 minutes, then add the cooked beans with a little of the cooking broth to moisten. Cook for a further 20 minutes, or until the beans are meltingly soft and no juices remain. Season with sea salt and freshly ground black pepper and serve.

CB

Black beans

GLUTEN FREE / DAIRY FREE / VEGAN

MAKES ABOUT 400 G (14 OZ/2 GENEROUS CUPS)

Black (turtle) beans, pinto beans and borlotti (cranberry) beans are all freely interchangeable, and are a great option for so many dishes.

200 g (7 oz/1 cup) dried black (turtle), pinto or borlotti (cranberry) beans,
soaked overnight in 2.5 litres (87 fl oz/10 cups) water, then drained
and rinsed well
a 5 cm (2 inch) piece of kombu

Put the beans and kombu in a large pot with enough water to cover by 10 cm (4 inches). Simmer over medium heat for 1½ hours, or until the beans 'give' easily and show a creamy texture when pressed on a board, and no hard, pebbly bits of starch remain. The beans are now ready to use. If freezing them, include some of the cooking liquid.

⊗

Dairy

Here are two very simple recipes for two staple dairy items to keep tucked away in the fridge: ghee and home-made organic yoghurt. Ghee is simply clarified butter and one of the most versatile fats for cooking as it has a high burning point. Organic yoghurt is very expensive to buy, yet so easy and inexpensive to make. ☙

Ghee

GLUTEN FREE

MAKES ABOUT 225 G (8 OZ/1 CUP)

Ghee is very simple to make, and as it is a saturated fat, is also very stable. Do give it a try as it adds such lovely flavour to your cooking and is an extremely health-supportive fat.

250 g (9 oz) butter, preferably organic and unsalted

Melt the butter gently in a small saucepan over low heat. Once it has melted, increase the heat so there is a gentle simmer — as the water evaporates, there will be a gentle gurgling sound and the butter will be covered with white foam. Continue to cook, uncovered, for 20–25 minutes, or until the milk solids start to brown on the bottom of the pan — tilt it to check — and there is little foam left on top of the butterfat. The time will vary for different butters as they contain differing water and fat ratios.

Remove from the heat and leave to cool until any milk solids left on top have sunk to the bottom. When cool, spoon off any remaining milk solids floating on top. Gently pour the butterfat into a bowl, stopping as you get to the solids. Discard the solids. To make sure all the milk solids are removed — this is especially important for people who are intolerant to the milk protein, casein — strain the butterfat through two or three layers of muslin (cheesecloth). Refrigerate until needed — it will keep indefinitely.

☙

Organic yoghurt

GLUTEN FREE

MAKES ABOUT 625 G (1 LB 6 OZ/2½ CUPS)

The only equipment you need for making your own yoghurt is a clean glass preserving jar or jam jar with a lid. The jar must be made of tempered glass that can withstand heat. A thermometer is handy, but not essential.

> 1 litre (35 fl oz/4 cups) organic, full-cream milk
> 1 tablespoon yoghurt — it must say 'live cultures' on the label

Wash your jar and lid well, then rinse out with very hot water and drain to dry.

Put the milk in a saucepan and bring to just before the boil — 82°C (180°F) on a thermometer — stirring occasionally. Turn off the heat and cool the milk to 43°C (110°F), or until it is still quite warm, but you can put your finger in it and keep it there. Stir a couple of times to prevent a skin forming.

Spoon the yoghurt into the jar and pour in a little of the milk. (Don't be tempted to add a little extra yoghurt to the culture, thinking more is better; the bacteria need lots of room to grow and play.) Stir to combine well, then add the remaining milk and replace the lid.

Leave the jar to sit overnight, or for at least 8 hours, in a warm — but not hot — place: approximately 20–25°C (68–77°F). (I wrap mine in a blanket and place it right up next to the fridge, where the engine keeps the side warm. I can also put it in the oven during the day, as my oven goes to a very low temperature.)

The next morning you should have lovely, thick yoghurt. Allow it to cool a little, then refrigerate.

❧

MANY PEOPLE ARE LACTOSE INTOLERANT OR ALLERGIC TO THE PROTEIN IN MILK AND OTHER DAIRY PRODUCE. GOOD-QUALITY YOGHURT CONTAINS LIVE BACTERIA THAT BREAK DOWN MUCH OF THE REACTION-CAUSING PROPERTIES OF MILK AND MAKE IT EASIER TO DIGEST

Grains

Good organic whole grains have as much as possible of their natural, edible parts intact and provide slow-release fuel and fibre that enables the body to run properly. They also provide nutrients as nature designed them — in the correct proportions for optimum usage. When preparing whole grains, as with beans, you need to be a bit organized as many need some pre-soaking for the best results.

Here you'll find information on preparing a large range of grains, and four lovely gluten-free recipes for everyday use. There are two quick ones: a fragrant white basmati, and nutrient-packed quinoa, and for days when you have a little more time, a polenta and deeply nourishing brown rice flecked with wild rice. ❧

SOAKING GRAINS

Most whole grains benefit from soaking. This is because grains contain phytic acid and enzyme inhibitors in the outer layer, or bran, which interferes with the absorption of many minerals, notably calcium, magnesium and zinc. During soaking and fermentation, lactobaccilli bacteria begin to break down the phytic acids and enzyme inhibitors, creating lactic acid as a by-product. The bacteria also break down gluten — a protein that is very difficult to digest. Because of this, soaking often increases tolerance to wheat, and increases the vitamin content in the grain, especially B vitamins. It can also dramatically reduce cooking times.

Whole grains are best soaked for 6–12 hours, though this isn't really necessary for buckwheat and hulled millet. I would recommend, however, soaking everything else, especially harder grains such as barley, rye, spelt and wheat. A useful routine is to soak them overnight in a large bowl with 2 teaspoons of whey, buttermilk or yoghurt stirred gently through. Soaking should be done at room temperature, allowing a little fermentation to occur.

COOKING GRAINS

The following basic techniques for cooking grains will give you a fluffy and generally intact grain, though some grains such as millet and buckwheat do tend to lose their form. The cooked grain can then be served with a meal, included in a stuffing or pattie mix, or used for a wealth of other applications limited only by your imagination. The yields given for cooked grains are approximate, and will vary depending on the age of the grain, growing conditions and other factors.

GENERAL METHOD FOR COOKING GRAINS

SERVES 4

If using soaked grains (see page 241), discard the water, drain well and pat dry. Pour the grains into a sieve and rinse under running water, shaking gently. If using unsoaked grains, rinse well and pat dry with a tea towel (dish towel). Put the drained grain in a heavy-based saucepan, add the required amount of water (see below), cover with a lid and bring to the boil. As soon as it reaches boiling point turn the heat down as low as possible (a heat diffuser is useful here). Begin timing from this point, based on the cooking times below.

Time saver

COOK EXTRA
GRAIN TO USE IN
PORRIDGE THE
NEXT MORNING,
IN A SALAD FOR
LUNCH, OR TO
INCLUDE IN A
STUFFING OR
DESSERT

220 g (7¾ oz/1 cup) pearled barley
  soaked, 560 ml (19¼ fl oz/2¼ cups) liquid, 50-70 minutes
  unsoaked, 625 ml (21½ fl oz/2½ cups) liquid, 60-80 minutes
  makes 680 g (1 lb 8 oz/3-4 cups) cooked

200 g (7 oz/1 cup) kasha (toasted buckwheat)
  soaked, 435 ml (15¼ fl oz/1¾ cups) liquid, 15-20 minutes
  unsoaked, 500 ml (17 fl oz/2 cups) liquid, 15-20 minutes
  makes 680 g (1 lb 8 oz/2½-3½ cups) cooked

200 g (7 oz/1 cup) hulled millet
  soaked, 435 ml (15¼ fl oz/1¾ cups) liquid, 15-20 minutes
  unsoaked 500 ml (17 fl oz/2 cups) liquid, 15-20 minutes
  makes 550-650 g (1 lb 4 oz-1 lb 7 oz/2½-3 cups) cooked

185 g (6½ oz/1 cup) quinoa
  soaked, 435 ml (15¼ fl oz/1¾ cups) liquid, 15-20 minutes
  unsoaked, 500 ml (17 fl oz/2 cups) liquid, 15-20 minutes
  makes 540 g (1 lb 3 oz/2 cups) cooked

200 g (7 oz/1 cup) wheat or spelt berries
  soaked, 1 litre (35 fl oz/4 cups) liquid, 2 hours
  makes 600 g (1 lb 5 oz/2-3 cups) cooked

200 g (7 oz/1 cup) long-grain brown rice
  soaked, 375 ml (13 fl oz/1½ cups) liquid, 30 – 40 minutes
  unsoaked, 435 ml (15¼ fl oz/1¾ cups) liquid, 40 – 50 minutes
  makes 450 g (1 lb/2½ cups) cooked

200 g (7 oz/1 cup) short- or medium-grain brown rice
  soaked, 435 ml (15¼ fl oz/1¾ cups) liquid, 30 – 40 minutes
  unsoaked, 500 ml (17 fl oz/2 cups) liquid, 40 – 50 minutes
  makes 450 g (1 lb/2½ cups) cooked

At the end of the cooking time (or about 5 minutes before, for longer-cooking grains), remove the lid and check if there is any water left by tipping the pot at an angle. If there is, replace the lid and continue to cook until no liquid remains. When the grain is ready, small steam holes should appear on the surface.

Take the pot off the heat and place a clean tea towel (dish towel) or sheet of paper towel over the grains (this helps absorb excess moisture, resulting in a fluffier, less 'wet' grain). Cover with a lid and leave to stand for 5 minutes, allowing the internal heat and steam to finish the cooking process.

ଓ

White basmati rice pilaff

GLUTEN FREE

MAKES ABOUT 675 G (1 LB 8 OZ/3 CUPS)

Sometimes you just want a beautifully fragrant white rice rather than a wholegrain. I turn to basmati! You don't have to sauté the rice in ghee beforehand, but you'll end up with a better result.

300 g (10½ oz/1½ cups) basmati rice
1 tablespoon ghee or unsalted butter

Put the rice in a bowl and fill with cold water. Swish the rice around and drain off the water — repeat a few times until the water is no longer cloudy with starch.

Put the ghee in a saucepan over medium heat. When the ghee is warm, add the rice, stirring constantly until the rice smells slightly toasted, but is not at all coloured.

Add 500 ml (17 fl oz/2 cups) water, a pinch of sea salt and bring to the boil. Immediately reduce the heat to very low. Cover and gently simmer for 15–20 minutes, or until all the water has been absorbed. Turn off the heat and leave to sit, covered, for 10 minutes. Fluff up the grains with a fork and serve.

ભ

Quinoa for dinner

GLUTEN FREE

MAKES ABOUT 480 G (1 LB 1 OZ/3 CUPS)

YOU CAN COOK THE QUINOA IN WATER INSTEAD OF STOCK

Quinoa is the best friend of the time poor. It is exceptionally high in protein, B vitamins, iron, potassium, zinc, calcium and vitamin E — all in 20 minutes of cooking. Rather than turning to couscous (which is only a small part of a grain, and generally refined) for a quick dinner grain, do give quinoa an opportunity to prove itself to you. If you soak it beforehand, you will ensure optimum absorption of minerals — and given it has so many, this is such a worthwhile option.

200 g (7 oz/1¼ cups) quinoa, soaked overnight if desired with 1 tablespoon
    yoghurt or buttermilk, or 2 teaspoons whey or lemon juice
560–625 ml (19¼–21½ fl oz/2¼–2½ cups) stock (any sort is fine)

QUINOA TAKES WELL TO SPICES SUCH AS CUMIN, CORIANDER, CINNAMON, TURMERIC, CARDAMOM AND GINGER ADDED TO THE COOKING LIQUID, AND ALSO TO TOASTED SEEDS AND NUTS TOSSED THROUGH THE COOKED GRAIN

Rinse the quinoa and drain well. Pat dry with a tea towel (dish towel), then place in a saucepan with 560 ml (19¼ fl oz/2¼ cups) stock or water if soaked, and 625 ml (21½ fl oz/2½ cups) if unsoaked. Add some sea salt if needed (remember there's already salt in your stock), then cover and bring to the boil. As soon as the quinoa comes to the boil, turn the heat down low.

Simmer for 15–20 minutes, or until the quinoa is soft. About 5 minutes before the end of cooking time, check if there is any water left by tipping the pot at an angle. If so, continue to cook until there is no water left. When the quinoa is ready, small steam holes should appear on the surface.

Remove from the heat, place a clean tea towel or piece of paper towel on top of the grain, then replace the lid. Allow to sit for 5 minutes before serving.

ભ

Polenta

GLUTEN FREE / DAIRY FREE

SERVES 4

The key to good polenta is to cook it for at least 20 minutes; this ensures a full softening of the grain. It also helps to use a deep, good-quality pot with a heavy base, and to stir the polenta with a large wooden spoon. The end result should be beautifully creamy.

> 1 litre (35 fl oz/4 cups) stock (or water) for a firm polenta — plus 250 ml
>   (9 fl oz/1 cup) for a soft polenta
> sea salt, to taste
> 150 g (5½ oz/1 cup) polenta

Using a large heavy-based saucepan, bring the stock or water and salt to the boil. Start adding the polenta to the water slowly, stirring as you go. Lower the heat to a gentle simmer and cook for 20–30 minutes, stirring frequently (especially as the polenta starts to thicken). Add your choice of flavourings and stir well.

VARIATIONS

Polenta benefits enormously from the addition of extra flavourings. After the polenta is cooked, stir in any combination of the wonderful accompaniments below.

> 2 teaspoons finely chopped rosemary
> 2 teaspoons finely chopped basil
> 1–2 tablespoons unsalted butter
> 25–50g (1–1¾ oz/¼–½ cup) grated parmesan cheese
> 1–2 tablespoons butter

ભ

Brown speckled rice

GLUTEN FREE

MAKES ABOUT 425 G (15 OZ/2½ CUPS)

Richer in protein, minerals and B vitamins than many other grains, wild rice adds a delicious nuttiness to what is simply cooked brown rice. If you can't find wild rice, or it's too expensive, just use 200 g (7 oz/1 cup) long-grain brown rice instead.

- 100 g (3½ oz/½ cup) long-grain brown rice
- 100 g (3½ oz/½ cup) wild rice
- 1 tablespoon yoghurt or buttermilk, or 2 teaspoons whey or lemon juice (optional)

If possible, soak all the rice overnight in water with the yoghurt, buttermilk, whey or lemon juice.

Put the rice in a sieve and rinse well. Pat dry with a tea towel (dish towel) and place in a small saucepan. Add 375 ml (13 fl oz/1½ cups) if soaked, or 435 ml (15¼ fl oz/1¾ cups) if unsoaked. Cover and bring to the boil. As soon as the rice comes to the boil, reduce the heat so no steam escapes through the lid (you may need to use a heat diffuser).

Cook for 35 minutes if soaked, or 45 minutes if unsoaked, or until the grains are tender. With wild rice, the cooking time often varies. If it isn't done by this time, or the liquid has run dry, add a little boiling water and continue to cook until tender.

ᛒ

Puff pastry

Puff pastry is a great example of the 'all things in balance and moderation' argument. I would qualify that by adding 'all things *made from real ingredients* in balance and moderation'. When made from organic butter and a less-refined flour, puff pastry has a rightful place in a wholesome diet. This puff, based on a recipe by American chef Michel Richard, is surprisingly easy to make. It's not hard or time consuming — it just needs to spend a lot of time resting and chilling between rollings. The reward is the best puff you have ever tasted — one you can make with spelt. Best of all, you have instant pastry on hand for many delicious somethings. ෬

Spelt puff pastry

WHEAT FREE

MAKES 4 SHEETS, EACH ABOUT 24 CM (9½ INCHES) SQUARE

The most important thing about making this pastry is to take care that the butter does not melt into the flour dough — the butter needs to be firm at all times. You are layering dough, butter and air, many times over. If, when rolling the butter, it starts to soften and smear through, immediately put your pastry on a tray lined with baking paper, cover this with baking paper, and put it in the fridge until it is chilled again. This is a great pastry to use in summer, but an easier one to make in winter. In summer I make it early in the morning, freeze my rolling pin (I have a copper one) and chill it well between rolls.

    300 g (10½ oz/2 cups) plain (all-purpose) white spelt flour
    185 ml (6 fl oz/¾ cup) iced water
    250 g (9 oz) unsalted butter, well chilled
    75 g (2½ oz/½ cup) plain (all-purpose) white spelt flour, extra

Place the flour in a bowl. Using a butter knife, gradually 'cut' the water into the flour. The dough should hold together, *but must not be at all wet* — you will be surprised how the spelt 'gives' as it sits for a couple of minutes. (You might need to use 1–2 tablespoons more water, as different batches of spelt flour absorb different amounts of water.) Form the dough into a ball — *do not knead or play with it* — and wrap in a tea towel (dish towel), then flatten a little and chill in the fridge.

Place the butter between two sheets of baking paper and beat with a rolling pin until it forms a rough 20 cm (8 inch) square, about 1 cm (½ inch) thick. You may need to lift the paper from both sides from time to time, to release and allow the butter to spread. It doesn't matter if the butter ends up more of a rectangle. Return the butter, between the paper sheets, to the fridge to chill.

Put the extra flour in a bowl near where you will be rolling, to use for dusting. Place the dough on a floured work surface. Sprinkle a little flour over the pastry and rolling pin. Roll the dough into a square, about 26 cm (10½ inches) — again, it doesn't matter if it ends up slightly rectangular. To prevent sticking, keep the pastry and rolling surface lightly dusted with flour, even turning the pastry from time to time.

Starting from the centre of your square, roll out each corner to make an 'ear', creating a kind of 'cross' shape.

Remove one piece of baking paper from the butter and invert it onto the centre of the pastry. Remove the remaining paper, and fold over the pastry ears, so they completely cover the butter — you should not need to stretch the pastry. They will overlap and that is fine. You should end up with a completely sealed parcel of butter. Pat the edges a little to make a nice, neat rectangle — the pastry should be right up against the butter. If the pastry and butter at this stage still feel cold and chilled, you can start to roll. If not, cover and place in the fridge to chill.

You are now commencing to *make turns*. (You'll be rolling the dough lengthways, so make sure you have plenty of space.) Making sure your rolling surface and pin are dusted with flour, begin to roll out the dough lengthways. When the butter is very chilled, this might take a couple of times where you simply press along the pastry to gently flatten it evenly. As the pastry begins to 'give', continue to roll out until you have a rectangle about 67 cm (26½ inches) long and 24–26 cm (9½–10½ inches) wide. You are only ever rolling lengthways.

As you roll, you need to continually move the pastry and dust with flour underneath and on top of the pastry. As you are moving the pastry, take care not to hold it for too long, as your body warmth will soften the butter. Work swiftly to prevent the butter softening. Try to avoid ending up with pointy, uneven bits at the two outside edges on the ends of the pastry, using the rolling pin to push (not press or roll) them back into a more even line. Otherwise you can incorporate the pointy ends into the fold (in the next step). You are now ready to commence the first turn.

Fold the pastry into three — the pastry up from the bottom, and down from the top. Repeat the rolling to make a rectangle about 67 cm (26½ inches) long, following the guidelines above. Fold the pastry as described, rotate so the closed fold is to your left, and mark it with two little dents. This lets you know you have completed two turns.

Place the pastry on a tray lined with baking paper, top with baking paper and cover, sealing so it doesn't dry out. Place in the fridge to rest and chill for 2 hours.

Repeat the above rolling and folding twice — you have now completed four turns. Mark the pastry with four little dents. Place on a tray lined with baking paper, top with baking paper and cover, sealing well. Chill in the fridge for another 2 hours.

Repeat the rolling and folding twice more — you have now completed six turns and the pastry is ready. Place on a tray lined with baking paper, top with baking paper and cover, sealing well so it doesn't dry out. Place in the fridge to rest and chill.

You can now freeze the pastry, but I prefer to cut it into quarters and roll the pastry into four sheets ready for use, each about 24 cm (9½ inches) square. To roll, keep the table, rolling pin and the top of the pastry lightly dusted with flour. Try to keep the shape fairly even as you roll, but don't worry too much as you can trim it to shape later. The pastry should end up about 2–3 mm (¹/₁₆–¹/₈ inch) thick. As each sheet is rolled, place it on a tray (I use a cake cardboard) covered with a sheet of baking paper, with a piece of baking paper between each pastry sheet. Top with a sheet of baking paper, cover and seal well with plastic wrap and freeze.

You will get the best 'puff' from the pastry in this form. However, no piece of puff should ever go to waste. As you trim pieces from the pastry you are using, fold or layer them on top of each other, then wrap and freeze until ready to use. You can then roll the scraps out again to a thickness of 2–3 mm (¹/₁₆–¹/₈ inch). You won't get the same puff, but you will still have fabulous, flaky pastry — excellent for pasties (see page 138), a quiche (see page 85), or cut into strips and baked with cheese or sesame seeds.

೮౩

Stocks

Home-made stocks are absolutely the cheapest, most nourishing food item available. They are an invaluable tool for good health and healing, a rich source of nutrients and goodness, not to mention one of the easiest ways to deliver flavour. If you want to get lots of minerals (for strong healthy bones) and aid digestion, make stocks.

Commercial stocks are overbearing in flavour, and those made from bones (such as fish, chicken and beef stock) carry none of the rich, nutrient-dense bounty of gelatine contained in your own home-made stock. When you have little money to spend on organic meat, make your own bone stocks.

Stocks are so easy to make, simply requiring a lovely big pot — and when using bones, some acid (such as wine or vinegar) to help draw all the gelatine and minerals from the bone. You can't muck them up, and they freeze brilliantly. ∞

Vegetable stock

GLUTEN FREE / DAIRY FREE / VEGAN

MAKES ABOUT 1.5 LITRES (52 FL OZ/6 CUPS)

This is the stock I invariably make. I like it, it works and it is easy. It has a great flavour and the sea vegetable enriches the broth with minerals. A great vegetarian or vegan stock.

1 medium–large brown onion, skin left on, quartered
1 small leek, rinsed well and roughly chopped
5 small–medium carrots, skin on, scrubbed and roughly chopped
1 medium–large orange sweet potato, skin on, scrubbed and
   roughly chopped
2-3 celery stalks, roughly chopped
5 small–medium dried shiitake mushrooms
a 5 cm (2 inch) piece of kombu, or 2 teaspoons agar flakes
3-4 parsley stalks, with or without leaves
1 fresh or dried bay leaf
2 thyme sprigs

IF LEEK IS NOT
IN SEASON, SIMPLY
LEAVE IT OUT

THE SWEET POTATO
IS ESSENTIAL TO
THIS VEGETABLE
STOCK AS IT ADDS A
SUBTLE SWEETNESS

Put all the ingredients in a stockpot with 3 litres (105 fl oz/12 cups) water and bring to the boil. Reduce the heat to low and gently simmer for 1–1½ hours, ensuring the stock is not boiling too rapidly. After 1 hour the stock will have reduced to about 1.5 litres (52 fl oz/6 cups).

Strain the stock, discarding the solids. Either use the stock as is, or continue to cook over a fairly rapid heat to reduce the stock for a richer, more concentrated flavour.

Place the stock in the fridge to cool before storing in containers to freeze.

VARIATIONS

To make a simple **beef** or **lamb stock**, add a selection of beef or lamb bones to a large pot — the amount you use will depend on your pot. I usually use about 2.5 kg (5 lb 8 oz) of bones in a good-sized stockpot. Do include a marrow bone — you may need to ask your butcher to cut it down the middle to expose the marrow. If desired, to deepen the flavour of the stock, you can slowly brown the bones in the stockpot before adding the other ingredients.

Add 1 brown onion (leave the skin on and cut it into quarters), 5 roughly chopped small–medium carrots (leave the skin on), 2–3 roughly chopped celery stalks, 3–4 parsley stalks, 3 bay leaves and 2 thyme sprigs. Add enough water to cover the bones well. Include also 60 ml (2 fl oz/¼ cup) white wine, or 1 tablespoon apple cider or white wine vinegar — the acid will help to leach the nourishing minerals, protein and cartilage from the bones, into the stock. The longer you cook this stock, the better the result. Simmer for 5–24 hours over a very low heat, checking the water from time to time and adding more as required, and skimming off any scum. Strain the stock, discarding the solids. Either use the stock as is, or continue to cook over a fairly rapid heat to reduce the stock for a richer, more concentrated flavour. Place the stock in the fridge to cool before storing in containers to freeze.

CB

Poached chicken and chicken stock

GLUTEN FREE / DAIRY FREE

MAKES ABOUT 2.5 LITRES (87 FL OZ/10 CUPS)

Organic chicken is expensive, so I like to gain maximum usage from every one I buy. This recipe gives you poached chicken, ready for a number of uses, as well as chicken stock, which is probably one of the most valuable items you can have in your pantry. Alternatively you could use 2–3 carcasses, or about 8 wings — the wings are especially good for stock, and if you happen to come across the feet, definitely use them also. I never remove the fat from stock, especially when the chicken has been raised on grass and scraps as well as foraging for insects. Chicken fat boosts immunity as it contains CLA (conjugated linoleic acid).

THE SIZE OF THE CHICKEN REALLY DOESN'T MATTER — IT WILL ONLY AFFECT THE QUANTITY OF BOTH STOCK AND MEAT. JUST MAKE SURE YOUR CHICKEN IS BARELY COVERED WITH WATER

1 organic chicken, giblets included (ask for them)
3 carrots, skin on, scrubbed and roughly chopped
3 celery stalks, roughly chopped
1 onion, cut into quarters
4 thyme sprigs
4 bay leaves
4 parsley sprigs
2 sage leaves
sea salt and freshly ground black pepper, to taste
2 tablespoons white wine, or 1 teaspoon apple cider vinegar

Put all the ingredients in a stockpot and add enough water to barely cover the bird. Simmer over medium heat, without heavy boiling, for 45 minutes to 1 hour, or until the meat is just cooked. The time will vary depending on the size and meatiness of the chicken. Skim off any scum that comes to the surface, but not the fat.

If using a whole bird, carefully remove it from the pot directly into a large bowl. (If using carcasses or wings, you won't be removing any meat, so disregard this step and keep simmering them in the stock.) Cut the breast meat, with any skin, from the frame and place in another bowl. Cut off the legs and wings, and place in the bowl with the breasts. Using tongs, return the carcass to the stock, and tip any remaining juices onto the meat. If the meat is not covered with the juices, remove some from the stock. Cover the chicken with a clean tea towel (dish towel), not plastic wrap. Allow to cool just a little, then refrigerate for later use.

Gently simmer the stock for another 1–3 hours, and then at a more rapid boil for 20 minutes to reduce and concentrate the stock, if desired. Strain the stock, discarding the solids. Place the stock in the fridge to cool before storing in containers to freeze.

CB

Fish stock

GLUTEN FREE

MAKES ABOUT 2 LITRES (70 FL OZ/8 CUPS)

Fish makes a surprisingly delicious stock, and fish stock has long been regarded in the East as a restorer of life force. It's particularly rich in minerals — especially iodine — and thyroid-strengthening substances. Avoid oily fish, as their flavour will overpower the stock.

1 tablespoon butter or olive oil
1 large brown onion, roughly chopped
1 carrot, roughly chopped
2 – 3 tablespoons white wine, or 2 teaspoons apple cider vinegar
a few thyme sprigs
a few parsley sprigs
1 bay leaf
1 fish bone (the whole body) — try not to use an oily fish
1 fish head, cut in half (or just use half a large fish head)

Melt the butter in a stockpot. Add the onion and carrot and cook over a gentle heat for 15 minutes, so they develop a little colour. Add the wine and allow to sizzle and boil, then add the remaining ingredients and about 2.5 litres (87 fl oz/10 cups) water, or enough to cover. Reduce the heat and simmer for 30–50 minutes, skimming off any scum. Strain the stock, discarding the solids.

Place the stock in the fridge to cool before storing in containers to freeze.

CB

Special little somethings

Here's a handful of very simple ways to add extra flavour and nutrients to your everyday meals — when you're busy, you will be so glad to find them in your fridge. Roasted or blackened capsicums (peppers) have a wonderful rich and sweet flavour that adds a whole new dimension to a tart, frittata, stew, pizza, salad or sandwich. Also included here are two versions — including a dairy-free one — of pesto (surely the best flavour-booster around!), as well as a nutrient-boosting nut and seed mix for a sprinkling of good health. ଔ

Roasted capsicums

GLUTEN FREE / DAIRY FREE / VEGAN

Roasted capsicums enhance the flavour of many dishes, especially tomato-based sauces and salads. Red ones have a lovely sweet taste and vibrant colour.

2–3 red capsicums (peppers)
olive oil, for brushing

Preheat the oven to 180°C (350°F/Gas 4). Wash the capsicums well and cut the tops off close to the stems. Remove the inner membrane and seeds. Stand the capsicums upside down in a baking dish and rub well with olive oil. Bake for 1 hour, or until the skin is well wrinkled and the top begins to blacken. Remove from the oven, place in a bowl and cover with a plate until cool enough to handle. Peel off the skins. The flesh is now ready to use.

ଔ

ROASTED OR BLACKENED CAPSICUMS KEEP VERY WELL IN THE FRIDGE — FOR SEVERAL DAYS IN A BOWL WITH A GOOD SEAL, OR 1–2 WEEKS IF COVERED WITH A LAYER OF OLIVE OIL

Blackened capsicums

GLUTEN FREE / DAIRY FREE / VEGAN

Blackening capsicums (peppers) is a step further than roasting or grilling them, giving a deeper, smokier flavour. Blackening requires blistering the skin over a flame — preferably a natural wood flame, but gas will also give a good result.

1 capsicum (pepper)

Put the capsicum on a rack over a wood fire and allow the skin to blacken for 10–15 minutes, turning with a pair of tongs every now and then to evenly expose all the skin. Alternatively, use a stovetop gas flame, setting a wire rack over the flame so the capsicum is not too close to the flame. Place the blackened capsicum in a bowl and cover with a plate until cool enough to handle. Peel off the charred skin, then remove the inner membrane and seeds. The flesh is now ready to use.

If you don't have a gas stove, cut the top off the capsicum, close to the stem. Cut the flesh into quarters and remove the inner membrane and seeds. Blacken under a hot grill (broiler) for 5–8 minutes, or until the skin is black and blistered. Place in a bowl, cover with a plate and leave until cool enough to handle. Peel off the charred skin. The flesh is now ready to use.

 C3

Time saver

BLACKEN SOME EXTRA CAPSICUMS AT THE SAME TIME FOR LATER USE

Pesto

GLUTEN FREE

MAKES ABOUT 250 G (9 OZ/1 CUP)

A house is not a home without pesto. It is incredibly quick to make, lasts well and can be used in so many ways, such as tossed through hot cooked pasta or steamed vegetables, spread on toast, or swirled into minestrone. Healthwise, it's a star — green leaves bursting with goodness, stacks of antioxidants from the extra virgin olive oil, and protein and fats from the pine nuts. Pesto will keep in the fridge for about 2 weeks.

2 handfuls of basil
50 g (1¾ oz / ½ cup) grated parmesan cheese
40 g (1½ oz / ¼ cup) pine nuts
3 garlic cloves, crushed
80 ml (2½ fl oz / ⅓ cup) extra virgin olive oil

Put all the ingredients in a food processor and pulse until well combined. Try not to blend for too long — pesto should be chunky, not a smooth, homogeneous blend.

To make a good pesto you need good ingredients — fresh parmesan cheese, fresh garlic, and the best-quality olive oil

Dairy-free pesto

GLUTEN FREE / DAIRY FREE / VEGAN

MAKES ABOUT 175 G (6 OZ / ⅔ CUP)

If you're vegan or on a dairy-free diet there's no need to give health-giving pesto a miss. Try this wonderful version.

100 g (3½ oz / ⅔ cup) pine nuts
3 large handfuls of basil
2 teaspoons shiro (white) miso
2 garlic cloves
1 tablespoon lemon juice
100 ml (3½ fl oz) extra virgin olive oil

Do not be tempted to add salt to the dairy-free pesto as shiro miso is quite salty

Put all the ingredients in a food processor and pulse until well combined but still a little chunky. Alternatively, use a mortar and pestle — pile all the ingredients, but only a small amount of the olive oil, into the mortar. Bash together until well combined, then work in the remaining olive oil.

VARIATIONS

Try lightly roasting the pine nuts for a more robust flavour.

Nut and seed mix

GLUTEN FREE / DAIRY FREE / VEGAN

MAKES ABOUT 185 G (6½ OZ/1½ CUPS)

This nut and seed mix supplies a wide range of valuable fats including the essential fatty acid, omega-3, and protein for cellular repair and growth. A little added at breakfast or to a smoothie vastly increases the nutrient density of the meal and will keep you going longer. Refrigerated in an airtight container to protect the valuable fats, it will keep for up to 4 weeks. The quantity given below is ideal for a family. If you want to make less, simply halve the recipe.

45 g (1½ oz/¼ cup) linseeds (flax seeds)
40 g (1½ oz/¼ cup) sesame seeds
30 g (1 oz/¼ cup) sunflower seeds
30 g (1 oz/¼ cup) pepitas (pumpkin seeds)
40 g (1½ oz/¼ cup) almonds or other nuts

Put the linseeds in a blender or nut mill and process — they are fairly hardy and need to have a bit of time by themselves first. Add the remaining ingredients and pulse until you achieve the desired texture.

☙

glossary

Don't be put off by some of these ingredients if you haven't heard of them before and think that they will be difficult to find — they're not. All of them can be found in healthfood stores, and many can also be found in the natural foods section of your local supermarket. ෫

Adzuki beans
Considered the king of beans in Japan and extremely nourishing for the kidneys, adzuki beans are also much easier to digest than other beans.

Agar
Also known as *kanten*, agar is a high-fibre, nutrient-rich, calorie-free jelling agent made from seaweed. It is sold in flakes, powder and bars, but I prefer using the powder or flakes as they are easy to measure out and give reliable results. *See also pages 34–35.*

Apple cider vinegar
Unfiltered apple cider vinegar (a naturally fermented vinegar made from apples) is a health-promoting vinegar, and an extremely rich source of potassium. It is the best choice for making chutneys and pickling.

Arame
Rich in calcium and iodine, arame is a thin, noodle-like sea vegetable traditionally used to treat high blood pressure, breast and uterine fibroids, and to normalize menopausal symptoms. It is popular for promoting good, wrinkle-free skin. It can be added to salads and stir-fries and is excellent in soups.

Arrowroot (gluten free)
Similar in appearance to cornflour (cornstarch), arrowroot comes from the root of a tropical plant and is gluten free. It can be used as a thickening agent for sauces, but I rarely use this product as true arrowroot is not readily available where I live. It is most often tapioca (cassava) flour, and this behaves a little differently to true arrowroot as it gives a more viscous and 'gooey' sauce.

Asafoetida
Also known as *hing*, this Indian spice is generally used as an altenative for garlic, in a stew or soup. Do take care when using it, as it really is very strong and smelly.

Balsamic vinegar
This is a sweet, low-acid vinegar with depth and richness of flavour. It is a good choice for Mediterranean-inspired salads, including those using root vegetables.

Barley

Barley is a high-starch grain — and wonderful for use in winter soups. As the soup cooks, the barley starch helps to thicken it, while providing flavour, texture and creaminess. For this reason, it is also a good alternative to rice for a winter risotto. The most commonly used barley has two hard inedible husks. Thus, most barley is milled to some degree to make it edible. There are three main types: naked, natural and pearled. **Naked barley** is an old variety, no longer popular due to its low yield. It naturally occurs with little husk, so when available it is less refined than pearled barley. **Natural barley** is most often a naked barley with the small amount of husk removed, so all of the germ and bran is left intact. Good organic or biodynamic **pearled barley** has had the outer husks removed, with most of the germ and bran left intact, and is brownish in appearance. Supermarket-bought pearled barley removes all but the inner white starch and is highly refined. I prefer organic or biodynamic pearled barley as it not quite as hefty as the natural or naked, but still has a large amount of goodness. Barley is also available as barley flakes (also called rolled barley) and barley meal. **Barley flakes** are made from barley that has been steamed, rolled and flattened so that it cooks more quickly. **Barley meal** is hulled barley that has been broken down into very small pieces, and requires only a short cooking time. Barley meal is excellent for porridge.

Black (turtle) beans

Deeply flavoured and delicious, these beans are particularly good in Mexican dishes. Be careful when soaking them, as they can stain.

Black-eyed peas (black-eyed beans, cowpeas)

Also called black-eyed beans or cowpeas, these peas are popular in the United States and are excellent in soups, stews, dips and salads.

Black pepper

Pepper is high in volatile oils that will quickly disappear once exposed to air — so for the best flavour, it should be freshly ground just before using. Freshly ground black pepper has a distinctive lemon smell that is quite delicious.

Borlotti (cranberry) beans

Borlotti beans are great for stews, and mash well for dips. When fresh, they take approximately 30 minutes to cook.

Broad (fava) beans

These vary greatly in size and are a good bean for Italian and other Mediterranean dishes. As they cook, their skins loosen. Remove the skins for the best flavour.

Brown rice (gluten free)

With the bran and germ intact, brown rice comes in long- and short-grain varieties. When buying brown rice, choose a brand that includes some green (unripe) grains, as this is an indication the grains have not been gassed to ripen them. Short-grain rice is generally stickier and is the best choice for puddings, sushi and rice balls, where the stickiness is an advantage. Long-grain tends to remain separate and is preferable for savoury dishes such as fried rice, pilaffs, or on its own. **Brown rice flour** can be used as porridge, and is the essential flour for gluten-free baking. *See also rice, sticky rice, wild rice.*

Brown rice vinegar

This vinegar is a perfect choice for Asian-inspired dressings and matches beautifully with sesame oil. It works well with sushi nori in combination with the rice and mirin. It is also good for pickling.

Buckwheat (gluten free)

Technically, buckwheat is not a grain at all, but rather a fruit related to the rhubarb family. Buckwheat is gluten free. Historically, it is a staple peasant food, most notably in the cold climates of Russia. When other crops failed, buckwheat was a grain that could be relied on, able to grow in the poorest soil. It has a distinctive nutty taste and an earthy quality that works well with root vegetables, onions and mushrooms. Buckwheat is high in protein (particularly lysine), is a rich source of B vitamins and a major source of the bioflavinoid rutin, which is good for the heart and circulation. Buckwheat has long been treasured as a health food in Japan, where it is known as **soba**. Technically, buckwheat is called **groats** when unroasted, and **kasha** when roasted. The unroasted groats are pale, almost light green and tan in colour, with a bland flavour that is enhanced by dry roasting. **Cracked buckwheat** is made from unroasted groats, broken down into smaller pieces. It can be used for porridge.

Butterbeans (lima beans)

These beans are delicate and delicious. Be careful not to overcook them as they tend to crumble and disintegrate easily. Baby limas are also available, and are wonderful in salads.

Cannellini beans
These are white beans with a soft, mellow flavour. Be careful not to overcook them as they can lose their shape.

Chickpeas
Technically a type of pea, chickpeas are most often categorized as a bean due to their long cooking time. They are excellent for dips, stews and salads, and work well with curry flavours.

Cocoa powder
Cocoa is really concentrated chocolate, and its natural acidity and tartness is increased when the fat is removed from it. As well as conventional cocoa powder you will come across **dutched cocoa powder**, used in this book. 'Dutching' is a process that uses an alkali to remove some of the acidity in cocoa, making it 'softer', darker, and less bitter and acidic. Many dutched cocoas use harsh chemicals in the alkalizing process, and some are more dutched than others. I use a moderately dutched cocoa — the organic, fair-trade Green & Black's. It is a beautiful, full-flavoured cocoa, with some of the aggressive acidity and bitterness removed.

Corn (maize) (gluten free)
Maize (corn) is one of the most loved of grains. 'Corne' was the Old English word for the predominant grain of the land, so when the English first landed in the Americas and saw the abundance of maize they named it 'Indian corne'. There are many varieties of corn products, and unfortunately they are often called by different names in different stores. Some varieties to look out for are **blue- or red-coloured corn**, which is usually ground into flour and used for tortillas in the United States and Mexico. Blue corn is higher in the amino acid lysine, and has a fabulous flavour. Corn is gluten free. *See also cornflour, maize flour, maize meal, masa, polenta.*

Cornflour (gluten free)
Check the packet when you buy cornflour (cornstarch) as it is often actually made from wheat. An extremely finely ground gluten-free starch, cornflour is used as a thickening agent and is particularly useful where some 'structure' is required in the finished product, such as in baked goods rather than a sauce. In small portions it is also used as a flour, to aid binding.

Great northern beans
These are white beans, larger than navy beans, with a beautiful creamy flesh.

Green split peas

Dried green split peas are quite sweet and an excellent addition to vegetable soups, providing flavour and body. Yellow split peas are not as sweet, but excellent for soups, dips and dal.

Kamut

Like spelt, kamut is a precursor to what we know as wheat today, and contains a more digestible form of gluten. Kamut is a deliciously flavoured grain — I especially like to buy pasta and spaghetti made from it. The flour (sometimes known as pharaoh's flour, or Egyptian flour) is also lovely in small amounts in a shortcrust pastry, mixed with white spelt, lending it a very nutty and 'short' texture.

Kombu

Containing glutamic acid, the safe and natural form of MSG, kombu is a wonder helper in the kitchen. It enriches and boosts the flavour of stocks, soups, stews and grains, and also tenderizes beans. Kombu is a high-protein sea vegetable, containing iodine, beta-carotene, vitamins B, C, D and E, calcium, magnesium, potassium, silica, iron, zinc and germanium.

Kudzu (kuzu) (gluten free)

Well known in Japan and China for its medicinal qualities, kudzu is made from the starch of the kudzu plant. It is used in cooking as a thickener, much like arrowroot or cornflour (cornstarch). It imparts a beautiful sheen to sauces, and will also set soft puddings. *See also page 34.*

Lentils

A large range of lentils (often called dal) are eaten throughout the world, and they are some of the best things to store in your pantry for a quick meal. **Black lentils** (also called caviar or beluga lentils) are less common than other varieties. They can be interchanged with green or brown lentils in recipes. **Tiny blue-green lentils** are small, hold their shape well and can be used in place of brown lentils. The best known tiny blue-green lentils are the French 'Puy' lentils. **Brown lentils** are larger than a **green lentil**, but they both have a strong, deep, astringent taste. They hold their shape well, but can easily be puréed. **Split red lentils** are small and a vibrant orange/red colour and break down easily when cooked. Best used in soups, they can also add flavour and help to thicken dals and pâtés. **Whole red lentils** are sold with their skins on, and resemble a small brown lentil, but inside are characteristically red. The skins of whole red lentils are quite astringent and need counterbalancing to soften the taste. They take longer to cook than the split red lentil. *See also page 28.*

Maize flour (sometimes called cornflour) (gluten free)

Made from 'flour corn', this looks like a fine wholegrain flour and is a beautiful pale yellow colour. The cornflour commonly sold as a thickener for making sauces is actually the white starch inside the highly refined grain.

Maize meal (gluten free)

Softer than polenta, this is a mix of a finer-ground polenta and maize flour. It makes good soft polenta or porridge, but is too soft for sturdier work.

Masa (gluten free)

Also called *maseca*, this is a flour made from corn and treated with lime. It is used for making authentic corn tortillas. When dried it is called *masa harina*.

Millet (gluten free)

Millet is vastly underrated, but is a superb, gluten-free grain. It has as much or even more protein than wheat, is high in phosphorous and B vitamins and very high in iron. **Whole millet** has the husk still intact and birds love it. It is difficult for humans to digest, but is good for sprouting. Whole millet should be ground and will take about 1 hour to cook. **Hulled millet** has a lovely sweet, buttery taste. It responds particularly well to dry roasting before cooking. Hulled millet is easier to digest than whole millet and is my preference when using millet. You can also buy **millet flakes**, which are the rolled (flattened) whole millet grains.

Mirin

This is a sweet and subtle wine, fermented from rice. It has an ability to harmonize harsh or discordant flavours and helps bring ingredients together. It is indispensable in lentil dishes, counterbalancing their astringency beautifully. True (unprocessed) mirin is fermented, producing enzymes and lactic acid bacteria traditionally valued for good health. It does, however, have an alcohol content of approximately 12% — and organic mirin higher still.

Miso

A fermented paste, miso is traditionally made from soya beans and salt, often with added grains. Koji (*Aspergillus orzae* culture) is added to cooked soya beans with salt and left to ferment. The longer this fermentation takes place, the stronger the flavour. Miso contains vitamin B12 and is an excellent alkalinizer. Unpasteurized miso is a rich source of live lactobacillus. Miso comes in a wide variety of flavours and colours. Two good misos are **genmai** (brown rice miso) and **shiro** (white rice miso). Pasteurized genmai is useful for adding flavour and depth to soups and stews, and unpasteurized genmai miso is great as a spread or for miso soup. Shiro miso works well in dressings and dips to soften and bring flavours together.

Mung (moong) bean

Probably the most widely known of the dal family, these are small and yellow and cook quickly. They are an easy-to-digest and nourishing legume.

Mung dal

When the mung bean is split and the skin is removed you have mung dal — though in many cases some of the skin is still visible.

Navy beans

Creamy textured and sweet, these are the classic white bean for baked beans.

Oats

Oats are higher in unsaturated fats than other grains, and are usually thought of as a winter grain. This higher fat content provides energy for warming, and hence their place in many cold-climate cultures, such as Scotland. This grain takes many different forms. **Whole oats** have the outer husk still intact and are generally sold for sprouting. **Oat groats** (oat kernels) are whole oats from which only the inedible outer hull has been removed. **Steel-cut oats** (sometimes called Scottish oats) are oat groats/kernels that have been cut into small pieces. **Rolled oats** (or oat flakes) are probably the most common form of oats; they are oat groats that have been steamed and flattened. If you see rolled oats referred to as 'stabilized', this means that they have been steamed to make rolling easier.

With their high fat content, oatmeal and oat flour are excellent alternatives to wheat, with a beautiful, mild taste. **Oatmeal** refers to the oat groat that has been ground to a flour, and is excellent for binding ingredients. It is available as coarse, medium and fine grinds — fine is the best for baking. **Oat flour** is very similar to fine oatmeal.

Pinto beans

Interchangeable with borlotti (cranberry) beans, pinto beans are excellent for any Mexican dish. They are sweet and lightly flavoured.

Polenta (gluten free)

Made from a hard corn, polenta is available as both a coarsely and finely ground meal, and can come in a variety of colours, but is mostly yellow or white. In many cases the skin and germ are removed to extend shelf life. Search and ask for polenta that is made from corn with the germ intact (this type should be stored in the fridge to avoid spoilage). In many North American cookbooks this is often referred to as cornmeal; in other countries it is called polenta.

Quinoa (gluten free)

Quinoa is technically not a grain, but a member of the *Chenopodium* plant family. Greatly revered by the ancient Incas, who called it 'the mother grain', quinoa boasts the highest protein content of any grain and is exceptionally high in B vitamins and calcium. It is a rich source of vitamin E and contains the amino acid, lysine. It is coated with saponin, a natural insecticide, and must be washed well before using. It is a wonderfully versatile grain with a delicate flavour, and requires only a short cooking time. Traditionally, all quinoa is pre-soaked or at least well rinsed before using, and when it is cooked a tiny, white spiral appears, encircling the grain. Quinoa comes in a variety of colours: white, red and blue. **Quinoa flakes, pasta** and **flour** are all commercially available.

Red kidney beans

One of the harder beans to digest, red kidney beans work best in dishes that cook for a long time. They have a deep, strong flavour.

Rice (gluten free)

For many people with allergies, rice is one of the most easily tolerated grains as it is gluten free. Generally speaking, brown rice has a nuttier, stronger flavour than white rice, and is more nutritious. **Basmati** and **jasmine rice** are two beautifully flavoured long-grain varieties. Unrefined brown basmati and jasmine rice are also available, but less common. *See also brown rice, sticky rice, wild rice.*

Sea vegetables

Sea vegetables (or seaweed) are an extremely concentrated source of nutrients, especially minerals. They are rich sources of protein, vitamins A and C, B vitamins, iron, iodine, trace minerals and calcium. *See also agar, arame, kombu.*

Shoyu

Similar to tamari, shoyu is a fermented soy sauce used to enhance flavour. Shoyu has a noticeably stronger fermented taste than tamari and contains wheat. Traditionally, shoyu was the liquid pressed from miso paste. When the weather is hot, shoyu is best kept in the fridge.

Soba noodles (gluten free)

Made from buckwheat flour, soba noodles are absolutely delicious in Asian-inspired noodle bowls, stir-fries or salads. Be selective when buying, however, as many soba noodles use half wheat flour.

Soy

Soy products are widely eaten in Asian countries and are a popular inclusion in vegetarian diets. *See also miso, shoyu, soy milk, tamari, tempeh, tofu; also see page 30.*

Soy milk

This is 'milk' made from unfermented, soaked and cooked soya beans. Many of the cheaper soy milks are made from soy protein isolate (SPI), with the addition of highly refined oil and sugar. When cooking with soy milk, keep in mind that the soy milk's quality (and therefore flavour) will be evident in the end result. Soy milk is low in fat and this also needs to be taken into account. If using, choose a soy milk that is simply made from whole organic soya beans, water, kombu sea vegetable and a malt of some kind — this is really the entire list of ingredients you want to see on the label. However, for gluten-free cooking, choose a soy milk that is malt free as most contain malt from barley, which is a gluten grain.

Soya beans

Soya beans have little flavour and are rarely served in their natural form. They are high in protein and nourishment and are used to make tofu and tempeh.

Spelt flour

Also known as dinkle or farro, this is an ancient, non-hybrid relative of modern wheat that is now very freely available. This grain behaves almost identically to wheat, but has a much lower gluten content. Spelt is remarkably water soluble, and more easily broken down in the body. Many people allergic to wheat and wheat products find they are able to enjoy spelt. You will find spelt sold as a berry, in a rolled form for porridges, and as a white or wholemeal flour.

The recipes in this book are all made using spelt flour, but you could also substitute wheat flour if you prefer, as this will not affect the end result.

Spices

Organic spices have a beautiful, vibrant flavour — much more so than their commercially produced counterparts. You may find you need to use a little less of organic spices in recipes as their flavour is often stronger.

Sticky (glutinous) rice (gluten free)

This rice can be both long- and short-grained, and has a high starch content a little like arborio, a rice used for making risotto. Sticky rice comes in black, white and even red grains; it is used for *mochi* and is the essential ingredient for sticky rice puddings.

Tahini

This is a paste made from sesame seeds, and can be — but isn't always — a rich source of calcium. Some people believe unhulled tahini is richer in calcium, but the calcium is bound in the oxalic acid in the hull of the seed, and is not readily available. For this reason I prefer to use the softer-flavoured hulled tahini, and include other calcium sources in my diet. Take care to buy good-quality tahini — for me this would be organic, since many conventional tahinis are made using seeds that have been hulled using a chemical process.

Tamari

A fermented soy sauce, similar to shoyu, used to enhance flavour. Tamari is widely assumed to be wheat free. This isn't actually so, although you can buy tamaris that are wheat free and salt reduced. Tamari is the soy sauce I most commonly use.

Tempeh

To make tempeh, soya beans are cooked, split and sometimes blended with other grains such as rice or millet. They are then inoculated with the *Rhizopus oligosporus* bacteria and spread on trays. Left to ferment for about 24 hours, the spores spread quickly, forming a thin fuzz (mycelium) over the beans, transforming them into a firm cake. Tempeh is probably one of the most body-compatible of the soy products. Fermentation delivers many benefits to the soya bean — it greatly reduces its oligosaccharides (the complex sugars that can cause flatulence), it makes the protein easy to digest and, most importantly, deactivates the phytates and enzyme inhibitors present. The flavours and texture of tempeh are deep and nutty, hearty and filling. For this reason most newcomers love it and find it extremely satisfying. Because tempeh uses the whole bean — unlike tofu — it contains all its nutrients and can be considered a wholefood. Tempeh also freezes well.

Tofu

This is a soya bean curd made from 'milk' pressed from cooked, mashed soya beans. The best-quality tofu is made from organically grown soya beans, which are then coagulated with nigari (calcium and magnesium salts derived from sea water). This binds the protein together to produce curds, and these in turn are pressed. While being pressed, the amount of whey discarded will determine the type of tofu — soft or silken tofu has a high water content, and the firmer ones less water. Tofu is not a 'whole' food but has been derived from cooked whole soya beans (and in many cases, soy protein isolate). Unfortunately, many vegetarians use it as a prime source for their protein needs, rather than relying on a wide and balanced diet.

Umeboshi vinegar

Technically, this is not a vinegar at all, but the brine resulting from the pickling process of the umeboshi plum. It has a delicious fruity flavour, is highly alkaline and is also known as an antibiotic. It is an excellent choice in a salad dressing and has a great fruit flavour.

Vanilla

Vanilla is enormously popular for flavouring cakes and desserts. **Vanilla bean seeds** are contained within the vanilla pod and impart a subtle flavour. Unlike vanilla extract, vanilla seeds do not affect the colour of the finished product, and so are preferable for some dishes. If using a **natural vanilla extract**, buy a good-quality one. Real vanilla extract will give a truer and more beautiful flavour, and basically just contains vanilla extractives and alcohol, whereas inferior ones contain corn syrup, glycerin, fructose, propylene glycol and preservatives. **Vanilla bean paste** is a paste of vanilla seeds suspended in a liquid — generally a sap such as inulin or tragacanth. One teaspoon of vanilla bean paste is the equivalent of one vanilla bean, and is a great option when you want a lot of vanilla flavour, without the colour that vanilla extract imparts.

Vinegar

True vinegar, traditionally produced, is the product of long fermentation over many months. Unpasteurized and unfiltered, it can be a rich source of many nutrients, and is very different to many instantly produced vinegars on the market today. Buy vinegar in glass — it is a solvent and will break down the polycarbons in plastic. *See also apple cider vinegar, balsamic vinegar, brown rice vinegar, umeboshi vinegar, wine vinegars.*

Wheat

Perhaps the most prevalent cereal grain grown and consumed today, wheat is one of the world's most valuable currencies. Because it is such an important crop, wheat is usually treated with a good deal of herbicides, pesticides and fungicides, both in its growing stages and during storage. It is this enormous exposure to chemicals that contributes to it being one of the most allergenic substances for many people. Wheat is usually referred to as 'hard' or 'soft'; the harder it is, the higher the gluten content. The high gluten content in hard wheat is essential for successful bread making, while the softer wheat, with lower gluten levels, is useful in cakes and pastries.

Whey

When milk sours, lacto-fermentation takes place. The end result is that the protein (which contains curds) separates from the watery — and extremely valuable — whey. (You will also end up with whey when making Labneh; see page 68). Whey is greatly beneficial for soaking grains, nuts and seeds as it helps make them easier to digest.

Wild rice (gluten free)

Strictly speaking, this is not actually rice, but an aquatic grass seed. Nutritionally speaking, wild rice has more B vitamins and protein than other rice, and has a very assertive flavour. It is best used in combination with brown rice, to soften the taste. Wild rice generally takes 1 hour to cook, with a ratio of 3 cups liquid to 1 cup wild rice. After cooking, allow it to sit and steam with the lid on for 10 minutes.

Wine vinegars

These are made from white or red wine, sherry or Champagne — and each variety has something to offer. Champagne vinegar has a delicate, sharp and light flavour, whereas sherry vinegar is assertive and highly acidic. White wine vinegar mixes well with herbs, while red wine vinegar will anchor a hearty salad.

ɔʒ

index

Published in 2008 by Murdoch Books Pty Limited

Murdoch Books Australia
Pier 8/9
23 Hickson Road
Millers Point NSW 2000
Phone: +61 (0) 2 8220 2000
Fax: +61 (0) 2 8220 2558
www.murdochbooks.com.au

Murdoch Books UK Limited
Erico House, 6th Floor
93–99 Upper Richmond Road
Putney, London SW15 2TG
Phone: +44 (0) 20 8785 5995
Fax: +44 (0) 20 8785 5985
www.murdochbooks.co.uk

Chief Executive: Juliet Rogers
Publishing Director: Kay Scarlett

Project manager: Desney Shoemark
Editor: Katri Hilden
Food editor: Katy Holder
Design concept and design: Vivien Valk
Photographer for cover and chapter openers: Michele Aboud
Stylist for cover and chapter openers: Sarah De Nardi
Photographer for page 8 image and inside cover images: Geoff Fisher
Production: Kita George

Text copyright © 2008 Jude Blereau
Photography and design copyright © 2008 Murdoch Books

National Library of Australia Cataloguing-in-Publication Data

Blereau, Jude.
Coming home to eat.

Includes index.
ISBN 9781921259906 (pbk.).

1. Cookery (Natural foods). 2. Quick and easy cookery.
I. Title.

641.563

A catalogue record for this book is available from the British Library.

Colour separation by Splitting Image Colour Studio, Melbourne, Australia.

Printed by 1010 Printing International Limited in 2008. PRINTED IN CHINA.

IMPORTANT: Those who might be at risk from the effects of salmonella poisoning (the elderly,
pregnant women, young children and those suffering from immune deficiency diseases) should
consult their doctor with any concerns about eating raw eggs.

CONVERSION GUIDE: You may find cooking times vary depending on the oven you are using.
For fan-forced ovens, as a general rule, set the oven temperature to 20°C (35°F) lower than
indicated in the recipe. We have used 20 ml (4 teaspoon) tablespoon measures. If you are using
a 15 ml (3 teaspoon) tablespoon, for most recipes the difference will not be noticeable. However,
for recipes using baking powder, gelatine, bicarbonate of soda (baking soda), small amounts of
flour and cornflour (cornstarch), add an extra teaspoon for each tablespoon specified.